# European Welfare Futures

# EUROPEAN WELFARE FUTURES

## Towards a Theory of Retrenchment

Giuliano Bonoli, Vic George and
Peter Taylor-Gooby

Polity Press

First published in 2000 by Polity Press in association with Blackwell Publishers Ltd

*Editorial office*:
Polity Press
65 Bridge Street
Cambridge CB2 1UR, UK

*Marketing and production*:
Blackwell Publishers Ltd
108 Cowley Road
Oxford OX4 1JF, UK

*Published in the USA by*
Blackwell Publishers Inc.
Commerce Place
350 Main Street
Malden, MA 02148, USA

A catalogue record for this book is available from the British Library.
Bonoli, Giuliano.
    European welfare futures: towards a theory of retrenchment /
Giuliano Bonoli, Vic George, and Peter Taylor-Gooby.
    p.    cm.
Includes bibliographical references (p.   ) and index.
    ISBN 0-7456-1810-3 (H/B: acid-free paper).—ISBN 0-7456-1811-1
(P/B: acid-free paper)
    1. Social service—European Union countries.   2. European Union countries—Social policy.   I. George, Victor.   II. Taylor-Gooby, Peter.   III. Title.
HV238.B66   2000
361.94—dc21                                                    99-39727
                                                                  CIP

Typeset in 10 on 12 pt Times New Roman
by Best-set Typesetter Ltd, Hong Kong
Printed in Great Britain by MPG Books Ltd, Bodmin, Cornwall

This book is printed on acid-free paper.

# Contents

# List of Figures

# List of Tables

# Acknowledgements

This book originated in our work for the Squaring the Welfare Circle project from 1993 to 1996. It was conceived at a time when European monetary union was an aspiration and when right and centre-right governments dominated the major European nations. Since then the European project has advanced through a number of stages, and so has our collaboration. We are grateful to the many colleagues both in the UK and elsewhere in Europe with whom we have worked on comparative research over the past five years. Particular thanks are due to Professor Paul Wilding for his valuable comments on chapters 3 and 5, to colleagues at the University of Kent, to the Leverhulme Trust for the award of an Emeritus Fellowship to Vic George that enabled him to work on the project and to Lynn Dunlop and David Held of Polity Press for their encouragement to persevere with the book. We are also grateful to the Economic and Social Research Council who supported the Squaring the Welfare Circle Project under grant no. R000234.711, to DGV of the European Commission (grant no. Soc 94 103019), the Netherlands government agency COSZ (grant no. 20237) and the Anglo-German Foundation (grant no. 1037); and to Social and Community Planning Research who facilitated access to the data analysed in chapter 4 and to the ZUMA agency in Cologne who supplied it. The errors and idiosyncrasies of the analysis are, of course, our own responsibility.

In addition, we are grateful to the following organizations for permission to reproduce copyright material:

International Labour Office, Geneva, for Table 3.2 adapted from data drawn on *World Employment 1995*, copyright © International Labour Organization, 1995.

OECD, Paris, for Table 2.1 from *The Growing Role of Private Social Benefits*, Labour Market and Social Policy Occasional Paper no. 32, 1998, © OECD 1998; Table 5.1 compiled from data in *Economic Outlook*, no. 56, December 1994, © OECD 1994 and in *Social Expenditure Statistics of OECD Member Countries*, Occasional Paper no. 16, 19976, © OECD 1976; Table 6.1 compiled from data in *New Orientations for Social Policy*, 1994, © OECD 1994; Table 6.2 compiled from data in *Historical Statistics 1960–1990*, 1992, © OECD 1992 and *Economic Outlook*, no. 62, December 1997, © OECD 1997; Table 6.3 from *Ageing Populations, the Social Policy Implications*, 1988, © OECD 1988; Table 6.4 compiled from data in *Historical Statistics 1960–1981*, 1983, © OECD 1983 and in *Economic Outlook*, no. 62, December 1997, © OECD 1997; Table 6.5 from *Revenue Statistics of OECD Member Countries 1965–96*, 1997, © OECD 1997; Table 6.6 from *Economic Outlook*, no. 65, June 1999, © OECD 1999; and Table 7.1 compiled from data in *Revenue Statistics of OECD Member Countries 1965–96*, 1997, © OECD 1997.

The Office of National Statistics for Table 5.2 from A. Richards and K. Madden: 'An International Comparison of Taxes and Social Security Contributions 1984–1994', *Economic Trends*, no. 517, 1996, Office of National Statistics, © Crown copyright 1996.

United Nations, Department of Public Information for Table 3.1 from *World Economic and Social Survey*, 1997, copyright © United Nations 1997.

Giuliano Bonoli
Vic George
Peter Taylor-Gooby

# Introduction

Throughout Europe, the dominant theme in contemporary social policy is the retreat of the welfare state. This book is one of the first texts in the field to examine systematically the pressures on government that have led to retrenchment. There is now general agreement that the bulk of the social legislation introduced in recent years is intended to reduce the role of the state in welfare. Policies that lead in the opposite direction play a subordinate role and this is true of the new legislation for the social insurance finance of social care in Germany, for the minimum income in France, for improved benefits for the unemployed in Greece or for wage supplements for low-paid workers in the UK.

This mass of restrictive social legislation consisted of several overlapping types. Some new policies have reduced the level of cash benefits, restricted entitlement and reduced the period for which the benefits can be paid. Other legislation increased the payments made by users of the health, education and social care services. Still other legislation made the provision or the administration of some of the cash benefits the responsibility of employers or other bodies or introduced market principles in the management of services. Finally, legislation privatized parts of the social services or many public utilities in their entirety.

Despite these attempts to reduce the role of the state in welfare, social expenditure as a proportion of GDP continued to increase during the past decade, although at a slower rate than before. This increase is the result of rising demand – more retirement pensioners, larger numbers of unemployed people or lone parents, more high-technology medicine and higher public expectations of the quality of services.

A large number of textbooks attempt to explain the *growth* of the welfare state. Paul Pierson provides a path-breaking analysis of the factors that constrain governments which have decided to pursue retrenchment policies in *Dismantling the Welfare State?* (1994). There are few attempts, however, to explain the forces that drive retrenchment policies or to understand why cut-backs have taken different forms in different countries. This book seeks to fill this gap. It deals with the question of why welfare retrenchment has come to be seen as necessary by governments in advanced industrial countries and by international bodies such as the Organization for Economic Development and Co-operation (OECD), the European Union (EU) and the World Bank. It also considers some of the factors that influence the pace and process of retrenchment.

## Key Factors in Explanation of Retrenchment

Four main factors are involved in current pressures for retrenchment. These factors have been discussed elsewhere. We wish to explore their interrelations and the way they give rise to conflicts in the development of welfare policy.

The four factors are, first, globalization which imposes an international competitive logic which different nation states cannot escape and which constrains national policies, particularly in relation to taxation and the labour market; secondly, the assumption of politicians and others that the public will not tolerate increases in taxes and social contributions to finance improvements in welfare (or indeed the maintenance of current standards as needs expand); thirdly, the neo-liberal approach to political economy, now dominant in the assumptive worlds of policy-makers, which argues the priority of market freedom over welfare intervention; and fourthly, the dilemma of 'squaring the welfare circle', which confronts all welfare states. This refers to the way governments now experience simultaneous and contradictory pressures from opposite directions. Increases in the numbers of older people, rising demand for education and training, rising unemployment and the expectations of citizens that social progress will involve higher standards of service press for higher spending. At the same time, concern about the impact of globalization, the logic of liberalism and fears of tax revolt demand the contraction of provision.

We argue that the institutional framework in different countries in the largest sense (including both the formal political institutions and the assumptions and expectations about the role of the labour movement, business organizations, finance capital, the voluntary sector, regional differences and other factors) plays a central role in deciding how these conflicts are played out and resolved. This approach places institutions centre stage in analyses of contemporary developments in social policy.

It also explains why social policies in EU member states fail to converge, although they face challenges that are broadly similar, and despite the aspirations of central policy-makers and the evident progress towards monetary and commercial union.

The process of retrenchment can only be understood by considering the options available to policy-makers and governments trapped in this dilemma to respond to the pressures they face. These options are strongly influenced by the institutional structures which form the immediate policy-making environment. Accordingly we seek to analyse the key differences in institutional structure which will exert a determining influence on the nature and direction of the response by different European governments to current pressures for retrenchment.

## The Structure of the Book

The first two chapters of the book deal with essential background material for our argument. The first reviews the various theories that have been used to explain the growth of the welfare state in order to demonstrate that these approaches have limited relevance to understanding the most important issue in contemporary welfare policy, which concerns retrenchment and restructuring. The chapter emphasizes the urgency of rethinking our explanatory approaches to today's welfare developments and stresses the importance of institutional frameworks in structuring the options available to policy-makers.

The second chapter considers the course of welfare state retrenchment in recent years. It provides a thematic rather than a country-focused approach. The object is not so much to show what happened in each and every country in Europe considered separately, but rather to highlight the methods that have been used to control the expansion of the various social services. This approach sets the scene for the following chapters that discuss the various factors that have influenced retrenchment and show how they contribute to government policy-making in this field.

Chapter 3 examines the importance of *economic globalization* and the growth of an increasingly competitive world market. This explanation emphasizes the importance of external factors that make it difficult for governments to sustain, let alone expand, generous state welfare provision. The argument here is that, in an increasingly globalized world economy, large firms will always have the option of moving their capital as well as their production and distribution to those countries that offer them the greatest economic advantage. The level of taxation, particularly on employers and capital, and the degree of labour regulation are two important considerations that will affect their decisions. Countries with high levels of state welfare provision will almost inevitably suffer in this process unless they can convince firms that the benefits to business outweigh the costs.

Research studies provide partial support for this thesis. Two main indicators have been used to measure the degree of openness of an economy to international pressures and hence of its dependence on events largely beyond the control of national governments: the share of the country's GDP accounted for by exports and imports; and the degree to which the economy relies on foreign direct investment.

Comparative research does not in general bear out the claim that the more open an economy the greater the degree of welfare retrenchment. Generally, the economies of small countries such as Belgium, the Netherlands, Austria and Sweden are more open to international pressures than those of larger countries. There is, however, no evidence that small countries either spend less of their GDP on welfare services or that they have been retrenching more severely in recent years than large countries.

Studies of the investment behaviour of large firms do, however, provide partial support for the idea that globalization limits the freedom of manoeuvre of national governments in welfare policy. They show that labour costs and labour regimes are taken into account by large firms in their investment plans. Other factors may also influence decisions. They may well override the significance of welfare factors depending on the specific situation. On the whole, however, the rising power of multinational enterprises militates against the generous universal welfare state and acts as a pressure for the containment, retrenchment and restructuring of the welfare state.

Chapter 4 deals with the argument that *electoral support for welfare provision is in decline*. The evidence of opinion studies is that, with minor upward or downward variations, public support for an interventionist state in the realm of employment and welfare was as strong in the mid-1990s as in the mid-1980s. Similarly, the level of public willingness to pay more tax for better services in the mid-1990s varied between countries: enthusiasm for welfare is highest in those countries (the UK and the USA) where social spending is relatively low; other countries exhibit rather lower but varying levels of support.

This evidence contradicts claims by theorists and social commentators that people are now disenchanted with state welfare or that more powerful groups press for welfare retrenchment because they perceive it as in their interest. It is difficult to attribute welfare retrenchment simply to a narrowing of the social conscience among more affluent groups or to a general disquiet with the principles of the interventionist welfare state. However there is some evidence that, in the higher spending countries, substantial numbers among those who favour increased state provision also believe that someone else should foot the welfare bill. The important point is not so much the continuing popularity of provision (despite the assumptions of liberal political economists) as the extent to which policy-makers presuppose that spending increases will invite tax revolt. In the context of the Maastricht Treaty requirements, which set very strict limits on state borrowing, the contradiction between welfare support and willingness to pay more tax means that it is extremely difficult to advance policies which do not constrain spending.

Chapter 5 discusses the *neo-liberal turn in economic policy* that has played an important role in driving and legitimating retrenchment, particularly in Anglo-Saxon countries, but also elsewhere. At the explanatory level, the central argument is that high levels of public expenditure undermine economic growth through their adverse effects on incentives to work, to save and to invest. Public spending has economic, social and political costs which no democratically elected government can ignore indefinitely.

It is the claims about the economic and social costs of public expenditure that have attracted most attention and concern. High levels of public expenditure affect adversely the economy of a country (it is claimed) because they undermine work incentives, cut the rate of saving or deter investment. The generous provision of social security benefits encourages recipients of working age to reduce their work effort and to increase the level and duration of unemployment. Knowing that their needs will be taken care of by the state, people in welfare states see no point in saving, particularly when such savings are highly taxed. The high levels of taxation needed to finance generous welfare services also drive employers' investments out of the country to the detriment of everyone, including those who benefit from state welfare.

The evidence to test these claims comes from two types of research: studies of human behaviour in individual countries and studies which compare trends in public expenditure and taxation with trends in rates of savings and economic growth. The overwhelming body of evidence from research on behaviour suggests that neither the level of benefits nor the level of personal taxation has any noticeable effect on work effort. The work ethic remains strong among the unemployed; the vast majority prefer income from work to income from benefits. There is no evidence of a culture of dependency fostering reliance on benefits and avoidance of work. As for the effects of taxation, most studies show that people's willingness to work is largely unaffected, either positively or negatively, by existing taxation levels.

The results of large-scale comparative studies are mixed partly because of methodological problems. Different studies examine different countries, compare over different periods, refer to different state services or use different definitions of the same services. The result is that they reach different conclusions. Such studies also tend to use aggregate measures of total welfare effort or spending at too high a level of abstraction to produce helpful conclusions. Two countries may spend the same proportion of their GDP on public services but may finance and provide them in radically different ways so that the effect on economic growth differs. The main research reviews confirm that no clear picture emerges. Atkinson reviews nine studies which examine the relation between social security spending and economic growth (Atkinson, 1995). Four out of nine find a negative relationship, three a positive relationship and two an insignificant relationship. Esping-Andersen examines studies of the relationship between total social spending and growth to show a similarly mixed picture (Esping-Andersen, 1994b). On this issue the jury is out and unlikely to return for some time. As an academic analysis, the liberal approach is controversial. However, it has exerted an important influence on policy-makers, and has played a major role in justifying retrenchment.

The sixth chapter deals with the dilemma that has come to be known as 'Squaring the Welfare Circle'. The point is that, on the one hand, democratically elected governments today find it very difficult to raise the necessary resources for the ever expanding public demand for welfare. Economic growth rates have slowed in recent years and there are doubts whether the electorate is willing to pay the necessary direct taxes for the finance of state welfare. On the other hand, demand for welfare has been rising because of demographic factors associated with the ageing of the population; labour market factors relating to the rise in unemployment and early retirement; social factors affecting the creation of rising numbers of one-parent families; and rising living standards which create a public demand for better-quality services. Governments are trapped between simultaneous pressures for welfare contraction and expansion exacerbated by their desire for re-election. The evidence of chapter 2 shows that they have tended to resolve these pressures in the direction of retrenchment.

This account does not seek to explain how individual governments have attempted to solve the problem that rising demand confronts restrictions on the resources available for welfare. It merely states that there is a problem which governments cannot ignore if they want to be re-elected. Retrenchment does not simply correspond to a structural gap between resources and demands for welfare but is politically mediated. The solutions different governments adopt depend not only on the state of the economy, demographic shifts and their own ideological perspective but also on the political and institutional structure which forms the environment of policy-making in their country.

Welfare retrenchment is a complex process. In this book we focus attention on the way in which interpretations of the impact of globalization, the belief by policy-makers that taxpayers will not support welfare spending and the dominance of liberal political economy have tilted state responses to the dilemma of squaring the welfare circle decisively in the direction of retrenchment. The process and degree of retrenchment is heavily influenced by institutional structure in different countries. This is the theme of chapter 7. This chapter attempts to explain why welfare retrenchment is handled differently in different countries. National political and institutional structures are crucially important in determining the shape and severity of cut-backs and constraint in welfare policy. Finally in chapter 8 we go on to look at some of the implications of our approach for understanding current and future developments in policy-making in the EU.

This book provides a systematic examination of explanations of how and why welfare retrenchment takes place. It builds on a growing body of evidence and scholarly work demonstrating that the traditional explanations of welfare expansion are of little relevance to the current welfare developments of restructuring and retrenchment. It considers the importance of the political and economic shifts associated with globalization as a qualitatively new force constraining policy-makers. It shows that attention to political frameworks as well as to objective constraints and the ideologies of governing parties is necessary to understand the process of welfare retrenchment in Europe. It also indicates that progress towards convergence in welfare policy at the EU level will require a measure of rapprochement in institutional frameworks which will take far longer to achieve than has convergence in monetary and fiscal systems.

# 1
# Explanations of the Growth of State Welfare

Europe has made three gifts to the world: industrial capitalism, the competitive market and the welfare state. The first two are everywhere triumphant. The last is subject to restructuring, revision and retrenchment. This book attempts to chart the reasons for the changes in welfare policy in the main European countries. In this chapter we review approaches that seek to understand the development of welfare states in a comparative cross-national context and argue that greater attention to political institutions and processes is necessary in order to give satisfactory accounts of current developments. The theories which provide the most convincing accounts of post-war welfare state expansion do not provide the best explanations of retrenchment.

The development of comparative theory in social policy over the past forty years has been influenced by two factors. First, the conflicts between different social science disciplines, anxious to claim or defend territory, have been particularly intense, as each strives to make the case for its own perspective. Secondly, theory has developed in the shadow of social change, responding to shifts in the climate of international relations and the understanding of global politics. Thus the era of confident capitalist expansion was also the period of the 'end of ideology' and of the dominance of convergence theory in social science. In comparative studies, approaches which tended to stress the similarity of the factors operating in different welfare states and to downplay national differences predominated. The development of intellectual critiques of this perspective from those who emphasized the role of conflict led ultimately to the development of approaches which combined the insights of different disciplines in a holistic theory of welfare state regimes. New challenges resulted from the reappraisal of traditional social science by feminism, postmodernism and other approaches. At the same time the stability which underlay consensus theory was threatened by the economic shock of the oil crisis in the 1970s and the intensifying competitive pressures of economic globalization, followed by the dissolution of barriers between East and West in Europe in the late 1980s. Comparative theory responded by opening the question of whether the frameworks appropriate to understanding the period of welfare expansion were appropriate to the new climate of uncertainty and retrenchment.

## The Development of Comparative Theory: Structural Explanations

The first self-consciously comparative studies of welfare states were carried out in the 1960s, in an intellectual climate which favoured convergence theory. The path-breaking work of Wilensky provided the first impetus. In a quantitative analysis of data covering sixty-four countries, Wilensky showed that

> economic growth and its demographic and bureaucratic outcomes are the root cause of the general emergence of the welfare state . . . In any systematic comparison of many countries over many years, alternative explanations collapse under the weight of such heavy, brittle categories as 'socialist' versus 'capitalist' economies, 'collectivistic' versus 'individualistic' ideologies, or even 'democratic' versus 'totalitarian' political systems . . . these categories are almost useless in explaining the origins and general development of the welfare state. (Wilensky, 1975, p. xiii)

The conclusion that welfare development is due to long-run structural factors is hardly surprising in a study based on a limited amount of data from a large number of diverse countries. The availability of resources, the increase in proportion of elderly people who tend to consume the most in terms of pensions, medical care and social care and the development of the bureaucratic apparatus to allocate state services are bound to play a major role in generating gross differences in welfare spending. In later work, Wilensky sought to refine his analysis by focusing on a smaller and less diverse group of the nineteen most developed OECD member countries. Here he includes political and institutional factors in his explanation of the development of welfare states and in particular of how they respond to demands for a reduction in the tax-burden. The analysis shows that three factors exert an additional influence on policy development in this group of countries – the extent to which the institutional and political structure allows the incorporation of trade unions and business interests in negotiations on economic policy, the maturity of the party structure and the visibility of taxation (Wilensky, 1975, pp. 43–5). However it is still the structural economic and demographic factors which predominate.

## Politics Matters

Wilensky's work raised a large number of issues which were pursued from different directions. Political scientists and sociologists expressed concern at the relative lack of importance accorded to social and political factors and in particular to working-class politics in Wilensky's model, and sought to demonstrate that 'politics matters' in the development of the welfare state. This approach was strongly influenced by Marxist political economy, which saw class-struggle as the primary force behind the development of capitalist welfare states. The conflict of interest between classes is played out through party politics at the parliamentary level and through trade union struggles. Working-class interests may succeed in gaining provision that serves them within a capitalist system, to a greater or a lesser degree. At the same time, capital is under strong pressure to provide welfare services in order to legitimate the inequalities and make the world safe for the exploitation of labour power (O'Connor, 1973; Gough, 1979).

Stephens also criticizes Wilensky's measures of corporatism and of the role of politics (Stephens, 1980, pp. 94–6) from a Marxist perspective. Using far more detailed analyses of developments in a smaller number of countries, he is able to show that 'the level of labour organisation and the strength of the socialist parties' influenced welfare state development in the post-war period. The terms of the compromise between capital and organised labour 'varied substantially according to the strength of . . . labour and of the socialist parties' with the result that 'the character of the political economies has diverged too, some countries moving towards a corporate collectivist pattern, others towards democratic socialism' (Stephens, 1980, pp. 195–7).

Korpi, writing mainly about the development of welfare in Sweden, in the context of comparative analysis, argues that the development of policy is to be understood in terms of the 'power resources' available to the bourgeoisie and to labour in 'democratic class struggle'. These include degree of organization, relationship to the mass media and expression through political parties (1978, pp. 317–19; 1983, pp. 208–11). A subsequent study of eighteen nations, directed in collaboration with Esping-Andersen, concludes: 'cross national comparisons indicate that the balance of political power is closely related to the extent to which the boundaries of social citizenship have been expanded' (Esping-Andersen and Korpi, 1984, p. 202).

Castles repeatedly emphasizes the importance of political factors. In an influential – and combative – series of papers, he locates the argument that the development of welfare states can be understood entirely in terms of economic development and the development of technical institutional structures firmly within post-war convergence theory and provides a thoroughgoing refutation of the approach in analysis of data relevant to the nineteen most developed OECD nation. The thrust of this work is to demonstrate that politics does matter, alongside other factors, and that the most significant political issues are the political complexion of the parties in and out of government and the degree of concentration of government power (Castles and McKinlay, 1979a, 1979b).

## The Role of Welfare Institutions

An alternative line of research, developed both in response to Wilensky's work and to the political science emphasis on the importance of political parties, seeks to direct attention to the importance of social institutions. Skocpol and Amenta argue that 'states may be sites of autonomous official initiatives and their institutional structures may help to shape the political processes from which social policies emerge. In turn, social policies, once enacted and implemented, themselves transform politics' (Skocpol and Amenta, 1986, p. 131). Thus US social policies since the New Deal have led to the creation of new bureaucratic and popular constituencies favouring expanded welfare programmes, especially those directed to the needs of women and children (Piven and Cloward, 1982). Similarly, the structure of funds administered largely by 'social partners' in unemployment, pension, medical and family benefits in France has produced a system of considerable inertia in the face of attempts at reform. The initial public housing programmes in Sweden set in motion 'a positive sequence of policy development' (Headey, 1978, ch. 9) by creating interest groups favouring further government interventions. Policy feedback is an important factor and approaches based purely on analysis of political or structural factors run the risk of ignoring it.

The 'politics matters' and the 'social institutions matter' approaches emerged in response to the blandness of structural convergence accounts. In addition to these new perspectives, methodological developments have called accounts which rest on a one-dimensional explanation into question. A number of careful analyses show that the conclusions different writers arrive at are heavily influenced by the conceptual framework and the measures of key variables with which they start out. For example, the widely used International Labour Office measure of welfare effort is likely to downplay the significance of working-class mobilization since it is skewed towards cash benefits rather than the provision of services in areas like health and social care or social housing, which also meet working-class needs. Work by Julia O'Connor shows that labour political involvement influences service provision more strongly than cash benefits (O'Connor, 1988, p. 277; O'Connor and Brym, 1988, p. 64). A number of detailed time-series analyses show that structural, political and social factors are all influential and the part played by each varies in different countries at different times. A good example is the work of Hicks and Swank, which is able to explain nearly 95 per cent of the variance in measures of income transfers, by taking into account the politics of government, the capacity of labour and capital to influence events, investment and economic growth (Hicks and Swank, 1984, pp. 100, 103).

One outcome of these methodological and theoretical debates has been that the most recent approaches to understanding the development of the welfare state attempt to link together analysis of the political history of institutions with more sophisticated statistical measurement of structural and economic variables and pay particular attention to accounts of welfare states as systems that develop over time. There has been a shift in interest away from quantitative measures of the size of welfare programmes to qualitative understanding of how welfare provision relates to different types of society. Thus Hage, Hanneman and Gargan (1989) use both detailed case-studies and extensive time-series statistics for Germany, France, Italy and the UK and show that different interactions between the various factors are important at different junctures in their development. The most significant work is that of Esping-Andersen, who draws together the disparate perspectives into regime analysis.

## Regime Theory

'To talk of a regime is to denote the fact that in the relation between state and economy a complex of legal and organisational features are systematically interwoven' (Esping-Andersen, 1990, p. 2). Thus Esping-Andersen starts out from an interest in states and markets. The core of his analysis is the notion of 'decommodification'. 'The outstanding criterion for social rights must be the degree to which they permit people to make their living standards independent of pure market forces. It is in this sense that social rights diminish citizens' status as commodities' (p. 3). Welfare states have been understood as responses to stratification in capitalist societies. Esping-Andersen takes this argument one stage further by arguing that, since social rights give individuals access to resources, welfare states themselves constitute systems of stratification in their own right. The 'policy feedback' identified by Skocpol and Amenta may thus function in relation to the interests generated by particular policies or pieces of legislation, and also in a more general sense, in relation to the interests of broader social groups.

In understanding of the differences between welfare state regimes, Esping-Andersen identifies three factors as of the greatest importance: 'the nature of class mobilization (especially of the working class), class-political coalition structures and the historical legacy of regime institutionalization' (p. 29). He groups regimes in capitalist society into three basic types: liberal, corporatist and social democrat. In the first, provision is limited to modest benefits for a clientele of low-income, usually working-class, state dependants. Reform has been circumscribed by adherence to work-ethic norms and the regime minimizes decommodification and encourages a strong market-oriented welfare system for middle- and upper-income groups. The archetype is the USA.

In the corporatist regime-type, social rights are granted much more widely. However, the preservation of status differentials predominated so that rights were attached to class and status. Private insurance and market welfare play a relatively small role, but the emphasis on upholding status differentials minimizes redistribution. In many corporatist countries there are strong links to the Church, and an emphasis on a Christian Democratic family ethic in social policy. Germany is the leading example of corporatism.

The third welfare regime is the most clearly concerned with decommodification. In social democracies, universalism is a basic principle guiding social reform and social rights have been extended to middle-class groups, with an emphasis on egalitarianism at a high standard of provision. The pattern is Sweden.

The different trajectories of welfare state development are accounted for largely in terms of the interaction between class politics and the development of state institutions, located within the framework of general structural factors. In social democratic regimes, a broad coalition between the industrial working class and the peasantry created pressure for universal provision into which social democratic government incorporated middle-class groups. Corporatist politics was concerned to preserve status divisions in order to weaken the development of a universalist working-class socialist politics, and thus fostered interests which enshrined the divisions in welfare policy. In liberal systems, the interests of industrial and agricultural employers blocked the development of universalist welfare and fostered an unequal social structure in which the forces supporting the development of welfare were relatively powerless (Esping-Andersen, 1990, ch. 1).

Regime theory seems able to solve two problems of comparative approaches to social policy. First, it offers a way of bringing together the different strands of analysis which have emerged over the past three decades of comparative work. Secondly, it analyses welfare states in a way which does justice to the differences of type as well as of level of expenditure between them. It also offers a certain adaptability since it is not exclusive: it is always in principle possible to imagine other constellations of political and institutional forces to account for further patterns of welfare state development.

We will go on to discuss some of the additional regime types that have been discussed by various commentators, before considering various criticisms of the approach that have been made – that it is too centred on Scandinavian debates; that it ignores the development of feminism as one of the most important creative forces in social science over the past two decades; that it is not well-adapted to encompass the postmodern development of industrial society; that it is also ill-adapted to understand the differences between welfare states in the politics of retrenchment; and that it does not pay sufficient attention to the political differences between consensus and majoritarian regimes.

## Additional Regime Types

Three variations to Esping-Andersen's model of welfare state regimes among advanced capitalist countries have been proposed. A number of writers have argued that the Mediterranean welfare states in Europe offer a fourth category. Leibfried draws attention to the relatively recent development of welfare systems in these countries, the lower levels of benefit and the lack of a comprehensive means-tested system (1990). Ferrera presents a more developed analysis, listing four characteristics: comprehensive or near comprehensive medical care and pension systems, much less developed social security for unemployed and sick people of working age, insurance finance (since the revenues from taxation are uncertain in a less developed state apparatus) and the use of welfare to reinforce a clientelistic social structure (1995). The last refers to a social system in which powerful individuals are able to direct benefits to their supporters. In the clan system of Ancient Rome, the relevant resources were controlled by rich families. In the modern Mediterranean welfare state, the resources involved are state welfare resources. Many commentators point out that much of politics in advanced societies involves the devising of policies that advantage likely constituencies of supporters (for example, Baldwin, 1990). The key feature of modern clientelism lies in the direct personal relationship between patron and client and the use of discretion to channel benefits such as disability and invalidity benefit to particular individuals within a category, rather than the wider redistribution by a political party to a social group which might support it, such as home-owners or those on lower incomes.

The second regime variation is proposed by Castles and Mitchell to underscore a distinction within the category of liberal regimes (1990). The liberal-leaning Anglo-Saxon countries (the USA, Canada, Australia, New Zealand and the UK) all tend to score relatively low on measures of welfare effort or expenditure. The lack of a strong structure of social insurance benefits for the bulk of the working class and the reliance on means-tested assistance programmes lead them to be categorized as members of the liberal regime family. However, the Australasian members of this group are distinctive in their history of labour government and the strength of labour unions, and the UK to some extent shares these characteristics. The argument is that these countries have tended to deploy the power resources available to the working class to secure rights within the labour market, rather than social bene-fits, so that a different trajectory has been pursued from Scandinavian social democracy, despite superficial similarities in welfare outcomes. The 'Labourist' welfare states tend to have good minimum wage legislation, strong enforcement of health and safety at work, strong tenure in employment and relatively high wages, so that they achieve a measure of social equality without resort to redistributive state benefits.

A third variant of the regime framework emphasizes the religious and cultural basis of policy in many of the corporatist countries and dis-cusses Christian Democracy as a distinct variant of corporatism (Van Kersbergen, 1991). This approach is based on Catholic social tradition and in particular on two features of it – the emphasis on subsidiarity and on the support for the nuclear family (Spicker, 1991, p. 3). Subsidiarity as defined by Pope Pius XI (1931) ranks institutions in a hierarchy – family, community, employer and state – and argues that social action should be located as near the beginning of that hierarchy as possible. Only when such approaches have failed should policies at a more general level be pursued. The stress on a strong family policy in countries like the Netherlands, the involvement of a wide range of semi-autonomous organizations in the delivery of social and health care and the role of employers in pensions in Germany can be understood in this context. This approach helps to fill in the cultural background to some features of corporatism.

Regime theory, as discussed so far, applies only to Western capitalist countries. Explosive economic growth in Pacific Rim countries, especially Japan and the 'little tigers' (Hong Kong, Korea, Singapore, Taiwan) which have moved from less developed status to attain per capita GDPs at least equivalent to European countries in three decades, has focused attention on this area. Esping-Andersen refers briefly to 'the Confucian tradition of familialism with its care obligations' and the stresses it faces in urbanizing and developing societies in his work for the UN (1994a, p. 8). In his more recent edited work, Goodman and Peng stress that much Western discussion of Pacific Rim capitalism has been hampered by difficulties in obtaining high-quality information. It is misleading to see developments in this region through Western spectacles – as variants of Western regime types. Even the most highly developed Pacific Rim countries are low spenders by Western standards – Japan's state welfare spending as a proportion of GDP is about half the UK's and a third of Sweden's (Goodman and Peng, 1996, p. 207). However, it may be more appropriate to see the role of government as a regulator of welfare from family and private sources, rather than as a provider. Some estimates indicate that, when these factors are taken into account, East Asian welfare spending is more nearly equivalent to Western levels (Kwon, 1995).

The three main characteristics of Japanese welfare systems according to Goodman and Peng are 'a) a system of family welfare that appears to negate much of the need for state welfare; b) a status-segregated and somewhat residual social insurance based system and c) corporate occupational plans for "core" workers' (1996, p. 207). Most accounts trace similar patterns in Taiwan and Korea. In Singapore the place of social insurance is filled by compulsory savings through the Central Provident Fund and in Hong Kong social security is discretionary (Jones, 1993, pp. 206–7). Social spending is oriented towards investment in human capital through education and training schemes and in all the countries under consideration education is highly valued and extremely well-developed, as is appropriate in economies seeking to develop from a low base with relatively undeveloped home markets, so that high value-added export is essential to economic success. Housing and the quality of urban infrastructure are major issues and in Hong Kong, Singapore and Taiwan there are substantial state social housing programmes. Subsidized health care schemes are available in most of the countries.

Pacific Rim welfare is often understood as underpinned by the ideology of 'Confucianism'. This is a complex philosophy with varying interpretations in different societies. The key features for our purposes are: an overriding emphasis on family loyalty and responsibility and on the cohesion and hierarchical structure of the group, to which the individual is subordinate, but which provides a place for him or her; the importance of diligence, dutifulness and lack of complacency; and the significance of entrepreneurship and meritocracy (Goodman and Peng, 1996, pp. 195–6; Jones, 1993, pp. 199–201). This ideology points to a disciplined society amenable to central direction in which the family can function as a major provider of welfare and in which the meritocratic ethos militates against support for the unsuccessful.

In many ways this approach appears to offer an accurate description of East Asian welfare systems. Welfare provision has been subordinated to the goals of nation-building and of economic growth with considerable success. However recent developments lead to conflicts (Gould, 1993, p. 86). The most important are the sharp increase in the proportion of women in full-time employment, which creates stresses in the strict traditional family system, and the increase in the proportion of elderly people, which imposes strains on the family's ability to care for its dependent members. As Western pension systems find it hard to cope with an increase in the ratio of retired to working population so the ideal typical Confucian family finds an increase in elderly to young members a problem. These stresses have become evident in the economic crisis of 1998/9 in which the collapse of markets due to abrupt devaluation left family-based welfare unable to cope, leading to destitution and street homelessness on a substantial scale.

Good information on welfare in the most populous nation, China, is hard to obtain. However, such accounts as exist indicate that there are similarities to the capitalist Pacific Rim in the emphasis on family and particularly on enterprise-based provision, or 'workfare' which achieves relatively high levels of provision for most inhabitants despite scoring relatively low on measures of direct state welfare expenditure (Walker and Wong, 1996, pp. 87–8). The impact of the social changes consequent on the freeing of the market and on shifts in population structure are currently unclear.

## Shortcomings of the Regime Approach

The most influential strands in regime theory have been criticized on the grounds that they direct attention to particular issues of concern to Western capitalism (as Walker and Wong point out above) or that they are even more narrowly concerned with the struggles within Scandinavian social policy. An ingenious article by Kemeny points out that the central division in Esping-Andersen's regime theory and in the other approaches that have followed from it concerns the extent to which workers are able to escape commodification – the dominion of the power of capital (1995). The question is whether it is the political struggles of the working class themselves that are most significant in achieving this or a negotiated truce between labour and capital. The former is the essence of the social democratic account of the development of the welfare state, the latter the basis of the corporatist account. Kemeny points out that the split between social democracy and labour corporatism is the central tactical division that has faced Scandinavian labour movements during the past twenty years. Other arguments imply that it is necessary to broaden the whole scope of the analysis.

## Broader Approaches to Comparative Analysis

A number of writers have approached the problem of comparing welfare states from a feminist perspective. Three distinct stages in such work can be identified. In the first stage, a considerable quantity of careful empirical work demonstrated that the face the welfare state presents to women does not neatly fit into the categories developed by Esping-Andersen. Thus the extent to which welfare states give women rights over their own bodies in relation to abortion, childbirth and women's health issues does appear somewhat greater in the liberal regimes of the US and Canada, in line with their greater commitment to an individualistic free-market ideology. However, there are clear differences between the rights possessed in principle and those which different groups of individuals are able to exercise in practice, since these are countries in which abortion is expensive. Regime theory does not give a satisfactory account of women's experience in such welfare states (Shaver, 1992, pp. 35–6). An authoritative study by Cass reviews evidence on the gendered division of care-work for the 'liberal market societies of Britain, Australia and the US . . . the social democratic Scandinavian welfare states . . . and the (post) command economies of Eastern Europe'. The study shows that: 'in each case, the obligation to provide care, to take care of consumption work and to provide private welfare is closely related to employment status and types of employment activity . . . and to the capacity to participate fully in the politics of the state and the authority structures of the work-place' (Cass, 1990, pp. 1–2). The same pattern is reported in the studies reviewed by Milkman and Townsley (1994, pp. 605–6). There is no clear pattern of divisions corresponding to the divisions in market relationships that forms the basis of regime approaches.

The second stage in feminist approaches sought to propose alternative categorizations. A number of writers have argued that welfare states can be classified according to the emphasis on and support for differentiation in gender roles between male breadwinner and female dependant: thus the UK, Germany and the Netherlands are identified by Lewis (1993) as strong male breadwinner regimes, Sweden and Denmark have developed into weak male breadwinner regimes where women have achieved more equal status as breadwinners and receive compensation for their unpaid work as mothers and carers, and France falls into an intermediate category, because women have gained some entitlements as citizen mothers and citizen workers. Daly takes the argument further by suggesting that women are to be understood as occupying different social positions in relation to income distribution than men: state and market are the chief sources of support available to men, whereas women also receive support from men. Thus the risks of dependency are

greater for women and the question of the extent to which state benefits are available to substitute when other sources of support are denied
is crucial (Daly, 1993, p. 18).

The third stage in analysis draws these approaches together into a distinctively feminist analysis. A path-breaking article by Shola Orloff
(1993) attempts to identify the principal ways in which the welfare state
influences women's interests from both the power resources and the
institutionalist approaches. The result is an account of women's position
in relation to the social rights of citizenship that reproduces the strategy
of bridging the politics, structure and institutions developed by the
regime approach.

The tradition which led to regime theory suggested three main dimensions along which welfare citizenship varies in different welfare states –
state versus market, stratification and decommodification. A critical
examination of these categories from the perspective of gender relations
extends comparative analysis. In relation to the first, traditional analysis
focuses on the extent to which social policy encroaches on the role of
the market and allows resources to be allocated according to different
principles. Orloff also draws attention to the additional role of the family
and its interaction with both market and state mechanisms of distribution, in a way that parallels Daly's approach. Here the principal issues
are the extent to which women's unpaid but socially necessary work in
the home is recognized both as grounds for the acquisition of social rights
(for example waiving of pension contributions for housewives with
young children) and as an activity which requires a degree of support
in the way that formal waged labour is regulated; the availability of
women for employment as a result of the provision of child-care and
other services; the extent to which women have real choices between
waged and unwaged work; the extent to which equal opportunities provision expands opportunities in employment, education and training; and
the extent to which the state intervenes in the distribution of power
within the family, by, for example, dividing household benefits equally
rather than directing them to an assumed male breadwinner.

In relation to the second dimension, stratification, academics such as
Esping-Andersen have pointed out that the welfare state is not simply a
response to the class divisions of capitalist society but itself imposes a
structure of stratification through citizenship rights. Welfare has a corresponding impact on gender hierarchies and two processes are of particular importance: 'privileging full-time paid workers over workers who
do unpaid work or who combine part-time paid work with domestic and
caring labour, and reinforcing the sexual division of labour in which
women do the bulk of unpaid work' (Orloff, 1993, p. 314). Both processes
deserve attention and are not captured in traditional approaches to the
welfare state.

The third dimension of the power resources approach is decommodification. This requires a corresponding attention to the extent to which welfare guarantees women access to paid employment and services that enable them to balance home and work responsibilities. The position of women needs to be considered not only in relation to the role of government in reducing their dependence on market relations, but also in terms of its role in reducing their dependence on family relations, a corresponding process which might be described as 'defamilialization'. Orloff also identifies two aspects of welfare states that bear specifically on women's experience. These are: access to paid employment, which reduces women's dependency on men, and the capacity to form and maintain an autonomous household, which would involve secure incomes for women engaged in domestic work and caring for children.

Taken together, these five dimensions of welfare states provide the framework for a classification of provision in relation to women's interests. The key issues concern independence both from the market and from the family, and this adds a new dimension to comparative analysis.

Welfare citizenship has also been analysed from the viewpoint of ethnicity and nationhood. Social policy plays a role in securing social cohesion. For example, the reunification of Germany from 1989 onwards was accompanied by 'social union' which resulted in large short-term transfers from West to East and improved benefit standards for pensioners and others while the mechanisms supporting equal opportunities in employment for women (collective child and social care, training and equal pay) were eroded (Leisering and Leibfried, 1998, ch. 8). This reinforced the transfer of West German patterns of household and gender relations to the East.

Inclusion implies the possibility of exclusion and welfare also forms part of the apparatus for rationing rights on grounds that are implicitly or explicitly racist. The existence of different traditions of citizenship among EU member states (broadly speaking, the exclusive conception based on kin ties and typified by Germany, and the more inclusive, residence-based approach, typified by the French revolutionary ideal) provides a further source of tension (Turner, 1990, p. 209; Bussemaker and Voet, 1998). These issues are becoming more obvious as the EU becomes increasingly subject to migratory pressures on its Mediterranean and eastern borders. Analysis by Williams traces the different emphases on nationality in entitlement to welfare in the first third of the twentieth century in the USA, the UK, France and Germany, and suggests that current shifts towards a more globalized international economy are likely to impose further pressures on the relationship between citizenship and nation (Williams, 1995, pp. 150–3; Deacon, 1997, pp. 210–11). Citizenship and its limitation is a powerful determinant of individual access within particular welfare systems and contributes to the reinforcement of status differences. These issues direct attention to the role of political processes and the capacity to participate in them in determining welfare outcomes, which is discussed further below.

## Postmodern Welfare States

Postmodern approaches in social science vary according to the conception of modernity involved and the social changes which are seen as transcending it. The modern world, it is argued, involved notions of rationwality and order in science (the Enlightenment), economic life (rational accounting and modern capitalism), the moral order (the ideals of scientific socialism and of rationally ordered progress), in art and aesthetics (order, pattern and representation) and in the state (rational bureaucratic administration – Bauman, 1987).

For a number of reasons the ideals of modernism no longer carry the force that they once did. The experience of mechanized war, of ecological crisis and of the oppressiveness of urbanism devalues science as the vehicle of progress. Social idealism is undermined by the disasters of 'scientific socialism' and of a rational liberal market capitalism. The bureaucratic state can be as much an instrument of oppression or at least an apparatus that ignores the wishes of individuals as a channel of liberation. In short, modernity has outlived its appeal. The traditional welfare state, as the application of a rational social science to the solution of the social problems thrown up by modernity, is modernism in practice, and has a strong interest in the view that the world-view on which it rests is obsolete.

The impact of this approach on social policy is twofold. First, it renders suspect the prioritizing of particular needs. The comparative tradition stressed social class inequality as the central axis of redistribution and social class forces as the primary motor of change, whether through democratic or revolutionary class struggle. Increasingly, other dimensions of inequality have gained attention – gender, disability, sexuality, age and ethnicity (Williams, 1992, p. 214), and also region and area of residence. Since there is no way to place these dimensions in a hierarchy, all must be taken equally seriously, so that the interests of the subject fragment.

The second issue to emerge from postmodernist social science concerns social cohesion – the glue that cements conflicting interests in market capitalism. If the world is irredeemably plural, it is of central importance to take seriously what all individuals think. The idea of democracy involves difficult problems since free expression, articulacy and access to the means and media to press home a point are unequally distributed (Doyal and Gough, 1991, pp. 120–2). The most profound attempt to resolve this problem lies in Habermas's concept of an ideal speech situation in which undistorted communication might be possible (Habermas, 1970, p. 372). However, practical arguments about how to realize such a situation are unconvincing and it remains simply a theoretical possibility. The postmodern world requires greater attention to what people say they want and what people say they do not want, and wider distribution of access to the means to attain it. From the perspective of comparative social policy, it is further reinforcement to the idea that welfare needs are plural and possibly mixed in different proportions in different countries, so that the slotting of welfare states into neat categories is difficult. The evolution of welfare states, and in particular the differences in trajectory between individual welfare states, requires serious theoretical attention.

The relevance of the postmodern critique is highly controversial (see Taylor-Gooby, 1994, 1997 for discussion). While policy debates are undoubtedly becoming more plural and it is hard to justify limiting the factors responsible for the development of welfare states simply to conflict between the working class and capital, there are also important structural forces shaping developments across nations. Some writers argue that postmodernism is simply an ideological smokescreen that disguises the growing power of capital in world markets (Callinicos, 1989). Others suggest that, while many of the dislocating processes identified by this approach are real at the level of people's experience, the forces that created the oppressions and opportunities of the modern world remain dominant. What remains is a hybrid 'high modern' society in which future directions are uncertain (Giddens, 1990).

## The Current Context

The most obvious feature of the international social policy climate at the turn of the century is retrenchment. In the thirty or so years after the Second World War, welfare programmes expanded in almost all advanced industrial countries, in some cases from a relatively low base. One authoritative study, published in the mid-1980s, summed up the general pattern as 'growth to limits' (Flora, 1986). Since the oil crisis of the 1970s and the recessionary shocks of 1980/1, 1991/2 and 1998/9, confidence in the desirability of further expansion in public programmes has been dealt a severe blow. Further pressures on government welfare spending arise from two factors: the growing realization that cheaper communications and the collapse of the barriers dividing much of the second and the first worlds are leading to rapid growth in world trade and international competition, and the commitment to the market model of international politico-economic relations enshrined in the policies of the EU and associations such as the North American Free Trade Area, and, more generally, in the 1993 Uruguay Round of the GATT treaty and the World Trade Organization. The first factor is often understood to demand retrenchment on the grounds that high levels of welfare spending constitute a burden not shared by competitors, especially in the newly industrialized world, although it is equally possible that spening in particular areas (and the most widely canvassed are education and training) may help improve the competitive position of a country (Atkinson, 1995; Esping-Andersen, 1994b; Pfaller, Gough and Therborn, 1991). The second restricts the freedom of government to act in ways that resist competitive pressures. The climate surrounding policy-making is thus generally understood to be one of retrenchment. The question arises of whether the comparative social policy frameworks developed to explain the growth of the welfare state are appropriate to deal with the new circumstances.

Pierson argues that the politics of welfare retrenchment are qualitatively different from those of expansion for two kinds of reason. First, the goals of policy-makers have shifted. Secondly there are changes in the context in which they operate (Pierson, 1996, p. 144). A shift in goals demands a new approach to welfare politics: 'retrenchment is generally an exercise in blame avoidance rather than credit claiming, primarily because the costs of retrenchment are concentrated (and often immediate) while the benefits are not' (1996, p. 145).

The groups which lose through the curtailment of programmes are likely to be better organized and informed than the diffuse generality of taxpayers who might benefit from lower taxes. At the same time there is some social psychological evidence that the pains of the loss of a given amount of welfare are more keenly felt than the addition of an equal welfare gain – so politicians lose more public esteem by inflicting cuts than they previously gained from a corresponding programme expansion. Very large numbers of individuals see themselves as current or potential beneficiaries from welfare programmes either as recipients of pensions, sickness, family and unemployment benefits, or as employees in health and social care services (up to half the adult population in some countries according to Flora – 1986, p. 154). Cut-backs as deliberate departures from previous policy are likely to be salient and well-publicized.

For these reasons the politics of retrenchment differ from those of expansion and cannot be understood in terms of the factors stressed in traditional theoretical approaches – the logic of industrialism, the power resources of labour and capital, the influence of regime type or the specification of men as independent breadwinners and women as dependent carers. The conclusion that organized labour is not important may result in part from the empirical focus on the UK and the USA where unions are weak. Elsewhere, for example in France and Germany, trade union struggle has had considerable impact in modifying proposals for reform in recent years. Nonetheless, current circumstances set a new agenda for policy-making and the influence of organizations like unions is severely curtailed compared to what it had previously been. Pierson argues that success in retrenchment can best be explained in terms of situational political factors, particularly the 'electoral slack' of the government (likely to be greatest in first-past-the-post constitutions which favour strong majorities), the skill with which politicians exploit budgetary crisis, the extent to which advocates of retrenchment can lower the visibility of reforms and the possibility of changing institutional structures to facilitate the process. For example, reforms can now be presented as required by an external agency such as the EU. The implication of this argument is that the grand theories of welfare policy are no longer appropriate – welfare development cannot simply be explained in terms of overarching features of society, such as class structure, or the pattern of service provision. Analysts must look much more closely at the detail of political arrangements and how they bear on policy-making. In short, the politics of welfare and the political processes which embody them deserve more attention.

## Welfare, Political Institutions and the Policy-making Process

One of the leading influences on the analysis of political structures and their role in policy-making in Western capitalist countries is the work of Lijphart (1984). In a path-breaking analysis of policy-making procedures in twenty-one industrialized democracies, he argues that governmental apparatuses may be understood as ranged along a spectrum from 'majoritarian' (in which the interests of the majority have the determining influence on policy) to 'consensus' (policy-making attempts to embrace the wishes of as many people as possible). In his work, the distinction is operationalized in an eclectic manner. The majoritarian ('Westminster') model of government is characterized by strong dominance of cabinet over parliament, bare majority voting, asymmetric bicameralism, a two-party system divided between left and right, first-past-the-post voting, unitary and centralized government, an unwritten constitution and the absence of referenda (1984, pp. 6–9). All these features magnify the power of the majority, or at least the party forming the government, over policy-making. In the consensus model, on the other hand, there is a tendency to 'over-sized' coalition (coalitions including more parties than is necessary to achieve a simple majority), a strong separation between legislative and executive powers, balanced bicameralism, with minority representation, a multi-party system, often split on multi-dimensional lines (for example, religion, ethnicity, region or language), proportional representation, federalism, a written constitution and a minority veto. All these features tend to allow minorities to exert an influence on policy-making and to characterize government as an inclusive rather than an exclusive activity.

Lijphart's approach captures much of the apparent differences in policy-making in European countries, and in particular the way in which the Westminster model appears to permit relatively rapid shifts in response to pressures for retrenchment while much less substantial shifts in policy take place more slowly in some of the main Continental powers. However, its eclectic approach and its focus on the formal apparatus of policy-making mean that the influence of interests which do not present themselves as formally organized political parties is not given sufficient attention. In a number of countries (for example, Germany and Switzerland) the corporate interests of capital, employers and of organized labour exert a strong influence on policy-making outside the formal political structure.

In a later article, Lijphart tackles this problem by drawing together the work of other authors and analysing empirical evidence to support the argument that 'corporatism is the interest group system that goes together with the consensual type of democracy, and that its opposite, the "pluralist" interest group system, goes together with majoritarian democracy' (Lijphart and Crepaz, 1991, p. 235). This approach establishes a direct link between the structure of interests in civil society and the opportunities for their expression available through political institutions. The link, however, appears to be complex, and subject to feedback in a way that is analogous to Skocpol and Amenta's analysis (1986) of how the development of particular policies tends to foster the growth of supporting social interests mentioned above. Institutions nourish the evolution of the interest groups that are most successful in achieving the objects of their members within a particular institutional structure, so that it is no surprise that we encounter particular and appropriate patterns of interest formation under different systems of government. This is brought out clearly in an impressive and detailed study of policy-making in the field of medical services by Immergut.

This study examines how approaches to health care have developed in three countries with very different opportunities for interest groups to influence policy-making. In Switzerland the possibility of referenda (which often produce negative results) gives an organized interest the possibility of blocking any proposal for change. In France, particularly under the Third and Fourth Republics, the complexity of government coalitions made the pursuit of new policy departures difficult. Any proposal for change ran the risk of prompting one or other group to defect. In Sweden the strength of the executive arm of government allows it to achieve radical change if it wishes. The study argues that the key features of medical provision in these countries (the development of a nationalized health service against the wishes of doctors in Sweden, the weakness of state control of doctors in France, resulting in the highest medical spending in Europe, and the failure of attempts to set up a social insurance health care system in Switzerland) can all be attributed to these differences in institutional context. Doctors' interest groups have developed in different ways in the different countries, being relatively weak in Sweden, influential to the extent of playing a major role in the administration of medicine financed through the state-backed system of social insurance in France and becoming a strong, cohesive, defensive interest group in Switzerland.

Different political arrangements give different opportunities to pursue and to oppose changes, which leads to different outcomes. In general

> political institutions do not neutrally transmit demands or merely ratify agreements previously worked out through pre-parliamentary interest-group bargains. Specific institutional configurations establish strategic contexts for political contests that determine those interests that can be effectively expressed and which ones will prevail . . . political institutions help to shape the definition of interests and their expression in politics. (Immergut, 1992, p. 5)

One influential approach to the explanation of the relative economic success of many of the smaller European nations (Denmark, Austria, Sweden, the Netherlands, and now, perhaps, the Czech Republic) is that their openness to world markets and their consequent economic vulnerability, which is felt at the level of government, of the firm and of organized labour, fosters the development of civil society institutions and of tight corporatist links between them and government that enable the efficient production and, most important, sustained execution of policy (Katzenstein, 1985). In a different context, the success of the Pacific Rim countries discussed earlier may be understood in terms of the way in which Confucianism legitimates a corresponding social and institutional discipline.

Similar arguments have led other commentators to suggest that the range of appropriate decision-making structures in modern Western nations is broadening. The difficulties of legitimating decisions when there is growing diversity of increasingly well-informed social interests suggest that, in addition to state, family and community, private interest associations may now be appropriate negotiating agencies in some contexts. However, the level which is appropriate to the exploration of possible solutions to a particular issue is very much a situational matter: 'the idea of a comprehensive corporative-associative social or political "system" is therefore fundamentally misleading . . . there is growing evidence that there is a certain range of policy areas for which institutions of group self-regulation may produce more socially adjusted and normatively acceptable results than either communal self-help, free trade or *étatisme*' (Streeck and Schmitter, 1995, p. 28). Which is appropriate is a matter for 'empirical research and reflection'.

The influence of private interest groups alongside national governments through lobbying at the level of the EU is also considerable. Examples of the significance of organized interest groups in lobbying are the Common Agricultural Policy (Streeck and Schmitter, 1991, p. 159), the development of interest 'cartels' in social policy (Room, 1994), the acquiescence in opt-outs to the Social Chapter of the Maastricht Treaty and the dilution of the EU's social policy from Green Paper to White Paper to Action Plan, so that the final stress is on consultation and information-sharing rather than innovation (CEC, 1996).

This brief review of discussion of the links between formal political arrangements and the private interests of civil society indicates that informal interests exert an important influence on policy-making. However, the way in which they organize and relate to government differs within different political institutional structures. The links are complex, and involve mutual feedback – political institutions influence the evolution of civil society and are themselves influenced by it. It is this complexity that has led to the difficulties in defining concepts such as 'corporatism' and the variety of definitions in use (Lehmbruch, 1982, pp. 2, 16–25). There is some suggestion that private institutions are of growing importance in a more complex world and one that is less firmly under the control of the nation state. The detail of the relation between formal political structure and informal institutional framework is very much an empirical matter. As Immergut puts it: 'political decisions emerge from highly complex combinations of factors that include both systematic features of political regimes and "accidents of the struggle for power"' (1998, p. 26; see also Hall and Taylor, 1996). Any approach to welfare policy-making must take seriously the role of corporate interests, and the way that this interacts with constitutional arrangements, political parties and the formal power structure of government, but cannot expect to read the relationship off from an *a priori* theory.

## Conclusion

Over the period reviewed, comparative social policy analysis has responded to two main forces. First, the various social science disciplines have staked their several claims to offer the royal road to understanding. Secondly, the changing climate of policy-making has exerted its own pressure on theory. The success with which the different approaches have advanced their individual claims means that any theoretical understanding must rely on a multi-disciplinary analysis, in order to grasp the importance of international economic forces expressed through the globalization of markets, the social structures that lead to interests in relation to welfare being recognized by different groups in different ways and the different capacities and opportunities to respond to them offered in different political systems both at a formal and an informal level.

The changing international political context implies that the approaches that have been successful at giving accounts of the expansion of welfare states are less likely to be successful at explaining retrenchment, since changes in external pressures and in the way interests are recognized and are able to express themselves are likely to lead to alignments in patterns of policy-making which differ from those recognized in current regime theories. The regime approach gives strong accounts of stability, and in particular of the differentiation of the welfare state in the post-war period of secure expansion. It is less successful at predicting the different trajectories pursued by welfare states responding to the pressures of expenditure containment and retrenchment. This is the challenge for contemporary approaches to comparative social policy analysis, which must include analysis of both the detail of public policy development and the role played by the decision-making structures, coalitions and interest groups of civil society.

# 2
# New Directions in European Welfare Policy: From Decommodification to Recommodification

The 1980s marked a watershed in social policy-making. During the previous three decades government intervention was generally geared towards improving the coverage of the public's needs by expanding existing programmes or by introducing new ones. Since then the overall direction of policy has generally been towards cost containment and often retrenchment. The change of direction took place first in English-speaking countries, the UK, the USA, Australia and New Zealand. Continental Europe and Scandinavia, until the early 1990s, had been largely spared retrenchment efforts. In fact, countries like France, Germany and Sweden kept on expanding their welfare states until the late 1980s. Serious cuts were adopted only as a consequence of the recession of the 1990s.

This situation is poorly reflected by most quantitative indicators. The most commonly used measure of welfare effort, social expenditure as a proportion of GDP, has not declined over the last few years, despite substantial cuts adopted by most governments (see chapter 6, table 6.1). As mentioned previously, this is partly due to the expansion of the population in receipt of benefits and services, as a result of demographic change, to rising health care costs, and to the fact that many of the retrenchment initiatives adopted can be phased in only slowly. This applies in particular to pension reforms which will only start affecting public budgets in some ten or twenty years.

Retrenchment is difficult to measure. If we want to gain some insight into what has been happening to welfare states during the last few years, we need to look at the legislative changes adopted in individual countries and assess the likely implications for the coverage, level and quality of welfare provision. This chapter tries to draw up a picture of the key social policy changes in some major European welfare states. It is based on information collected by the OECD (Kalisch et al., 1998) as well as on conference papers, which provide the most up-to-date information on a rapidly changing subject matter. The chapter concentrates on the core social policy areas of old age pensions, health care and unemployment compensation but also looks at developments in other areas. In the final part we try to assess what the implications of these changes are for social policy. Have the functions of the welfare state been undermined by the recent wave of retrenchment? Are we seeing a dismantling of the post-war social contract? These are some of the questions we will try to deal with.

## Old Age Pensions

Old age pensions stand out among the various areas of welfare state activity as one which has been subjected to strong pressures in recent years. First, pensions are the most costly single item in governments' social budgets. As a result pensions are likely candidates for the saving initiatives which characterize the current era of austerity. Secondly, expenditure on pensions is related to the age structure of the population. The expected increase in the proportion of older people, a development which will affect virtually all European countries, puts additional pressure on policy-makers to achieve savings in the area of pensions.

The twin pressures of budget balancing and demographic ageing have already had an impact on pension policy. Virtually every country in Europe has taken some steps towards reducing state expenditure on old age pensions (Taylor-Gooby, 1999; Myles and Quadagno, 1997; Kalisch et al., 1998). In the 1980s, and even more so in the 1990s, the direction of change in pension policy has reverted from overall expansion to retrenchment. As a result, in the current situation, the term pension reform is increasingly used as a synonym for cuts in old age pensions.

Pension reforms have taken various shapes in different countries. Besides their common objective, which is the achievement of savings or the containment of rising expenditure, there is little similarity among the measures taken. On occasions, governments have adopted highly visible, straight cuts in the level of benefits. This has been the case, for example, in the UK's 1986 reform, and to some extent in the German 1999 reform. In both instances, change has been controversial and cuts have had to be imposed in the face of strong opposition.

In general, however, governments have shown a preference for 'low visibility' reforms, which can be seen as part of a 'strategy of obfuscation' (Pierson, 1994, pp. 19–22). Examples are changes in the indexation of benefits which have little impact in the short term, but (as in the case of the UK's basic pension) can result in substantial reductions in the replacement rate of a benefit over the long term (Atkinson, 1994). Complex changes in the method of calculation of benefits have also resulted in lower benefits, without being easily identifiable as retrenchment. Italy and Sweden, for instance, have both shifted from a defined benefit to a defined contribution system, a change whose implications are far from easy to assess for non-specialists. These reforms are discussed in more detail below.

*The UK*

Britain was the first major European country to adopt new pension legislation with a view to reducing the level of state intervention in provision for retirement. The British pension system was transformed as a result of two important policy decisions which affected the basic pension and the second tier of provision respectively. In the early 1980s the Thatcher government decided to shift the indexation of pensions from earnings or inflation (whichever was higher) to inflation only. The impact of this measure was limited in the short run but in the long term it constitutes a serious reduction in the significance of the scheme. According to Atkinson (1994), the value of the basic pension expressed as a proportion of average income has declined from 32 per cent in 1983 to 22 per cent in 1993. Moreover, the relative value of the pension is expected to decline further in the future, and, in Glennerster's words, 'become an irrelevance and . . . be abolished' (1995, p. 182).

The second important change was adopted in 1986, as part of the 'Fowler Reviews' of the UK's social security system. The value of the State Earnings Related Pension Scheme (known as SERPS) was cut by a change in the formula. The benefit, instead of being calculated as the 25 per cent of the best twenty years of earnings, was to be scaled down to 20 per cent of lifetime earnings. At the same time employees were encouraged through tax reliefs and contribution rebates to opt out from SERPS (and from occupational pensions, for those who had one) and buy an individual personal pension. The key result of these changes has been an overall reduction in the level of state provision for retirement and an important expansion in the role of the private sector. By 1993 some five million employees had left SERPS and moved into private pensions.

To a large extent as a result of these changes, the UK is one of the few industrial countries which does not have a financing problem of public pensions due to population ageing (OECD, 1995a). Instead, the key issue in pension policy now is the lack of adequate coverage for those on low incomes, whose earnings are insufficient to make it worth buying a personal pension, and find the reduced levels of state provision inadequate (Nesbitt, 1995; Waine, 1995).

*Italy*

For much of the post-war period, Italy has had one of the most generous pension systems in Europe. Before the 1990s, the statutory age of retirement was among the lowest in the continent, at fifty-five for women and sixty for men. In addition, Italians were able to retire at any age if they had paid contributions for thirty-five years with a pension equal to 70 per cent of average salary over the last five years. For civil servants, only twenty contribution-years were enough for a full pension. Obviously, such a generous system proved extremely costly for the public purse, and as the government budget deficit reached worrying proportions in the early 1990s it became clear that cuts in the area of pensions were needed.

The system was reformed in two stages. First, in 1992, the statutory age of retirement was increased to sixty for women and sixty-five for men; the reference period was to be extended from the last five years to the last ten years (and to lifetime earnings for those who started working after the adoption of the reform). Finally, early retirement based on twenty contribution years for civil servants was abolished (the period was extended to thirty-five years, as for private sector employees). All these measures were not enforced immediately, but were meant to be phased in over a fairly long period, with some of the measures becoming fully effective only in 2002 (Ferrera, 1997a, 1997b). The 1992 reform introduced further cost containment measures, which did not impact on public spending in the following years because of the long phasing-in period. Even with all the measures in place, Italian pensions remain among the most generous in Europe.

That is why pension reform came back on the political agenda towards the mid-1990s. In 1995 a politically difficult reform was adopted with the support of the trade unions (Reynaud and Hedge, 1996). On this occasion, change was more radical. The key modification was a shift from a defined-benefit system, where benefits are expressed as a proportion of earnings over a given number of years, to a defined-contribution system. Benefits now depend on the total amount of contributions paid by workers. Upon retirement, this is converted into an annuity whose value depends on the age of the person, on how the country's economy is performing and on the number of pensioners. The last two adjustments are meant to allow the government to keep pension expenditure under control. The system remains financed on a pay-as-you-go basis, which means that the shift to defined contributions is *de facto* fictitious.

A number of other features of the old system were also changed. First, the notion of a statutory age of retirement has been abandoned, and employees are now able to retire between fifty-seven and sixty-five years of age, with more or less generous benefits according to age. The option of retiring after thirty-five contribution-years has been maintained until 2008, but with the additional requirement that the claimant must be at least fifty-seven years old (Ferrera, 1997a, 1997b; Artoni and Zanardi, 1996).

The 1995 reform has introduced an element of uncertainty in pension policy due to the fact that benefits can now, in theory at least, fall to very low levels. Italy has one of the lowest birth rates in Western Europe, and since the value of the pension will depend on demographic developments the result may well be a significant reduction in the level of state pensions.

## Sweden

Minor changes to the pension system were introduced in the early 1990s (OECD, 1994c, pp. 95–6). It was not, however, until 1994 that a major reform was implemented with support from all political parties. The reform was also based on a fictitious defined-contribution principle. The earnings-related component of the Swedish pension system, known as ATP, was modified in 1994. Under the new legislation, the pension is to be based on lifetime contributions re-valued according to changes in real wages, and calculated on the basis of the life expectancy of the relevant cohort. These measures are supposed to mitigate the impact of ageing on pension expenditure. As a result of the change, the amount of the standard pension is expected to decline from 65 per cent to 60 per cent of gross earnings. The reform has also introduced a funded element in the system. Contributions, which amount to 18.5 per cent of gross earnings, are split between a pay-as-you-go scheme (16.5 per cent) and a new funded scheme (2 per cent), which, according to current projections, should compensate employees for the reduction of the standard benefit (Stahlberg, 1997; Palme and Wennemo, 1997).

Many of the parameters that will determine the value of pension benefits in the future, like life expectancy, wage growth and returns on capital for the 2 per cent contribution to a funded scheme are not known at present. As a result it is not possible to ascertain whether the Swedish reform constitutes an instance of retrenchment, expansion or simply continuity. The new scheme was designed so as to deliver the same benefits that are paid today, if demographic and economic developments follow the central government projection. If they do not, future benefits could be lower or higher than at present. However, the most significant change implied by the Swedish (and Italian) reforms is that employees have lost some of the security in their pension entitlements that was guaranteed under the previous system.


*France*

In France the 1980s have seen a growing concern over the issue of financing pensions. Between 1985 and 1993 a series of government-mandated reports were published. All of them took a rather pessimistic view of the future of pension policy in France, and called for saving measures to be adopted. The reform of pension, though, was widely perceived as a politically sensitive issue, so that throughout the 1980s governments of the left and of the right tended to procrastinate. It was only in 1993 that the newly elected right-wing government managed to adopt a reform of the main basic pension scheme, covering private sector employees. This was made possible by a carefully designed reform package, which included both cuts and concessions to the trade unions with regard to their role in the management and control over pensions (Bonoli, 1997).

The changes adopted in 1993 fall under three categories. First, a 'Fonds de solidarité vieillesse' has been created, which has the task of funding non-contributory benefits. Secondly, the qualifying period for a full pension is extended from thirty-seven and a half to forty years and the period over which the reference salary is calculated is extended from the best ten years to the best twenty-five years. These are being introduced gradually over a ten-year transition period. Finally, the indexation of benefits is based on prices (as opposed to earnings) for a five-year period (Ruellan, 1993, p. 919).

In the long term, the impact of the reform on pension expenditure could be quite substantial. According to projections by the administration of the old age insurance scheme (CNAV), contribution rates in 2010 would have had to be increased by around 10 percentage points if the 1993 reform had not taken place. This figure is expected to fall to between 2.73 and 7.26 percentage points after the reform, if indexation according to prices is maintained. The 1993 reform will also have an impact on the amount of pensions and on the actual age of retirement. Because the qualifying period has been extended to forty years, it is expected that some employees will delay their retirement in order to receive a full pension despite the reform. The extension of the period over which the reference salary is calculated will have an impact on the level of pensions. The impact of this measure is a reduction in benefits by 7 to 8 per cent for high salaries, but does not affect those on the minimum wage, as they receive the minimum pension ('minimum vieillesse'), which has not been modified by the reform (Ruellan, 1993, p. 922).

In 1995, the Juppé government attempted to extend these measures to the pension schemes of public sector employees. This measure was kept secret with no negotiation with the trade unions. The result was a massive protest movement, led by a rail workers' strike, which forced the government to abandon its plans (Bonoli and Palier, 1996; Bonoli, 1997). Finally, in 1997, a new law was adopted to encourage through fiscal incentives the introduction of pension funds at the company level. These are meant to supplement existing state provision, and not to be alternatives to it.

## Germany

Finally, Germany has also reformed its pension system twice in the 1990s. First, the *Rentenreform 1992* (designated by the year it came into force) was explicitly designed to respond to the expected increase in pension expenditure due to population ageing. The main changes were a shift in the indexation of pensions from gross earnings to net earnings and an increase in the cost of early retirement for the worker. The change in indexation was seen as introducing an element of self-regulation in pension expenditure: under the post-1992 system, if contributions are increased to finance increased pension expenditure, this will reduce net earnings and as a result pension payments. The goal is to achieve an equitable share between workers and retirees in bearing the cost of population ageing.

Early retirement had become a common practice in Germany. Only a minority of workers waited until the statutory retirement age, which in the pre-1992 system was set at sixty-five and sixty for men and women respectively, to quit the labour market. The rules concerning early retirement were particularly generous, as they took into account only the missing contribution-years and not the longer period for which a pension needs to be paid. As a result of the 1992 reform, the cost of early retirement has been increased, though it is still lower than it would be if actuarially determined. The pension is reduced by 0.3 per cent per month of anticipation. The statutory age of retirement of men and women has been equalized at sixty-five, though this will occur over a fairly long transition period to be completed in 2012 (Schmähl, 1993).

The 1992 reform was adopted by the Christian Democrat government with the support of the Social Democrats and the trade unions. At that time it was felt that the pension problem had been dealt with, for a few years at least. However, towards the mid-1990s, amidst concern for rising rates of unemployment, an ambitious reform programme was launched, with the intention of creating a more favourable environment for job creation, particularly by reducing social insurance contributions. Initially, this programme was to be carried out in a characteristically German consensual manner: negotiating change with the Social Democrats and the trade unions and employers. However, after the left, worried by the overall direction of reform, abandoned the negotiations, the government decided to go ahead on its own. As part of the first set of measures, adopted in 1996, the phasing in of the retrenchment measures agreed in the 1992 pension reform was accelerated: instead of 2012, the transition will be completed by 2004.

The most significant changes, however, were passed in 1997, as part of the *Rentenreform 1999*. The most important, and controversial measure, was certainly the introduction of a 'demographic weighting' of pension benefits. Basically, if life expectancy increases, benefits are reduced so as to counter the effect of demographic pressures. This will affect both new benefits, via changes in the formula, and benefits already in payment, via indexation. On the basis of current demographic projections, it is expected that the standard replacement rate will be gradually lowered from 70 to 64 per cent of average earnings. This measure was adopted against the Social Democrats, then in opposition. At the time, their policy was to reverse this part of the reform.

Other measures introduced in the *Rentenreform 1999* were less controversial, and included an increase of the federal subsidy to the pension scheme (paid for by a 1 percentage point increase in VAT) and the improvement of contribution credits paid to those with caring responsibilities. The earnings basis of the credit was increased from 75 to 100 per cent of the average salary, and the credit will not be reduced if the carer is involved in paid work (Hinrichs, 1998).

Pension systems are being reformed virtually everywhere. Change is seldom path-breaking, but consists mainly of adjustments in the various parameters that define the level of benefits. In most cases, the measures adopted have a fairly long phasing in period, sometimes up to twenty years, which means that the full effects of reform will not be felt until well into the next century. For some countries, where the pension formula has been adapted so as to reflect economic and demographic developments, the effects of policy change will not be known until the reform is fully implemented. Pension trends, thus, are mixed. On the one hand, there have been cuts in the level of benefits, on the other, there has been an increase in the uncertainty associated with pension provision.

# Health Care

Together with pensions, health care is also an area of social policy in which there is concern with the issue of cost. Health expenditure is related to the age structure of the population, since health care consumption increases with age. As the proportion of older people is projected to rise over the next few decades in virtually all Western countries, governments expect significant increases in the demand, and hence in the cost, of health care. In addition, health care is subject to other financial pressures. Demands for better care by patients and technological advances that make new, and generally expensive, drugs and treatments available are trends that are likely to contribute to push up health expenditure.

Virtually all European countries have been responding to these pressures for some years now. Broadly speaking, the direction of policy change can be summarized under three headings: measures that encourage a more efficient use of resources; measures that control the price of services and drugs as well as their volume; and measures which transfer some of the cost of health care to patients (user charges or co-payments). In their review of recent developments in health care policy, Kalisch et al. (1998) found that OECD countries adopted these measures in various combinations. The study shows that, with the exception of increases in user charges, these measures do not necessarily result in lower quality or extent of health care coverage. In practice, however, there are limits to the feasibility of efficiency gains, so that beyond a certain point measures designed to increase efficiency can result in a lower quality of service.

Financial pressures on health care systems exist in virtually all advanced industrial countries. However, the sort of problem generated by such pressures can be substantially different depending on the institutional design of a health care system. In general, countries which rely on a state-controlled, mainly tax-financed system (UK, Nordic countries, southern European countries) have been better able to control the rise in health expenditure over the last few years. In these countries, the key problem in health care is not so much the increase in expenditure, which can be controlled by budget capping, but the inability of the system to meet patients' demands with limited resources. This leads to such outcomes as long waiting lists and the introduction of other rationing devices.

In contrast, in countries like Germany or France where health care is provided by self-employed doctors, with a mix of public and private hospitals, and is paid for by a national health insurance scheme, the government has had more problems in controlling health expenditure. Until the recent reforms, in these countries the level of expenditure was determined by demand for health care, with little or no mechanisms to control it. As a result, in these countries, there are generally no waiting lists, but individuals are asked to contribute more to the financing of health care through increases in contributions or user charges (Jobert and Steffen, 1994).

Similar socio-economic trends (ageing, rising expectations, and so on) are translated into different problems by different institutional arrangements. As a result, the solutions that governments develop to deal with these problems are also likely to be related to the institutional design of a country's health care system. In a state-controlled system, the main challenge facing policy-makers is to increase efficiency so that demands can be met with a limited amount of resources available. In contrast, what is needed in an insurance-based system is an effective strategy for cost containment.

## State-controlled systems

Recent developments in heath policy confirm this view. In Britain, for instance, tight control over the National Health Service budget during the 1980s meant that the pressures for increases in health spending were resisted relatively successfully. However, the result was what has been termed 'underfunding'. The consequences of that were increasing numbers of patients being forced on to waiting lists. The number of individuals awaiting hospital treatment increased from 622,000 in 1982 to 915,000 in 1992 (Holliday, 1992, p. 31).

The response of the government to the funding crisis of the NHS was to increase the funds available, but also, with the 1990 reform, to introduce an internal market in the system designed to introduce market mechanisms into the operation of the NHS. The cornerstone of the reform is a split between purchasers and providers of health care. General practitioners can elect to become purchasers of services for their patients and, with a fixed budget, shop around and get the best deal from a variety of competing hospitals and consultants (Klein, 1995). The Labour government, which came to power in 1997, has confirmed its intention to stick to the purchaser–provider distinction in the delivery of health care. However, the purchase of services will not be up to individual practitioners, but will be made by a 'Primary Care Group', an institution which will buy services for all patients resident in a given area. This measure can be seen as a response to concerns about the possible development of a two-tier system under the regulations previously in force (Powell, 1998).

In Italy, during the 1980s, the main instrument for containing health care expenditure was the imposition of spending ceilings on the health service by the central government. The annual budget bill was used to assign a limited health care budget to the regions, and to determine the amount of user charges payable by patients. The savings in public funds thus achieved were made good by increases in user charges, or cuts in services. For instance, co-payments on drugs, which were virtually non-existent at the beginning of the 1980s, had reached 30 per cent by 1989. Other areas of health care (medical tests, consultation of specialists) also saw an increase in the amount charged to service users. The strategy proved successful in stabilizing health expenditure for a while, but was undermined by a rather generous exemption policy on user charges, which being moreover not strictly enforced, allowed increasingly large numbers of patients to have access to free treatment. The shifting of health expenditure from the state to patients was a cost containment strategy which had its own limits (Ferrera, 1997a, 1997b).

More fundamental change was introduced with the 1992 health reform. On that occasion, local health units were given more autonomy and *de facto* converted into public enterprises. They are now run by a general manager (instead of a committee of political appointees, as was the case prior to the reform) on a five-year contract, renewable subject to performance. Hospitals can opt out of health authority control and become independent providers of health services. The new system aims at introducing an incentive structure for health care professionals which will make them more responsive to patients' needs and which will reward cost containment (Ferrera, 1997a, 1997b).

Sweden has also developed an internal market in its public health care system where the counties receive block grants based on the socio-demographic characteristics of their population and purchase services for them. The Swedish internal market is particularly far-reaching, as it covers 'space', with a system of internal rents, and lending, with an internal bank. Like Britain, Sweden has been struggling to get to grips with the waiting list problem. A major step in that direction was taken in 1991, with the introduction of a 'maximum waiting-time guarantee', which entitles patients awaiting an operation in a number of areas to be treated within three months. If the hospital responsible for the operation is unable to respect the three-months deadline, it has to buy the service elsewhere, from another state hospital or the private sector. After the introduction of the guarantee only a few hospitals were not able to provide treatment within three months (Jönsson, 1996).

## Insurance-based systems

A different course has been taken by reforms in countries with insurance-based health care systems. In France the traditional approach to rising health expenditure has been to increase the rate of contributions so as to bring more resources into the system. At the same time, given the demand-led character of health expenditure in insurance-based systems, efforts have been directed at moderating the pressure from service users. This has been done by introducing, and subsequently increasing, a user charge, known as *ticket modérateur*, on most drugs and treatments. This measure, however, succeeded in containing expenditure only temporarily. As a result, in the 1990s the emphasis has been moved towards spending capping and reducing the level of medical consumption which is believed to be excessive and to include substantial amounts of waste (Letourmy, 1994). In 1990 providers, insurance funds and the government reached agreement on a *convention médicale* which established spending targets. This strategy was strengthened in 1995 by the introduction of a government power to adopt sanctions against providers if the spending targets are not respected (Bonoli and Palier, 1998).

Germany followed a similar path, with the adoption of two major health care reforms in the space of only four years in the late 1980s/early 1990s. The 1989 reform increased the level and the scope of user charges. The objective, as with the French *ticket modérateur*, was primarily to induce cost-awareness among patients. More ambitious proposals, which included direct control over health expenditure, were abandoned after the opposition of health care providers. The effect of the 1989 reform was short-lived. Total expenditure on health declined by 4.4 per cent in 1989, but increased by 6.9 per cent and 10.5 per cent in 1990 and 1991 respectively (Hassenteufel, 1994). This prompted policy-makers to re-open the debate on health care. The resulting 1993 reform included more far-reaching provision. First, it temporarily froze payments to providers at the 1991 level, and introduced a rule whereby, if the volume of services and prescriptions exceeds a set threshold, the payment for each individual service is reduced. Secondly, the reform introduced a competitive market among providers of health insurance by allowing people to move between health insurance funds and by introducing a risk-equalization system, whereby funds with a good risk structure (determined, for example, by the average age of the insured population) have to subsidize those who are worse off (Hinrichs, 1995).

The health care systems of France and Germany, both based on similar social insurance programmes, have been reformed in very similar ways. First an attempt was made to contain demand by increasing user charges. When this strategy proved unsuccessful, measures were pursued which tightened the grip of the state over health expenditure. This contrasts with the approach adopted in countries where health care is provided by the state, like the UK, Italy or Sweden. There, measures have tended to focus on efficiency gain, within the limits of easily controllable resources. Whether changes in either system constitute retrenchment, or are simply a step towards modernizing the health care system is obviously a difficult question. It is certain that the generalized increase in user charges (Kalisch et al., 1998) implies a reduction in the level of coverage of public provision. However, the impact of other measures, such as increased controls over the supply of health care or the introduction of more competition, is more difficult to assess. The fact that expenditure on private health care has increased in most countries (see table 2.1 below) suggests that public health programmes are less successful than in the past at meeting citizens' health care needs.

## Unemployment Compensation

Benefits for unemployed people are a central part of the interface between social and economic policy. These benefits influence the supply and cost of labour, and as a result constitute a key parameter in the regulation of an economy. For this reason, and because expenditure on unemployment benefits is generally not as high as in pensions or health care, the direction of reform in unemployment compensation has not been affected by financial considerations so strongly as in other areas.

In adopting the measures reviewed below, the reduction (or containment) of expenditure was only one of the objectives pursued. What has also been important is an attempt to strengthen work incentives, pursued by cutting benefits, by tightening eligibility criteria and by co-ordinating unemployment compensation with in-work benefits, so as to make sure that 'work pays'. The 1990s have also witnessed a generalized shift from passive compensation towards active labour market policies. These are no longer a specificity of the Nordic countries but have been developed in various welfare states. Among others, Britain and Switzerland have introduced large-scale active programmes in the late 1990s (Kalisch et al., 1998; on Britain, see below).

*Benefit cuts*

One overall theme in the reform of unemployment compensation systems has been the reduction in the level and sometimes the duration of benefits, which can be seen as a response to both financial concerns and work incentive problems. For instance, in 1993 Germany reduced unemployment benefits by 1 per cent and 3 per cent for claimants with and without dependent children respectively. The duration of unemployment assistance benefits for those who had not previously been on the contributory scheme, was also reduced to one year, after which they need to rely on a locally administered social assistance system (Clasen, 1997).

A more substantial cut was adopted in Sweden, where in 1995 benefits were cut from a generous 90 per cent of earnings to 75 per cent (the cut also affected other earnings-related benefits, like those for sickness and disability). In 1997, however, the cut in the replacement rate was partially reversed to 80 per cent. Sweden has also introduced a six-day waiting period before a benefit can be drawn and a time limit of three years on insurance benefits (which can be extended to four years for those with a long contribution record). Eligibility has been tightened by excluding participation in 'recruitment support' programmes (an active labour market programme for new entrants to the labour market) from the range of activities which are counted as work for the purpose of qualifying for insurance benefits (Palme and Wennemo, 1997; Kalisch et al., 1998; Stahlberg, 1997).

In Britain unemployment compensation policy has been characterized by three trends: downward pressure on the level of benefits, increased targeting and an attempt to recommodify recipients. Levels of benefit have been modified on numerous occasions. Atkinson and Micklewright (1989) provide a list of the main changes adopted in benefits for the unemployed between 1979 and 1988. Measures adopted included the removal of the earnings-related supplement on the unemployment benefit (insurance) in 1980; the removal of statutory indexation of benefits (in 1986); and the taxation of unemployment benefits, which was removed by the Major government in 1992 (Glennerster, 1995, p. 185). Altogether, Atkinson and Micklewright identify some thirty-four individual measures adopted in the ten-year period they cover, of which they see twenty-three as disadvantageous to the unemployed, seven as having undetermined effects and four as favourable (1989, p. 21).

In relative terms, cuts on the insurance unemployment benefit were more substantial than those affecting the assistance benefit, income support (see also Pierson, 1994, 102). The two benefits have been subjected to the same erosion process but the insurance benefit has also been subjected to more radical cuts. As mentioned above, the earnings-related supplement was abolished in 1980. In 1996, the maximal duration of the insurance benefit was reduced from one year to six months (Erskine, 1997, p. 138). The result of the differential treatment of insurance and assistance benefits has been a dramatic increase in the role of means-tested provision in supporting the unemployed. In 1997/8 only 5 per cent of benefit expenditure for the unemployed was expected to come from insurance benefits (Erskine, 1997, p. 138).

Finally, British policy towards the unemployed has been directed at the recommodification of recipients. This has been pursued in two ways:

first by 'making work pay', a slogan which refers to the removal of marginal tax rates of 100 per cent or more for unemployed people who enter employment on low incomes (Hills, 1993). This was one of the key objectives in the 1986 Social Security Act when some adjustments were made through the introduction of in-work benefits (Family Credits). This was an attempt to reconcile two key objectives of Conservative income support policy: increase targeting and strengthen work incentives. More recently, the Labour government has been going in the same direction by planning the introduction of a Working Family Tax Credit (similar to the American EITC), and various other means-tested benefits available to those who are in work, such as child care vouchers (DSS, 1998, pp. 57–62). The goal of recommodification has been pursued also by strengthening the 'availability for work' requirement as a condition for the receipt of benefits. This was done in 1996 through the transformation of the Unemployment Benefit in a Job Seekers' Allowance, and more recently, through the introduction of a Welfare to Work scheme by the Labour government for youth and long-term unemployed (Convery, 1997; DSS, 1998).

France has a complex system of unemployment compensation, with insurance benefits set at different replacement rates according to age, length of contribution record, and duration of unemployment. The system provides also various kinds of means-tested benefits for the long-term unemployed and those with no contribution record. The main reform of the unemployment insurance system was adopted in 1992 on the basis of an agreement between trade unions and employers as 'social partners'. The different unemployment insurance benefits were replaced by only one 'digressive' benefit (which decreases with time) known as the *Allocation Unique Dégressive* (AUD).

The new unemployment insurance benefit is payable only for a limited period of time, which depends on the contribution record. The amount of the benefit decreases with time. For instance, a person who had worked at least fourteen months of the last twenty-four receives a full benefit for nine months, then loses 17 per cent of the benefit at six-monthly intervals (the intervals were four months between 1992 and 1996). Claimants with a shorter contribution record may be awarded benefits for a shorter period. While entitlement to the main unemployment insurance benefits runs out after thirty months, a variety of measures exist to extend the cover provided by the unemployment insurance fund. Most important of these is the *Allocation de Solidarité Spécifique*, which is subject to a means test, but is still contributory (Join-Lambert, 1997).

Besides these reforms, France has also developed various forms of active labour market policies, which generally aim at favouring reinsertion into work of the long-term and young unemployed. The cornerstone of this effort was the introduction in 1988 of a new non-contributory scheme: the *Revenu Minimum d'Insertion* (RMI). Its main features are the guarantee of a minimum level of resources to anyone aged twenty-five or over, which takes the form of a means-tested differential benefit. The rates, which vary according to family size, are rather low, generally set below the level of the minimum wage. The RMI has also a reinsertion dimension, in the form of a contract between the recipient and 'society'. Recipients must commit themselves to take part in reinsertion programmes, as stated in a contract, signed by the recipient and a social worker. Such programmes can be either job-seeking, vocational training or activities designed to enhance the recipient's social autonomy. The Jospin government also passed legislation in 1998 to enforce a maximum thirty-five-hour working week, designed to encourage more efficient use of labour and also increase the number of jobs.

Retrenchment has certainly figured prominently in the reforms of unemployment benefits adopted in most European countries. Cuts in benefits (levels, duration, eligibility) have been adopted in virtually all countries, with the exception of southern European countries, where unemployment compensation was an underdeveloped area of the welfare state at the beginning of the 1990s (Ferrera, 1996). As a result, there has been some expansion here, as part of a catching-up process with their northern European counterparts (Kalisch et al., 1998). Benefit cuts, however, have not been the only theme in unemployment insurance reforms. Concern with the optimization of labour supply has resulted in the expansion of active labour market policies in a large number of countries.

## Other Benefits

The three areas reviewed above have been at the centre of political debate and reform initiatives in virtually all European countries. Policy changes, however, were by no means limited to these areas. Cuts were adopted in other cash benefits, generally as part of an effort at controlling expenditure. Sickness benefits, for instance, were reduced in Germany, where the replacement rate for the first six weeks was cut from 100 per cent to 80 per cent of earnings, and in Sweden, from 90 per cent to 75 per cent and then back to 80 per cent (Hinrichs, 1998; Palme and Wennemo, 1997). As part of an effort to encourage employers to monitor awards of sickness benefits, responsibility was transferred to them in a number of countries. This was the case in the UK, where the transfer occurred in two stages: first only the administration of the benefit was shifted to employers (1986) and subsequently also the financing of it (1994). Similar measures were adopted in the Netherlands (Kalisch et al., 1998).

In some countries benefits for the sick and the disabled have been subjected to radical change, mainly because of perceived widespread abuse in the past. This was the case in the Netherlands, where disability benefits had been used as a substitute for unemployment insurance. The problem was dealt with first in 1992 by reducing the level of benefit and by requiring beneficiaries to undergo a medical re-examination. The result was a reduction in the number of claimants from over 800,000 in 1992 to 722,000 in 1997. A second reform came into force at the beginning of 1998 and introduced differentiated contribution rates for each branch of industry. This means that, depending on the risk of disability, insurance contributions can vary across sectors of industry (Visser and Hemerijck, 1997; Kalisch et al., 1998).

In Italy benefits for the disabled were subject to increased controls, and eligibility has been somewhat restricted. In 1990, medical commissions were introduced in each USL (Local Health Unit), with the task of reassessing eligibility of disability benefit recipients. In 1991 it was decided that invalidity benefits could not be combined with other social security benefits such as war pensions, old age or survivors pensions. Recipients had to choose the most favourable option. About 20 per cent of invalidity benefit beneficiaries were affected. In 1994, to a large extent as a result of these measures, some 3,000 claimants lost their entitlement to invalidity benefit, and about 1,500 gave it up spontaneously (Niero, 1996).

## Expansion of provision

Together with the retrenchment measures discussed in this chapter, European welfare states have also adopted some measures of expansion over the last few years. These mainly concern policy areas which respond to emerging new needs and aspirations of the public. Two examples are particularly relevant: social care for elderly people and policies to reconcile work and family life. Germany, for instance, introduced a brand-new social insurance scheme to pay for long-term care in the early 1990s (Ruppel and King, 1995). Other countries, mainly in northern Europe, have adopted and reinforced a series of measures directed particularly at women, aiming to make it easier to reconcile work and family life. The measures adopted range from child care provision to parental leave schemes (Kalisch et al., 1998). These elements of expansion, however, remain limited and concern new objectives of welfare states rather than its classical functions of protection from market-based uncertainty.

## Trends in Welfare Retrenchment and Reform

Differences in welfare institutions and in national political configurations are such that one would not expect a great degree of consistency in the trajectories that individual welfare states have been following in the 1980s and the 1990s. To a large extent this is what emerges from the brief review presented above, particularly if one looks at the details of policy across countries. Striking contrasts are, for example, the introduction of market mechanisms in health care provision in Britain against the increase in state intervention in France and Germany, or the expansion of protection for the unemployed in France against its strong curtailment in Britain.

These contrasts suggest that the quest for consistency must take place at a higher level of abstraction. If we want to understand what is happening to European welfare states, we should not limit our analysis to legislative changes, but also look at what the implications of these changes are in terms of outcomes. It appears that European welfare states, faced with similar challenges, develop different solutions depending on the welfare institutions and political configurations of each country, to attain similar outcomes. In the rest of this chapter we highlight some of these policies.

### *Privatization*

Some of the reforms reviewed above highlight the increased scope for private provision in social protection. This can occur as a result of explicit transfers of responsibility from the state to the private sector, as was the case with sickness benefits in the UK and in the Netherlands, as a result of the introduction of incentives for people to opt out of state provision (1986 British pension reform), or, in a more subtle way, by reducing or failing to upgrade state provision in line with rising public expectations and perceptions of need, so as to create a 'social protection gap' which is filled by private provision. This is arguably what happened most often in the reforms discussed above.

The extent to which individuals rely on the private sector to meet their social needs has increased significantly since the 1980s, as shown in table 2.1. The increase is not dramatic, as in all countries (except the USA, but there private provision has always played an important role) the private sector still covers only a very small proportion of the social protection effort. However, what is probably more important is the fact that the trend towards a bigger role for the private sector seems to be generalized across industrial countries. The sample covered by table 2.1 is rather small, but includes countries belonging to each welfare regime, which suggests that similar changes are taking place elsewhere too.

**Table 2.1**  Expenditure on private provision[a] as a percentage of GDP

| | 1980 | | 1993 | |
|---|---|---|---|---|
| | *Health* | *Total* | *Health* | *Total* |
| Denmark | 0.04 | 0.29 | 0.12 | 1.21 |
| Sweden | 0.07 | 1.27 | 0.09 | 2.34 |
| Germany | 0.56 | 2.83 | 0.66 | 2.88 |
| UK | 0.14 | 2.09 | 0.33 | 3.80 |
| USA | 3.05 | 4.85 | 5.34 | 8.28 |

[a] Private provision refers to both compulsory and voluntary benefits within the traditional areas of competence of the welfare state (pensions, health care, sickness insurance) provided by the private sector.
*Source*: Adema and Einerhand, 1998, table 4, p. 25.

An expansion in private provision is not necessarily the result of welfare retrenchment. We can expect other developments to be playing a role in this trend. For example, the increase in inequality experienced in most industrial countries over the last two decades might account for the increasing difficulties that the state has in meeting the high standards of provision demanded by the affluent, in a context of budgetary restraint. As a result, dissatisfaction with state provision due to rising expectations (and not to declining quality) could be the force behind the expansion of private provision. This argument is developed in the UK context by Glennerster and Hills (1998, p. 325).

### Shifting the burden of uncertainty to the individual

The expansion of private provision means that individuals will be more exposed to risks, such as those resulting from the market performance of their pension funds. Many pension schemes use the funds to purchase annuities on the date of retirement. Variations in the price of annuities across time can result in substantial differences in the level of benefit produced by similar contributions for people retiring on different dates. Future pensioners are not necessarily going to be worse off than those retiring today, but they will not have the same level of security. This shift of the burden of uncertainty from the state to the individual has not taken place only through the expansion of private provision but also as a result of direct government interventions. This has been the case, for instance, in the pension reforms adopted in Italy, Germany and Sweden. In these countries, the state no longer guarantees a given replacement rate for old age pensions. Instead, the amount paid out will depend on developments which are only partially predictable, such as the age structure of the population and economic growth. In so doing, governments are not necessarily reducing the level of provision – in fact, benefits under the new Swedish system could rise. What they are reducing is the level of risk-protection that these schemes provide, since the outcomes are less secure than in the past.

Developments in employment policy reflect a similar trend. The deregulation of labour markets, a trend that can be observed in virtually all industrial countries, has reduced the extent of control over wages and dismissals, leaving individual workers more exposed to uncertainty, even though not necessarily worse off. Similarly, the end of the guarantee of full employment, which until the 1990s was still upheld in countries like Sweden, means that the state takes no responsibility over whether or not someone has access to employment.

## Conclusion: The Trend to Recommodification

As Esping-Andersen (1990) has persuasively shown, many welfare states were successful in reducing people's dependence on labour market participation in order to afford a decent living during their phase of expansion. This process, which he calls decommodification, was experienced to a different extent by different welfare states, being most advanced in the Nordic countries. Recent changes, such as those reviewed above, seem to engage in the opposite process, recommodification, by increasing people's dependence on the market.

Recommodification seems to be the intentional outcome of the reforms of unemployment benefits. In this area, cuts in benefits have often been justified by the need to restore work incentives, and increasingly, cash is handed out only to those who are willing to reciprocate, by taking part in welfare-to-work programmes, training, and so forth. Recommodification is not incompatible with the expansion of provision in some areas, such as family policy. The measures adopted here, in fact, are generally designed to facilitate entry into the labour market particularly for women and single parents (child-care, parental leave).

In other areas, such as pension and health care, recommodification is not intentionally pursued, but is a by-product of governments' initiatives. The increased uncertainty introduced by the pension reforms can be counterbalanced by private insurance, a strategy available only to those who have sufficient income. The restrictions imposed in health care provision could result in a two-tiered system, in which good-quality and rapid health care will be available only to those prepared (and able) to pay. This, if anything, is likely to increase people's dependence on the labour market, from which they will need to extract sufficient resources to cover their health care needs.

Bearing in mind the problems involved in identifying general and supranational social policy trajectories, recommodification seems to be the most consistent trend in social policy-making in the 1990s, across both countries and policy areas. The balance between state and market in meeting people's needs seems to be shifting towards the market, in a reversal of the tendency that dominated social policy-making during most of the post-war period. How can we account for this new trend? What can explain this substantive change in the relationship between the state and its citizens? In the next three chapters we will assess some of the more influential approaches to the new developments in welfare.

# 3
# Globalization and the Welfare State

All the approaches discussed in the following chapters attempt to give accounts of the trend to constraint in state welfare in advanced industrial societies on the basis of national, internal, endogenous factors. Recent changes in the world economy call for a new approach: one that takes account of international as well as national factors. The relationship between the forces of globalization – the external factors on one hand and the internal factors within a country on the other – is the most useful framework for understanding current and future trends in welfare provision in Europe.

This chapter discusses (a) the notion of globalization as a process and as an ideology; (b) the two major strands of economic globalization – trade and finance – and their effects on the European welfare state; (c) the effects of globalization on the distribution of power within countries and the consequences of this on the welfare state; (d) the effects of globalization on the sovereignty of national governments and the consequences for the welfare state; (e) globalization and future welfare state developments; and (f) conclusions.

## Globalization as a Process and as an Ideology

Globalization is one of the most widely used terms in the social science debates of the 1990s. 'Every age has its defining phrases', writes Kapstein, 'and globalization is surely one of ours' (Kapstein, 1996, p. 351). It is sometimes used to describe the *process or the trends* in the internationalization of capital, production, technology, culture, family life, and so on. On other occasions it is used to refer to *the ideology* behind these trends and the desirability of these trends on societies.

The various definitions of globalization can be placed under three main headings in terms of breadth or inclusiveness. First, there are those which see globalization in predominantly one-dimensional terms though acknowledging the possibility that its effects may be spread more widely. Stressing its economic aspects, Bonturi and Fukasaka define globalization as 'the increasing inter-dependence of markets and production in different countries through trade in goods and services, cross-border flows of capital, and exchanges of technology' (Bonturi and Fukasaka, 1993, p. 146). McLuhan's exploration of the effects of electronic media on local cultures led him to the formulation of the notion of 'the global village' (McLuhan, 1964, p. 93). Still others emphasize the political implications of globalization stemming from the emergence of trans-national agencies that reduced the power of the national state (Burton, 1972).

Secondly, there are those definitions that see globalization as a multi-dimensional process spanning economic, social and political changes. Writing from a political science perspective, Strange emphasizes the economic and the political but also adds that 'the most important factor in all aspects of "globalization" is perceptive. Those affected perceive themselves to be living and working in a world-wide context, instead of in a local, national one' (Strange, 1995, p. 293). Similarly, Held and McGrew state that globalization 'is evident within a number of key institutional domains – the economic, political, military, cultural, legal etc.' and that globalization 'is essentially concerned with the reordering of time and space in social life' (Held and McGrew, 1993, p. 263).

Thirdly, some writers see globalization in all-embracing terms as a process that affects every aspect in the life of a person, community or nation. For Robertson, globalization refers 'to both the compression of the world and the intensification of consciousness of the world as a whole' (Robertson, 1992, p. 8). In a similar vein, Giddens sees globalization as '*action at distance*' and it 'is really about the transformation of space and time' (Giddens, 1994, p. 4). Globalization creates actively reflective individuals who 'cannot rest content with an identity that is simply handed down, inherited, or built on a traditional status. A person's identity has in large part to be discovered, constructed, actively sustained' (Giddens, 1994, p. 82).

The causes of globalization as a process are also much in dispute. Marxian writers stress the changes in the organization of international capital which have implications for the methods of production and distribution. Capital has to continually reorganize and regroup if it is to survive. As Wilkin puts it, for Marxists, 'the driving mechanisms of globalizations are to be found in the structure of capitalism as a world-system and its logic, which drives it towards both increased exploitation and the appropriation of capital' (Wilkin, 1996, p. 229). Weberians stress the multiple sources in the economy, the culture and the polity behind the process of globalization. Some of them pay particular attention to the technological changes in the area of mass media that help to spread ideas so rapidly across the world and thus influence the behaviour of individuals, agencies and governments.

For both Marxists and Weberians globalization is a process that is very much influenced by political forces – by decisions taken by governments or by international bodies. Functionalist and neo-liberal writers, however, see globalization as technologically determined and, as such, it is both inevitable and beyond the scope of politics. Governments, sooner or later, have to accept it.

These differences in the perception of globalization as a process are reflected in the debates concerning the origin of globalization. The various approaches can be placed in one of three groups. Those which see globalization as going back to 'the dawn of history'; those which place it with the onset of 'modernization and the development of capitalism' but with a recent acceleration; and those which consider it as 'a recent phenomenon' of the post-war era (Waters, 1995, p. 4). A minority of writers remain very sceptical of the very notion of globalization as a process or as an explanatory tool of what is happening today in the economies and welfare provisions of the various countries (Hirst, 1995).

It is, however, globalization as ideology that excites most passion. As ideology, the notion of globalization sits very comfortably with neo-liberal, monetarist, anti-welfare state thinking. New Right writers perceive globalization as a force that is beneficial to all, individuals and states, in all parts of the world. In their eyes, globalization practices benefit efficiency, raise economic growth, improve living standards for all, and liberate the individual from government planning and controls. Fukuyama's claims of the natural and beneficial effects of globalization are indicative of the position of many in this group: 'The unfolding of technologically driven economic modernization creates strong incentives for developed countries to accept the basic terms of the universal capitalist economic culture, by permitting a substantial degree of economic competition and letting prices be determined by market mechanisms' (Fukuyama, 1992, pp. 96–7).

Many on the left, however, see globalization as the most recent attempt by private capital to resolve its inherent economic and political contradictions; as of benefit to the upper groups in society, to the multinational companies and the affluent world; and as detrimental to the satisfaction of public needs. For Laxer, globalization is the very antithesis of such current public aspirations as 'belonging, security, equality, respect, personal development and freedom. These can best be fulfilled in socially supportive, democratic and egalitarian communities. Globalisation by the transnationals is not indifferent to these needs and aspirations; it is hostile to them' (Laxer, 1995, p. 308). Rinehart views globalization as a force for the perpetuation and accentuation of inequalities within and between groups of countries for the benefit of multinationals and the upper classes. Its constant emphasis on increased competitiveness involves 'a race to the bottom' (Rinehart, 1995, p. 22).

Piven Fox finds that many of the claimed economic trends associated with globalization are not new but, at the same time, warns that 'right or wrong, the explanation itself has become a political force, helping to create the institutional realities it purportedly merely describes' (Piven, 1995, p. 108). In a similar vein, Hirst and Thompson concede that even though globalization as a process is a more of a myth than a reality, one of its effects has been 'to paralyse radical reforming strategies' (Hirst and Thompson, 1996, p. 1).

This chapter concentrates on the economic and political claims of the globalization thesis as they relate to the welfare state in the advanced industrial countries of Europe. Most of the literature emphasizes the adverse effects of globalization on welfare provisions made by governments in industrial societies. A minority view, however, insists that globalization necessitates bigger rather than smaller government.

## International Trade and the Welfare State

One of the central claims of globalization writings is that the low labour costs in developing countries are a threat to the industries, the employment situation and the welfare state of the advanced industrial countries or Developed Market Economies (DMEs) of Europe. Even the European Commission, which sees unemployment as the result of a multiplicity of structural and personal factors, referred to the competition from developing countries as one of the causes of structural unemployment: 'Finally and more especially, the countries of the south are stirring and competing with us – even on our own markets – at cost levels which we simply cannot afford' (CEC, 1993a, p. 11).

Industrial production in affluent countries is based on advanced technology and on guaranteeing high-quality goods, high productivity and high wages. What has happened in recent years, it is argued, is that the fourth link in the chain is no longer necessary. Today, 'it is possible to have high technology, high productivity, high quality and *low* wages' (Schwab and Smadja, 1994, p. 41). The cost of a worker in manufacturing in most developing countries is lower than the corresponding cost in Europe even after taking into account differing productivity rates. This is the majority view but Golub's study of unit labour costs in the USA in the manufacturing sector found that they were surprisingly lower than those in India, the Philippines and Malaysia but higher than those in South Korea, Thailand and Mexico in 1990 (Golub, 1995, p. 142).

Similar arguments have been used in relation to the cost of industrial workers in the former Soviet bloc countries in Europe. In 1993 average monthly wages in Hungary, the Czech Republic and Poland were only one-ninth, one-thirteenth and one-twelfth of the level in West Germany (Lansbury et al., 1996, p. 109). A more specific example which takes into account productivity rates reaches the same conclusion. The wage of an industrial worker in the Volkswagen–Skoda factory in the Czech Republic is about ten times lower while the productivity is 60 per cent that of a worker in the company's plant in Germany (Schwab and Smadja, 1994, p. 42).

There are, of course, other factors that determine industrial investment, and the notion of competitiveness is controversial even though growth in productivity is generally considered as its main indicator (Porter, 1990, p. 6). Despite these caveats, once this pattern of production (high productivity, high quality and low wages) is established, companies and countries in advanced industrial countries are under pressure to reduce production costs. If this cannot be done through higher productivity rates resulting from improved technology, it has to be done through reductions in labour costs – employment, wages, and social security costs.

The abstract logic of the first part of the argument – the pressures emanating from low-wage and high-quality production – seems convincing. It is the second part of the argument – that low-priced imports inevitably mean unemployment and reductions in living standards – that is more open to question. It is true that many consumers will buy low-priced goods imported from Newly Industrialized Countries (NICs) but many other buyers in advanced industrial societies may be prepared to meet the higher prices of goods produced in their countries rather than purchase cheaper goods of objectively similar quality produced in far-off lands for a variety of personal reasons.

Whatever the theoretical merits of the argument, empirical evidence points to two very different conclusions. *From the short term* point of view, imports from the NICs of South and East Asia pose no major threat to European industry, as table 3.1 shows. Most of the world trade in terms of both imports and exports – about two-thirds – is accounted for by the activities of the advanced industrial countries, and this proportion has not changed much over the past twenty years. Moreover, most of this trade is between the advanced industrial countries. In 1980 64.5 per cent of all imports of advanced industrial countries came from other such countries; in 1995 the corresponding proportion was 70.6 per cent. Though the proportion of imports from the rest of the world declined correspondingly, the pro-

**Table 3.1**   Direction of world trade: imports (%)

| Origin | DMEsᵃ | Economies in transition | Latin America | Africa | W Asia | E + S Asia | Other Asiaᵇ |
|---|---|---|---|---|---|---|---|
| | | | *Destination* | | | | |
| **DMEs** | | | | | | | |
| 1980 | 64.5 | 40.6 | 62.9 | 70.4 | 66.3 | 55.4 | 73.7 |
| 1995 | 70.6 | 55.3 | 70.7 | 66.9 | 67.0 | 53.5 | 57.2 |
| **Economies in transition** | | | | | | | |
| 1995 | 3.4 | 35.8 | 0.8 | 1.5 | 4.4 | 0.8 | 4.5 |
| **Latin America** | | | | | | | |
| 1980 | 5.6 | 3.0 | 15.0 | 2.0 | 0.9 | 1.2 | 2.9 |
| 1995 | 5.1 | 1.1 | 17.0 | 2.0 | 2.3 | 1.4 | 2.1 |
| **Africa** | | | | | | | |
| 1980 | 5.5 | 2.1 | 1.7 | 4.4 | 1.0 | 0.9 | 0.5 |
| 1995 | 2.2 | 0.7 | 0.8 | 9.8 | 1.5 | 0.8 | 1.0 |
| **West Asia** | | | | | | | |
| 1980 | 8.9 | 6.0 | 8.7 | 5.2 | 9.8 | 12.8 | 0.4 |
| 1995 | 2.3 | 2.0 | 1.0 | 3.5 | 7.1 | 3.7 | 1.5 |
| **Eastern and southern Asia** | | | | | | | |
| 1980 | 6.1 | 1.3 | 1.1 | 2.1 | 3.9 | 14.7 | 3.4 |
| 1995 | 8.8 | 2.5 | 5.0 | 8.2 | 7.1 | 19.3 | 26.3 |
| **Other Asia** | | | | | | | |
| 1980 | 0.7 | 1.9 | 0.5 | 0.8 | 1.0 | 5.1 | 1.6 |
| 1995 | 3.9 | 1.2 | 1.5 | 2.1 | 1.8 | 12.4 | 1.4 |

ᵃ DMEs = Developed market economies which include S. Africa.
ᵇ Other Asia = China, S. Korea, Mongolia and Vietnam.
Data do not add up to 100 per cent because of incomplete information.
*Source*: UN, 1997, table A.16, p. 247.

portion from South and East Asia increased from 6.1 per cent in 1980 to 8.8 per cent in 1995. A similar picture emerges if one looks at the origin and destination of exports.

More significantly, however, South and East Asian countries have replaced the advanced industrial countries as the main source of imports for other countries in Asia including China with its huge population. This small group of countries provided 26.3 per cent of the imports of Other

Asia, which includes China, in 1995 compared to only 3.4 per cent in 1980. The proportion of imports of Other Asian countries coming from advanced industrial countries, on the other hand, experienced a substantial decline from 73.7 per cent in 1980 to 57.2 in 1995.

*From the long-term* perspective, therefore, the threat to European industry seems more real. A number of reasons account for this. First, three-quarters of the world's population lives in Asia and will continue to do so in the future. Secondly, while rates of economic growth during 1985–95 averaged to 2.6 per cent per year in the DMEs the corresponding figure for South and East Asia was 6.0 per cent and for China 9.9 per cent (UN, 1995, tables A.2, p. 300 and A.4, p. 301). During the same period, improvements in per capita incomes have also been faster in South and East Asia (an annual average of 3.9 per cent) and China (an annual average of 8.3 per cent) than in DMEs with an annual average of only 2.0 per cent (UN, 1995, table A.1, p. 299). This differential growth of incomes per capita may be accentuated in the future as population growth rates in Asia ease. Though most people in Asia will continue to live around the bread line for many years to come, an increasing proportion will have incomes high enough to spend on consumer goods. Thirdly, production of the 'new' products such as office machinery and data processing equipment, telecommunications equipment and electronics components is increasingly being concentrated in Asia. While in 1980, exports of these products from developing countries, mainly from South and East Asia, accounted for only 11.5 per cent of all such exports by 1992 the corresponding proportion rose to 28.2 per cent (UN, 1995, table XI.2, p. 173). This very substantial rise in the production of the 'new' products in South and East Asia has been the result of the relocation of production during the 1980s: 'Japan and the United States to the NIEs and from the Asian NIEs and Japan to Malaysia and Thailand' (UN, 1995, p. 175).

In brief, the potential for expansion of exports and imports is so much higher in Asia than elsewhere in the world that this region is increasingly being seen as the world's leading market of the future to eventually replace the USA and Europe as the dominant world trading bloc. The financial problems that these countries experienced during 1997 and 1998 do not alter the above scenario even though they indicate the complexities of economic issues at an international level.

Despite the relatively small size of the imports from the developing countries, their effects on job losses in advanced industrial countries is real. Wood estimates that 'the cumulative effect up to 1990 of the changes in trade with the South was to reduce the demand for labour in manufacturing by about 9 million (plus or minus 3 million) person-years – or by about 12 per cent of actual employment in Northern manufacturing' (Wood, 1994, p. 167). He also found that the bigger the increase in the country's imports, the greater the loss of jobs and the higher the rise in wage inequalities between the unskilled and other workers. A study of employment trends in the USA supports these findings – a drop of 6 per cent in demand for unskilled workers during 1978–90 as well as a major factor in the increase of wage inequalities between the low-skilled and other workers (Sachs and Schatz, 1994).

Similarly, the International Labour Office, which is very supportive of the overall positive effects of free world trade to all countries, concludes: 'It is not, however, unreasonable to conclude that trade with the South has been at least partly responsible for the loss of unskilled jobs and the widening wage differentials in the North' (ILO, 1995, p. 53). The same conclusion is reached by the World Bank, which adds the important rider that job losses in DMEs resulting from imports from developing countries may be higher than current estimates if one takes into account the job losses resulting from labour-saving technological changes that were introduced 'perhaps partly because of increased international competition' (World Bank, 1995, p. 56).

In brief, world trade has been one of the factors that has contributed to the rise in unemployment in Europe in recent years and this has had some adverse implications for welfare state developments.

## Multi-National Enterprises and the Welfare State

A major strand of economic globalization is the growth of financial flows across the world almost free of government controls and often with government encouragement. The reasons behind this range from the attempts by Multi-National Enterprises (MNEs) and other enterprises to evade high taxation regimes, to investment in new products, to diversify production, to exploit primary products in developing countries, to relocate enterprises to countries where they can maximize their profitability, and so on.

The increasing economic and political importance of MNEs is both one of the outcomes and one of the causes of the rising gobalization of the world economy. Their economic importance is shown by the fact that in the late 1980s, 'one third of all output, three quarters of commercial technological capacity and about the same proportion of trade is controlled or influenced by MNEs' (Dunning, 1992, p. 12). The result is that MNEs have become the 'central organisers of economic activities in an increasingly integrated world economy' (UN Center on Transnational Corporations, 1992, p. 1).

During the past forty years or so there has been a very substantial growth in the financial power of MNEs shown by trends in the volume of Foreign Direct Investment (FDI) in world markets and, secondly,

**Table 3.2**   Average annual stocks and flows of FDI, 1970–1992

|  | 1970–80 | | 1981–85 | | 1986–90 | | 1991 & 1992 | |
|---|---|---|---|---|---|---|---|---|
|  | *(US$ bn)* | *(%)* | *(US$ bn)* | *(%)* | *(US$ bn)* | *(%)* | *(US$ bn)* | *(%)* |
| **Stocks** | | | | | | | | |
| All countries | 313 | 100 | 618 | 100 | 1,173 | 100 | 1,897 | 100 |
| Developed | 243 | 78 | 474 | 77 | 933 | 80 | 1,503 | 79 |
| Developing | 70 | 22 | 144 | 23 | 240 | 20 | 394 | 21 |
| **Flows** | | | | | | | | |
| All countries | 21 | 100 | 50 | 100 | 155 | 100 | 138 | 100 |
| Developed | 16 | 76 | 36 | 72 | 129 | 83 | 98 | 71 |
| Developing | 5 | 24 | 14 | 28 | 26 | 17 | 40 | 29 |

*Source*:  ILO, 1995, table 10, p. 43 and table 11, p. 44.

noticeable changes in the location of MNEs. Table 3.2 shows both the stock and the flow of FDI over the past twenty years or so. Clearly the bulk of FDI stock is still held in the developed countries but during the past couple of years the proportion of FDI flowing to developing countries increased; if this trend continues, 'annual flows of FDI into the third world could, in the medium term, exceed those into the developed world. This would represent a major structural shift in the pattern, not just of investment, but also of the production and trade that arise from it' (ILO, 1995, p. 43). For the time being, however, both trade in goods and flows of capital remain intra-regional, mainly in Western Europe and Asia (Duffus and Gooding, 1997, p. 29).

As far as the country location of the origin of FDI is concerned, in 1960 US firms were the source of 48 per cent of FDI; by 1990 they accounted for only 26 per cent of the total. In 1960, European firms accounted for a similar proportion of FDI as the US and Japan was insignificant. By 1990 European firms accounted for a proportion double that of the US while Japanese increased their proportion to equal half of that of the US-based firms. All this happened during a period when the stock of FDI rose by twenty-four times, an exceptionally high rise which is 'of substantial importance for public policy' (Scaperlanda, 1993, p. 606).

MNEs create jobs in both the developed and the developing countries, and estimates show that the number of such jobs account for about 3 per cent of the total labour force in the world. If to this one adds the jobs generated indirectly, the proportion rises to at least 6 per cent. Most of these jobs are in the developed countries but 12 million jobs were in the developing countries, amounting to only 2 per cent of their labour force or 4 per cent including the indirectly created jobs (ILO, 1995, p. 45).

It is impossible to know the exact number of jobs exported from the developed to the developing countries. Country estimates do not always distinguish between the export of jobs to developing countries and other developed countries. Frobel and associates estimated that between 1966 and 1975 German textile industry doubled its foreign employment through subsidiaries and subcontracting, while domestic employment increased by only a quarter. Similarly, between 1961 and 1976, the number of foreign subsidiaries for German manufacturing increased fourfold. Though most of all this relocation of jobs was to low-wage economies, some of it was to other industrial countries for purely commercial reasons (Frobel et al., 1980). Arthuis estimates that in the case of France over a million jobs are threatened as a result of the delo-calization of firms in electronics, footwear and clothing to Asia and Central Europe (Arthuis, 1993). In Sweden large industrial corporations 'have been moving a large part of their production capacities to other countries' with lower labour costs during the 1980s (Kasvio, 1995, p. 44).

Again the problem may not be that severe at present but it may intensify in the future. An illustration of this is the recent establish-ment of car plants in India by many of the European and American car companies in order to satisfy the rising local demand for cars. This will prove of benefit to India in terms of jobs and to the compa-nies in terms of profits, but it can only exacerbate the problem of unemployment in Europe particularly among the unskilled and semi-skilled workers.

The fact that MNEs can relocate their production activities to suit their drive for profitability creates a pressure bordering on threat to gov-ernments and organized labour in industrial countries that they should contain and preferably reduce the welfare burden in terms of taxes, insurance contributions and the like that falls on employers. Govern-ments in some of the DMEs are ideologically happy to reduce labour costs as an industrial policy. As a recent government white paper in the UK put it: 'Excessive regulation stifles growth, destroys jobs, raises prices and drives companies elsewhere' (Department of Trade and Industry, 1995, p. 18). But even those who see high taxes as necessary to maintain high levels of welfare provision cannot indefinitely be immune to the dangers, particularly in countries where employers bear a large share of social protection costs. Many MNEs can choose where to locate their activities and 'this choice will, in part at least, be influenced by the taxa-tion policies of the authorities' (Dunning, 1993, p. 511).

Finally, the actual mobility of MNEs may well be lower than its theoretical possibility but this does not much change the implications outlined above. So long as their potential mobility is accepted, govern-ments and trade unions will respond submissively to their demands. Again, this can have adverse direct and indirect effects on the generosity of welfare state provision in advanced industrial countries. There is substantial evidence showing that competition between governments to please MNEs 'has given rise to a variety of reforms since the 1980s in areas like business taxation, infrastructure provision, the labour market, competition policy, and regulation' (Bureau of Industry and Economics, 1993, p. 174).

## The Balance of Power between Labour and Capital and the Welfare State

All the evidence suggests that globalization has been one of the factors that has shifted power away from labour organizations towards those of the business community. Trade union membership has declined and trade union power has weakened during the past twenty years in most advanced industrial societies. 'The 1980s was a period of deunionization', writes Standing, 'not only in the United States . . . but in most industrialized economies' (Standing, 1995, p. 172).

While capital is very mobile today, labour is still largely rooted in its own country. If 'financial markets are the most globalized' of all the forces of globalization, 'labour markets are the least so' (Waters, 1995, p. 89). International law and technological advances have vastly increased the mobility of capital. Immigration legislation has reduced the mobility of labour and most of what is taking place is within countries of the same regional pact. Moreover, 'migration from developing to developed countries translates into 1.5 new immigrants per thousand inhabitants (1995), the same as in 1970' (Duffus and Gooding, 1997, p. 34).

The result of this imbalance between the mobility of capital and labour is that, as Wilding puts it: 'Capital can more easily go where costs are lower and workers are more compliant. It knows this – and so do the workers' (Wilding, 1997, p. 416). The ILO concurs with the above view. The ability of firms 'to raise and spend money anywhere in the world increase the locational freedom of firms and thereby shift the balance of power away from labour to capital' (ILO, 1997, p. 70). This obviously undermines the ability of trade unions to carry out satisfactorily their traditional role of protecting and improving wages and working conditions for their members.

Some express this growing power of capital over labour in more stark terms. Rinehart sees it as tantamount to blackmail by MNEs: 'More and more, competitiveness is used as a form of blackmail. Corporations and financial capitalists threaten to withhold or relocate investment if workers refuse to grant concessions or if government regulations and spending on social programs are too great' (Rinehart, 1995, pp. 14–15).

This increased power of capital *vis-à-vis* labour weakens the forces within a country in support of state welfare. Despite all the debates concerning the relative contributions of labour and capital towards the creation of the welfare state in European countries, there is no doubt that today it is labour organizations that are attempting to protect the welfare state against the constant pressures from capital to reduce its scope. The numerous strikes by trade unions in several European countries in recent years in defence of the welfare state are a testimony to this. Evidence from comparative research also shows that respondents of labour organizations argue for the preservation and extension of welfare provision while respondents of capital support the containment and contraction of welfare (George, 1998, table 1, p. 21).

In addition, empirical evidence of welfare developments in several countries shows that organizations of capital have played a significant part in recent years in the reduction of welfare provision. In the UK the institutions of capital played a significant part in the reorganization of retirement pensions in the late 1980s that brought about a greater role of private provision at the expense of the state sector. In Sweden, during the late 1980s, the twenty-three largest Swedish companies increased their labour force abroad by 27 per cent and contracted their labour force within Sweden by 24 per cent, so that they employed twice as many workers abroad as in Sweden (Olsen, 1996, table 2, p. 14). In this way, argues Wilks, Swedish businesses have played a major part in undermining the traditional social democratic model that was the mainstay of generous welfare provision in Sweden (Wilks, 1996).

The rise in unemployment, due partly to the forces of globalization, is the second reason why trade unions have lost industrial and political power while the business lobby has increased its power. This has happened at slightly different times and to different degrees in European countries during the past twenty years but it is a common feature today in Europe.

Thirdly, globalization has contributed to the creation of a business ideology stressing the importance of such practices as constant competitiveness, downsizing, flexibility and so on, all of which involve labour obedience or compliance to the demands of management for increased efficiency. Though such demands are made in the name of efficiency, the results often benefit management and shareholders at the expense of workers' jobs and wages.

In all these three ways, the industrial and political power of organized labour has suffered and this involves an undermining of the forces supporting the role of state welfare in society. It may be argued, however, that this decline in trade union power and support of the welfare state has been offset by the rise in the power of social movements. Though there is some truth in this argument, two riders have to be born in mind: several of these social movements are divided in their loyalties to state welfare; and they rarely combine into a broad pro-welfare alliance for maximum effect. New social movements are primarily guerrilla groups trying to extract maximum sectional advantages without a broader view of the role of the welfare state.

## Management Ideology and Welfare Provision

One of the central strands of the ideology of MNEs and of globalization is the constant stress on profit maximization through 'mean and lean' forms of management. This type of management style has spread to public services with mixed results in terms of the quality of service provided to the public. On the one hand, it has sharpened up lethargic styles of public service management and made the public more aware of the cost of services. On the other hand, it has led to excessive reductions of personnel in the public services, more use of direct payments by service users and a greater emphasis on private provision.

There is ample evidence showing that direct payments by service users has risen in many European countries in recent years (Ploug, 1995); that such management practices as separating the providers from the users in health care systems has spread considerably; and that the role of the private sector in social protection has increased. As chapter 2 has shown, Adema and Einerhand produce evidence showing that as a percentage of GDP, private social expenditure rose in all the six countries that they examined: from 0.29 per cent in 1980 to 1.21 in 1993 in Denmark; 1.27 per cent to 2.34 per cent in Sweden; 2.83 per cent to 2.88 per cent in Germany; 2.09 per cent to 3.80 per cent in the UK; 1.27 per cent to 4.33 per cent in the Netherlands; and 4.85 per cent to 8.28 per cent in the USA (Adema and Einerhand, 1998, table 4, p. 25). Moreover, the ratio of private to public social expenditure also increased in all six countries.

## Government Sovereignty and the Welfare State

In the past, policy developments in advanced industrial societies were seen as the result of government action mediated through the dominant power relationships within a country. Governments were sovereign in their countries even though they had to exercise their authority through the network of class, elite and pressure group activity.

Today, however, there are at least three broad schools of thought concerning the sovereignty of governments in DMEs. First, the technological, almost deterministic approach which sees the forces of globalization as the inevitable result of technological changes over which governments have no control. Wriston, for instance, dismisses the importance of political actors in the globalization of financial markets and attributes it all to the inexorable forces of technology. 'Our new international financial regime differs radically from its precursors in that it was not built by politicians, economists, central bankers or finance ministers ... It was built by technology ... [by] men and women who interconnected the planet with telecommunications and computers' (Wriston, 1988, p. 71).

Similarly, Strange argues most strongly that the globalization forces 'have to a large extent emasculated state control over national economies and societies' and, as a result, 'the differences that used to distinguish government policies from opposition policies are in process of disappearing'. The pretence of politicians that they can decide and shape government policies means that 'Disillusion with politics, disdain for politicians is a common phenomenon' (Strange, 1995, pp. 298, 291 and 291–2).

On the other hand, there are those who reject the notion that globalization has made the national governments redundant. As Cable puts it, 'The truth is much messier' (Cable, 1995, p. 38). While not denying the influence of technology on the growth of globalization, they do not reject the influence of politics. They see the interaction between technological and political factors as far more complex, varying between countries as well as between areas of government policy.

In a detailed study of the globalization of the economy of Singapore, Ramesh not only accepts the influence of political factors but he attributes them the primary role. In his words, 'the high level of globalization of the island's economy is not an outgrowth of some larger systemic process but the result of deliberate efforts by the state' (Ramesh, 1995, p. 243). It was the government that went out of its way to offer the kind of tax and labour market policies that would attract MNEs to Singapore. Globalization affected different government policies differently. Education and training were protected because they were seen as conducive to economic growth while social security benefits were curtailed – a government policy approach that 'confirms the fears of the radical critics of economic globalisation' (Ramesh, 1995, p. 258).

Similarly, Helleiner, while accepting the influence of technology on the growth of the globalization of financial markets, stresses also the role of governments through a series of political decisions that made it easier for private capital to operate freely in the world market. For him, the growth of global finance 'was not a product solely of market and technological developments ... state behaviour and political choices have also played an important role in the process' (Helleiner, 1995, p. 334). Others in this group feel that while governments in Europe may not have been made redundant by international forces in all respects, they 'no longer control national economies in Western Europe' (Wallace, 1994, p. 67).

The third school of thought includes those who maintain that globalization is not a new force and its power has been exaggerated as well as those who accept the dynamics of globalization but claim that reformist governments can withstand such pressures. We have already referred to those who consider globalization as nothing new and hence not as serious a problem for reformist governments as it is made out. Tabb, for example, argues that globalization is neither new nor more widespread today than in the past. The idea that the state cannot control globalization forces is pure ideology – it 'is a powerful tool of capital' (Tabb, 1997, p. 28). Governments have the technical ability to control capital and it is, therefore, a political not a technological issue as to whether globalization forces are allowed to have their devastating effects on workers' living standards.

Others in this group are less dismissive of the problems involved in dealing with the globalization forces. Miliband, for example, accepts that in an increasingly capitalist integrated world the power of capital has increased but he still argues that 'the prospect of achieving radical change in any given advanced capitalist country is not nearly as bleak and hopeless as is made out' (Miliband, 1991, p. 230). This is because the various components of capital can be divided and the pro-reform groups are still strong and, provided a determined government handles the situation with skill and determination, radical socialist changes are still possible. Still others believe that no one government can withstand the forces of globalization. Only international or regional government action can do this. Benoist, for example, argues that 'the nation-state is simply no longer able to take on global problems by itself', while the idea of 'a world state is a pipe dream', and concludes that regional governments such as the EU 'could effectively confront globalization' (Benoist, 1996, p. 136).

The reduction of government sovereignty has been seen by many as a threat not only to the welfare state but to the democratic process as well. While this may be the case with respect to the reduction occurring as a result of the action of MNEs, it is not necessarily so with regard to the growing power of international or regional bodies. There are occasions when in fact it leads to a strengthening of the democratic forces: when regional or international bodies undermine the power of authoritarian governments; or when the decisions of international bodies correct decisions by democratic governments that are contrary to international law. Similarly, it is not necessarily a recipe for ineffective government for 'many goals cannot be met by governments acting alone: in tackling environmental degradation, international crime and drugs trafficking, the interests of individual nations can be protected only by co-operation with others' (Washington, 1996, p. 24).

The globalization of finance, of manufacturing and of the economy in general has been universally accepted by governments. The view that there should be a return to trade protectionism and finance controls is still voiced by some writers but it carries no weight with governments. Even parties of the left, such as the Labour party in the UK, have jettisoned policies that aimed at controlling the free global flow of finance and the activities of MNEs (Green, 1995). The result of this is that a return to trade protectionism appears most unlikely at present. As the World Bank puts it: 'Governments are increasingly seeking to improve the international competitiveness of their companies rather than shield them behind protective walls' (World Bank, 1995, p. 51). In the short term, this has implications for government sovereignty not only for economic policy but for social policy as well.

In brief, the consensus of opinion is that globalization has reduced the power of governments. There are no voices claiming that globalization has increased government power. Clearly, this has implications for welfare developments which will be examined in the following section.

## Globalization and Welfare Futures

There is general agreement that the forces of globalization have important implications for the volume, the generosity and the composition of contemporary European welfare state provision. As Dunn puts it: 'The central challenge of global economic liberalization is to the Keynesian conception of the welfare state; the promise . . . to take full responsibility for the economic welfare of a given population through the deft exercise of the power of the state' (Dunn, 1994, p. 12).

Conceptually, four different positions have emerged in recent years regarding the appropriate welfare state response to globalization pressures. The first three accept that individual countries can no longer isolate themselves from the global economic environment and hence their welfare states need to adapt to this new situation. They differ on the kind of adaptation that is necessary.

### Competitiveness requires state welfare

The first approach claims that globalization necessitates more, not less, government provision of public services for two interrelated reasons. First, industrial societies in a globalized economy have no option but to compete with one another. In order to maintain and improve their competitive position, countries need to provide first-class education and training services for all their citizens. Only then will they be able to create a highly skilled labour force that is necessary for higher productivity, lower unit labour costs and greater competitive advantage. This can only be done largely by the state. Second, a globalized economy involves labour flexibility at the national level, that is, acceptance by workers that they will lose their jobs several times in their working life and that they may have to take on part-time or low-paid jobs. Workers need to be compensated for this for reasons of both social justice and social harmony. Again this can only be done largely by the state through social protection policies of the kind that exist in many European countries today. Without such social protection measures, inequality, poverty and social disharmony will increase to the detriment of both the good life and economic competitiveness.

This is the position taken, for example, by Kapstein, who argues that both technological change and international trade competition are exacerbating unemployment, low wages and poverty in advanced industrial countries. This necessitates more government services to help those so badly affected. The paradox is that most governments are doing the exact opposite. In his words: 'Just when working people most need the nation-state as a buffer from the world economy, it is abandoning them' (Kapstein, 1996a, p. 16). If this continues, he argues, social strife, opposition to free trade and demands for protectionism will follow.

Until recently governments in countries that were most exposed to international trade were able to make the most generous provisions for their citizens. Evidence for this comes from the work of Katzenstein (1985). He shows how governments in several small European countries – Sweden, Austria and the Netherlands – tried successfully during the 1960s and 1970s to cope with the pressures of globalization by extending their public services. Being small countries, they were more open to the pressures of free trade than big countries in Europe and they had to spend a greater proportion of their GDP on public services in order to sharpen their competitiveness and secure the support of their workforce. Katzenstein's work, however, refers to the period when economic growth was high, unemployment was low and state welfare expansion was generally welcomed.

More recent work by Rodrik both supports and contradicts Katzenstein's findings. Rodrik's research shows that there is a positive correlation between the volume of public expenditure in a country and its exposure to trade or more accurately its exposure to external risk – level of trade and volatility in the prices of traded goods. He bases his conclusion on cross-country evidence from twenty-three OECD countries during the early 1990s. 'At one end of the continuum', he writes, 'are the United States and Japan, which have the lowest trade shares in GDP and the lowest shares of government spending. At the other end are

Luxembourg, Belgium, and the Netherlands, economies with very high degrees of openness and large governments' (Rodrik, 1997, p. 52). The reason is that 'exposure to external risk has resulted in demands for a more active government role in the provision of social insurance' (1997, p. 58). But there is a sting in the tail of Rodrik's study. More detailed examination of a smaller number of countries found that globalization was making the survival of big government increasingly difficult because of the pressures exerted on governments by MNEs with their drive for maximum competitiveness. To quote him again: 'globalization reduces the ability of governments to spend resources on social programs, it makes it more difficult to tax capital, and labor now carries a growing share of the tax burden' (1997, p. 64).

If Rodrik's findings are confirmed by other studies, we are in a para-doxical situation. Globalization requires high public spending if free trade, on which globalization depends, is to survive but globalization makes high public spending levels very difficult.

## Globalization against welfare

The second approach is based on the theoretical premise that globaliza-tion has intensified the problems created by high levels of public ex-penditure. Put simply, it is the neo-liberal view, discussed in chapter 5, which sees high levels of social expenditure and labour protection mea-sures as antithetical to economic prosperity. These have to be substan-tially reduced if such problems as unemployment, low rates of economic growth and such like can be dealt with satisfactorily. As Schwab and Smadja put it:

> there is no way that the Western European nations will be able to ease their enduring unemployment problems without dealing with the struc-tural rigidities in their labour systems, even though such an undertaking will require a kind of cultural revolution for Europeans accustomed to the notion of an ever-expanding welfare state. (Schwab and Smadja, 1994, p. 42)

We shall examine this approach in chapter 5. Suffice it to say here that some research on globalized industries lends support to the view that globalization pressurizes governments to reduce social protection measures. This is best brought out in Aspinwall's research using as its theoretical framework the notion of the 'unholy social trinity', that 'capital mobility, free trade and social/labour market policy auto-nomy' cannot be sustained simultaneously by a government for long (Aspinwall, 1996, p. 130). Since all countries are anxious to maintain and improve economic growth, governments find it impossible not to give in to the demands of MNEs or other firms for lower labour costs and a freer hand in labour relations. Aspinwall's case-study of shipping, a labour-intensive industry, in Norway, Germany and Denmark found supporting evidence for the 'unholy social trinity' thesis. It concluded that 'the social dumping argument has merit' (Aspinwall, 1996, p. 125) since governments in his study were forced to lower welfare costs and employment conditions to those prevailing for Asian and East European crews. It was a case where economic pressures overrode political preferences.

## Compromises between welfare and competitiveness

The third approach steers a middle course. While accepting the positive contribution of welfare provision to the social, economic and political life of a nation, it argues that the forces of globalization make certain adjustments and modifications to existing welfare provision necessary. It suspects that as at present constituted social welfare provisions can discourage work incentives and it argues that active rather than passive forms of social protection measures are, therefore, needed. This entails more emphasis on technological education, training and retraining measures, social protection regulations that make the payment of benefits more conditional on employment requirements and at least slight reductions in the generosity of benefits. It is the approach favoured by both the EC and the OECD in their attempts to satisfy the competing demands of their member countries. Thus the EC, while stressing the positive aspects of social policy, argues that the cost of labour, particularly the unskilled and semi-skilled, should be reduced in order to encourage employment (CEC, 1993a, p. 18). Similarly the OECD paints a picture of existing welfare provision that contains both positive and negative strands but needing certain reforms to boost employment. It claims that existing benefits 'have drifted towards quasi-permanent income support in many countries, lowering work incentives' (OECD, 1994, p. 48) and they need to be made more conditional to employment.

The general tone of this third position is that European countries can deal with the globalization pressures with only some fine tuning to their public services in order to improve competitiveness. It is not unexpected that it is this approach that commands most support among governments in Europe for, if for no other reason, welfare containment is electorally unpopular and has to be gradual and incremental. It does, however, raise the serious question of where the process of gradual retrenchment and restructuring is likely to lead to in the long term. Minor reductions in state welfare can have a major impact on the public in the long run because of their cumulative effects. Moreover, each minor reform may well be a form of fine tuning but taken as a whole they may constitute a more serious form of welfare restructuring.

## *The limits to economic globalization*

The fourth approach to globalization and welfare differs from the other three in the sense that either it does not see globalization as a major constraining force or, if it does, it believes that governments can stand up to MNEs provided they have the public backing and the will to do so. Most writers in this school of thought recognize the immense political problems of their position at least in the short term. Many also accept that parties of the left and trade unions can no longer protect the welfare state on their own. Robinson, for example, shows how globalization has increased poverty and inequality and how major political parties, 'tied all too closely to corporate interests', are unlikely to pursue the radical policies that are needed to reverse this process. He therefore feels that 'the array of social movements and non profit organisations' are the alternative vehicles for the radical project assisted by a regeneration of radical ideology that will demonstrate to the public that 'the neoliberal form of globalization is not natural, inevitable, or desirable' (Robinson, 1995, p. 379). Others, as we saw earlier, stress the importance of regional government blocs such as the European Union as the best way of controlling the power of international capital.

As pointed out above, while globalization had a constraining effect on state welfare, it had an expansive effect on private welfare. The net result may have been that though the total volume of welfare may have been unaffected, a greater proportion of that is taken up by private welfare provision. All the available evidence shows that a country's ranking on total welfare effort can differ from that of its state welfare sector. By international standards, the USA, for example, is a welfare laggard on state welfare but it ranks very high when private expenditure is included so that total welfare effort is compared (Leuven and Tuijman, 1996, p. 12). This has implications not only for the ranking of countries on the international comparative tables but, more importantly, for the distribution of welfare among different groups in society. Though middle and upper groups consume their fair share of state welfare, they undoubtedly consume the lion's share of private welfare.

## Conclusions

Bearing in mind the difficulties involved in the validity of international empirical data on the complex issues raised by globalization, a series of tentative conclusions can be drawn.

1   Economic globalization is a reality today irrespective of whether it is a new phenomenon or an old one that has accelerated during the past twenty years or so. This does not mean that we live in a totally integrated world economy but, rather, that we live in a world where world economic processes are becoming highly integrated. The same applies to political and cultural processes.

2   Imports of manufactured goods from developing countries have been one of the many factors that contributed to the rise of unemployment in DMEs. Such imports were initially in such areas as clothing, shoemaking and toys but more recently they have expanded to cover such technological products as radios, tvs, computers etc. The rise in unemployment can only exacerbate the problems faced by the welfare state in advanced industrial societies.

3   The activities of MNEs during the past two decades have also contributed in a small way to the rise in structural unemployment in DMEs. Though there are many reasons for the growth of unemployment and the spread of low wages, it is equally important not to ignore the part played by globalization both as a process and as the ideology of aggressive individualism.

4   Most hardship so far has fallen on unskilled workers in terms of both unemployment and low wages, while most of the benefits of trade with developing countries and the activities of MNEs have gone to the technologically skilled and the affluent sections of DMEs.

5   While the standard of living in a small number of NICs has improved, living conditions in most developing countries remain pitifully low. Indeed, as Deacon points out, the current social welfare achievements of the DMEs 'may not be replicable on a global scale given the finite energy and other resources' (Deacon, 1997, p. 26).

6   Globalization has also had beneficial effects on DMEs – it has expanded export markets and it has provided low-priced imports for consumers in DMEs. It has also benefited economically some NICs, particularly their elites.

7   There is ample evidence supporting the proposition that globalization has altered the balance of power within countries away from trade unions towards the employer's associations – a trend that has adverse implications on the maintenance of generous, universal, state welfare provision.

8   The sovereignty of national governments in advanced industrial societies has suffered to a greater or lesser extent. It would be just as wrong to write off the power of national governments as to ignore the fact that MNEs today exert more influence on government decisions concerning national economic and social issues than before.

9   The overall effect of globalization on state welfare provision has been one of containment and reduction. It has strengthened those inter-

nal factors that make for the contraction of state welfare provision. The extent and nature of this contraction has varied from one country to another depending on internal factors that we discuss in chapter 7.

10   Though there are differences of opinion among the supporters of state welfare as to how best governments should respond to the globalization pressures, the dominant view is that governments should marshal support from as many quarters as possible. It is, however, accepted that a certain degree of gradual restructuring is inevitable and in some cases necessary. As shown in chapter 2, the welfare state in European countries has been adapting to this new situation mainly through incremental containment and contraction of its provisions during the 1990s in ways that are in line with the national institutions of each country.

11   It is important to assess the effects of globalization on welfare developments over time rather than from a very short-term perspective. It may well be that what appear to be minor changes at first may gradually become more serious over time. Vice versa, some welfare cuts that had to be introduced in order to satisfy the demands of global forces can later be restored. As Hinnfors and Pierre point out in the case of Sweden, some of the welfare cuts introduced in the aftermath of the kronar devaluation in 1992 were partially restored in 1997 when the economy recovered and the globalization pressures eased (Hinnfors and Pierre, 1998, p. 114).

12   Though 'the general notion of an inexorable globalization pressure to shrink welfare states is untenable' (Rieger and Leibfried, 1998, p. 364), the belief that globalization pressures can be easily dealt with by national states is too simplistic. On present evidence, the forces of globalization will continue and possibly intensify in the foreseeable future, thus maintaining the pressures on state welfare provision. The main dilemma facing all governments is how to combine business competitiveness with social harmony and the satisfaction of adequate minimum standards of living for all in society. Globalization has made this task more difficult.

# 4
# Welfare Politics: The Narrowing of the National Conscience

One of the most obvious features of contemporary politics in the Western democracies is that parties are unwilling to endorse policies that involve an increase in public spending because they fear that they will lose electoral support. The whole climate of political debate about welfare policy has undergone a radical transformation since the three decades of confident expansion that followed the Second World War. The UK Labour party manifesto setting out the programme which led to a landslide victory in the UK in 1997 promised: 'There will be no increase in the basic or top rates of income tax over the next five years' (Labour Party, 1997, p. 5). In Europe, the winning parties in elections from 1997 to the end of the century in Germany, France, Sweden and Italy – all left or left-centre coalitions – succeeded on a platform that included tax cuts or at least a promise not to increase taxation. The OECD report *New Orientations for Social Policy* (1994a, p. 8) stresses that 'social policies cannot be developed outside the reality of budgetary considerations'. A similar perspective is adopted in the EU's *Social Policy* green paper (CEC, 1993a, p. 13) and in more considered language in the 1995 *Social Protection* report (CEC, 1996, p. 12).

A basic premise of current welfare policy-making is that taxes cannot be raised. The implications for constraint are sharpened by the Maastricht Treaty strictures on state borrowing, which effectively eliminate alternative sources of finance for expansion. At the level of party politics, welfare cut-backs are justified by the assumption that people will not tolerate tax increases. This chapter considers the theoretical accounts which support this position and goes on to examine evidence from attitude surveys on the dominant themes in public opinion. There is substantial and simultaneous support for reducing the level of taxation and social contributions and for maintaining and increasing spending on the main welfare services in most countries. This implies peculiar political difficulties for governments which seek to cut expenditure.

A number of influential writers have argued in recent years that governments are now able to pursue welfare retrenchment with little effective resistance because key groups in the electorate no longer support the pattern of state welfare spending that developed during the long boom and are unwilling to pay the taxes necessary to sustain it. There are two main variants of this view. One argues that, for various reasons to do with the development of distinctively modern social forms and the experience of living within them, a general cultural shift against state welfare has taken place. A clear exposition of this approach is to be found in the recent work of Giddens – for example: 'the welfare state project has foundered, partly because it came to embody what turned out to be the failing aspirations of socialism and partly because of the impact of wider social changes' (1994, p. 149). The theme of the obsolescence of state welfare is also be found in Inglehart, Glennerster, Etzioni and Jessop, as well as in writers who adopt the 'risk society' perspective such as Beck and Lasch.

The second variant is more closely concerned with social divisions, and argues that policy has swung decisively against state welfare because groups who see their interest in terms of low taxes and low public spending are increasingly able to dominate the political agenda. This position is clearly expressed by Galbraith:

> in past times, the economically and socially fortunate were . . . a small minority . . . They are now a majority of the citizens . . . who actually vote. . . . The future . . . is thought effectively within their personal command. Their anger is evident . . . when government and the seemingly less deserving intrude their needs and demands. This is especially so if such action suggests higher taxes. (1992, pp. 15–17)

It can also be found in writers such as Hutton (1996) and is reflected in much contemporary discussion of class and welfare policy.

A third approach to the relationship between political culture and welfare policy focuses on the inertia of advantaged groups. The main point is that, in a climate of retrenchment, those who think they will lose out if welfare is cut back protest vigorously and may be in a position to damage the government electorally. Politicians who wish to contain spending must move carefully if they are not to lose votes. The politics of welfare retrenchment differ radically from those of expansion (Pierson, 1994).

The claim that social change has generated forces that turn the contemporary climate of opinion firmly against state welfare is particularly influential in politics in the UK, where Anthony Giddens has developed close links with policy-makers and has been the leading academic contributor to a series of prime ministerial seminars from 1997 onwards. He was invited to present similar ideas to Clinton at a conference in February 1998. Ulrich Beck has attained considerable prominence in the German media with a broadly comparable set of ideas.

## Theoretical Accounts of Developments in Welfare Values

*The obsolescence of state welfare: theories of cultural shift*

The view that traditional state welfare is increasingly out of tune with dominant strands in modern culture is reinforced by arguments from a wide range of perspectives. It has become the common sense of the political economy of public debate and builds on theoretical accounts from at least five directions. First, influential analyses by Giddens (1994, 1998), Beck (1986), Lash (Beck et al., 1994) and others argue that a distinguishing feature of the way people think about their lives in modern societies is a qualitative shift in the apprehension of insecurity, which they refer to as the development of a '*risk society*'. The way this development has taken place makes traditional state-centred welfare services obsolete. The point is not that modern life is intrinsically more risky. In a material sense, most people are more secure than ever before. They live longer, and are better nourished, sheltered and fed. The distinguishing feature of a risk society is that the source and nature of uncertainty has changed, not that the amount of risk has increased.

Before modernity, risk was understood largely in terms of external factors – the displeasure of the gods, plague, drought, the barbarians at the gates. As scientific understanding of the genesis of problems developed, the idea that progress could be achieved through human interventions, whether technical (antibiotics, modern farming) or social (housing projects, employment policy, the NHS), gained a stronger hold. However, increasing awareness of the shortcomings of progressive solutions – the technology that leads to the hole in the ozone layer, Chernobyl, new variant CJD or genetically modified foodstuffs, the social interventions that produce high-rise slums, the great car society or the medicalization of health in the interests of professionals – has led people to see risk more as 'manufactured uncertainty'. The term refers to the notion that the risks we now face result as much from previous attempts to apply technology or social policies to practical problems as from external factors. Thus people tend to be more wary of professional and expert solutions to the problems they encounter and increasingly aware of the insecurities associated with developments elsewhere in society. It is in this sense that the modern world has moved towards a 'risk society'.

The incidence of manufactured uncertainty reaches across all social groups, and it is increasingly difficult for advantaged groups to insulate themselves against the risks of, for example, technological changes leading to unemployment among professionals as well as manual workers, the health problems that technical changes affecting diet may bring or the impact of planning or transport policy decisions taken elsewhere on the value of their homes. At the same time, people are inclined to be suspicious of the claims of official policy-makers. The development of modernism goes hand in hand with a jaundiced attitude to state welfare.

A second approach argues that the explanation is to be sought in *politico-economic rather than ideological changes*. The Beveridge-inspired welfare state developed in times of relatively high employment (sustained by a clear government commitment) and stable patterns of family life and of the gender division of labour. The accepted boundaries between government, family and private responsibilities rested on these assumptions. Jessop and others have pointed out that these conditions no longer apply (Jessop et al., 1991; Jessop, 1994). The state can no longer guarantee full employment and the availability of jobs over the working life. Family patterns are characterized by greater flexibility in relationships; the division between women's responsibility for domestic and child-care work in the home and men's responsibility as breadwinner in paid employment is outdated. Thus confidence in traditional welfare declines because the social relations that sustained it have become obsolete.

A third strand in argument also suggests that the basic assumptions underlying social policy-making have changed, but approaches the issues in terms of *economic 'rational actor' theory*. The policy-makers and planners responsible for creating the post-war welfare state were assumed to be active, altruistic and authoritative while the beneficiaries (the same people who also pay for welfare provision through the tax system) were deferential and acquiescent – a world of knights and pawns, as Le Grand puts it (1997, 2000). Politicians and civil servants devised and enacted policies in the common interest; citizens recognized this and were happy to pay the required taxes and to accept the standard range of services – and the gaps in provision – that the state offered. This corresponds to the dominant model of the 'civic culture' of the 1960s as combining the deference necessary to ensure stability with the (none too demanding) proactivity to engage in periodic elections (Almond and Verba, 1965).

More recent approaches to state welfare provision have been influenced by the rational choice approach that applies the model of the self-interested, individual actor of neo-classical economic theory to social and political contexts. They assume that policy-makers, providers, service users and taxpayers are both self-interested and proactive. Thus politicians design policies not for the common good, but to win elections. Officials and professionals tend to deliver services in ways that avoid the inconvenience of dealing with awkard cases or permit them to enlarge the sphere and influence of their operations (and hence their status and salaries). Taxpayers are unwilling to pay (unless they think public services are a better bargain) and punish politicians who ask them to do so at the polls. Service users devise strategic combinations of subsidized private and state services, use their social contacts and cultural capital to chart pathways through the state system or scrounge entitlement to benefits and subvert the collective goals to their own advantage. From this perspective the traditional welfare state is becoming obsolete – over-vulnerable to individual manipulation and thus likely to be mistrusted by citizens (see Taylor-Gooby, 1998b, ch. 11, for more detailed discussion).

A fourth, slightly different approach emphasizing *diminishing returns to welfare spending* is advanced by Inglehart and others in relation to a wider range of countries. Inglehart's approach rests not so much on an account of the impact of maldistributed prosperity in the context of a particular political framework as on the idea that the obsolescence of state welfare stems from its success. The welfare state has worked itself out of a job: 'the consensus [mass support for welfare statism] is dissolving. It no longer seems self-evident that the expansion of state authority constitutes progress – even to those on the left.' This is due to three factors: first, 'the welfare state has reached a point of diminishing returns ... this does not reflect failure ... but the fact that it has succeeded in alleviating those problems it can most readily solve'; secondly, decentralization in economic, industrial and administrative practice following the information technology revolution; and, thirdly, the claim that 'advanced industrial societies are undergoing a gradual shift from emphasis on economic and physical security toward greater emphasis on belonging, self-expression and quality of life' (Inglehart, 1990, pp. 9, 10). The recent work of Etzioni contains similar arguments, although here the driving force behind a tendency to reject interventionist state welfare is a desire for a simpler life resulting from the experience of material affluence, expressed in such developments as 'voluntary downshifting' (Etzioni, 1998).

A fifth approach, in recent work by Glennerster, develops the idea of the *fading glamour of state welfare* from a different angle. In an authoritative review of developments in the UK over the past two decades he demonstrates that welfare spending as a proportion of GDP remained at roughly the same level in 1995/6 as in 1975/6 (25.8 as against 25.7 per cent). The social wage is now directed more accurately at the poor. The puzzle remains that 'despite the steady but gradual improvement in rates of treatment in the NHS, much greater participation in post-school education and improved housing standards, dissatisfaction with the welfare system grew' (Glennerster and Hills, 1998, p. 325). The welfare state in fact costs roughly the same and achieves rather more – arguably a success story. The explanation for welfare disillusion lies outside the state sector: 'performance and quality standards were rising even faster in the rest of the economy . . . No wonder a one per cent per annum increase in the performance of the NHS in the 1980s caused frustration' (p. 325). People experience substantially improved standards of consumption in the marketed sector of the economy. Real wages have risen (for most), many more people have central heating, foreign holidays, cars, telephones, video machines and central heating. The welfare state simply cannot keep up.

These theories draw on different sociological and politico-economic traditions. They have in common the claim that public attitudes have shifted against willingness to support state provision in a way that makes the traditional welfare state simply obsolete. Welfare states do not fit with the development of modern society and must be discarded. The sheer weight and variety of arguments that buttress this position ensure that it becomes conventional wisdom – the default position in popular debate and dominant analysis in the assumptions of politicians across the political spectrum. This raises the question of why politicians still maintain welfare states if no one wants them. Before considering what people do in fact want, we will consider other theoretical frameworks.

## The obsolescence of the welfare state: theories of conflicting interests

The second cluster of approaches to the politics of state welfare adopts a different perspective. The core argument here is not that society as a whole has shifted against state welfare, but that particular groups, who see their own interests as best served by the contraction of the welfare state, have gained a dominant position. Probably the best-known exponent of this view is Galbraith in a recent development of his influential analysis on the *social impact of mass affluence*. His argument is simple and forceful and can be stated briefly: social change has enabled relatively advantaged groups to command an electoral majority which they use to maintain their own privileges and to constrain taxation and welfare spending.

This argument is set in the context of US public policy and low electoral turn-out. However, similar points are made in relation to other countries by authors such as Hutton, who argues that Galbraith's 'comfortable majority' can be roughly equated with the proportion of the workforce who have access to secure full-time employment (1996, p. 14) and that the risk of exclusion, enhanced by retrenchment, makes the desire to join this group ever more urgent (p. 217). Similar points are implied by the accounts of the 'new poverty' which is seen to divide the interests of those whose needs are not met by existing welfare systems within advanced economies from more established groups. The 'new poor' include one-parent families, many categories of immigrants, those without access to secure employment, many unskilled, low-paid workers, people with disabilities and others (Room and Berghman, 1990). The development of a 'one-third/two-thirds' society, erecting divisions between insecure and affluent, is subject to intense debate (Leisering and Leibfried, 1998, ch. 10). The fear that these shifts will condemn a sizeable group within the population of advanced countries to long-term social exclusion has also informed policy debate at the level of the EU (CEC, 1994b, p. 11).

The principal difference between this position and that reviewed in the previous section concerns the role of social divisions. This model is essentially conflictual. The comfortable majority uses the political power with which a particular electoral framework endows it to establish a policy regime in which it is advantaged by lower taxation and a weakening of any policies which might redistribute resources in the direction of poorer groups. The former approach operates in terms of an overall shift in social values. Those who emphasize risk and manufactured uncertainty argue that people have lost trust in the welfare state: 'the welfare state, once seen as the core of democratic politics, today creates almost as many problems as it solves' (Giddens, 1998, p. 16). From the perspective of Inglehart and those associated with him, it is the success of the welfare state in reducing inequalities over much of the century which leads to secular decline in the divisions of interest between social groups (1990, p. 258) and to a narrowing of commitment to major social interventions. Similarly, Glennerster sees rising expectations as characterizing the experience of the mass of the population. While both approaches agree that the current political climate will favour retrenchment, they differ in their account of the distribution of current inequalities and insecurities, on the trajectory whereby societies have arrived at the contemporary settlement and on the likely prognosis in response to any retrenchment which would increase inequalities.

All these approaches imply that citizens will no longer support government in taking a dominant role in the provision of welfare. They disagree in their account of this development. Jessop, Beck and Giddens believe that social changes outside the sphere of welfare have rendered state interventionism obsolete in the face of changing patterns of need and risk, Glennerster emphasizes the part played by rising expectations, fuelled by developments outside the state sector, Le Grand argues that ideological approaches to welfare have undergone secular change, Inglehart argues that it is the success of state welfare in meeting need that has undermined its relevance and Galbraith emphasizes the self-interest of the comfortable mass versus needy minorities. The key difference is whether the withdrawal of support is seen as confined to a self-interested and comfortable electoral majority (Galbraith) or as a broader social trend, as the other authors argue.

## Entrenched opposition and welfare cut-backs

An additional and contrary approach to welfare politics has opened up new areas for research and debate, by focusing attention on the process of retrenchment rather than the factors that influence policy-making. The influential theory that the dominant political currents constrain rather than advance retrenchment associated with the work of Paul Pierson and others was discussed towards the end of chapter 1. The central point here is that, for a number of reasons, the damage caused by welfare cut-backs tends to be more visible than the benefits. The benefits are spread across many taxpayers, while cut-backs are concentrated on particular groups who may then protest against the losses they experience as a result of school or hospital closures, benefit cuts or a hike in the pension age. The benefits may in fact consist of a small reduction in tax rates or the deferring of planned increases. Such gains are of low visibility. In addition, it is claimed, there is considerable psychological evidence of 'loss aversion', mainly from carefully controlled behavioural experiments (see Tversky and Kahneman, 1981). In general people feel the loss of something they had more keenly than they value the benefit of an equivalent good which they gain. To lose £5 from your purse, it is claimed, reduces happiness more than winning £5 in a lottery increases it. Thus, the theory goes, welfare cuts cause greater disquiet than equivalent tax cuts can compensate.

These factors mean that the politics of retrenchment (which essentially involves taking services they previously enjoyed away from people) is fundamentally different from the politics of the welfare expansion of the three post-war decades. Modern welfare policy-making is subservient to a politics of blame avoidance, where cut-backs must be concealed, approached with stealth, attributed to outside forces or presented as the inevitable consequence of policies established in the past.

This argument opens up fresh approaches to contemporary developments in welfare and has enjoyed considerable attention. One problem is explaining the different pace and character of retrenchment in different countries and the extent to which, in some circumstances, politicians appear able to proceed without manoeuvring to escape the blame for their actions. In relation to the climate of public opinion, the key issue is whether identifiable groups advantaged by the status quo resist change in a way that inhibits welfare reform – the converse of Galbraith's claim that those advantaged by retrenchment are able to secure a decisive policy shift in that direction.

We will now examine survey data to see how well these theories correspond to the opinions that people actually hold.

## Public Opinion and the Future of Welfare

Many national opinion studies exist and projects such as the International Social Survey Project (ISSP), the Cross National Electoral Project, the World Values Study and the EU's Eurobarometer link studies across countries. In this section we illustrate the argument through data from the ISSP, although a similar case could be based on other studies (see, for example, Coughlin, 1980; Kaase and Newton, 1996; Svallfors and Taylor-Gooby, 1999; Svallfors, 1997; Evans, 1996; Ferrera, 1993). This survey is chosen because it is of the highest quality, is conveniently available, covers the countries in which we are most interested, permits comparisons outside Europe and has been repeated on an annual basis, so that we can trace attitude change over time since the mid-1980s. Unlike many surveys, it includes questions which allow us to examine views on what services governments should be providing as well as on the level of service they do provide. It is important to distinguish the two, since immediate political debates can influence responses to questions dealing with the latter issue and such practical factors may confuse our understanding of the broader issues of principle with which discussion of the erosion of support for welfare in Europe is concerned.

The analysis is necessarily broad-brush. Attitude surveys rely on the answers to structured questions which may be understood and answered in different ways by different people. If these idiosyncratic differences are randomly distributed, they cancel each other out in a large sample and can be ignored. The problem in cross-national work is that national differences may introduce systematic variation. The translation of questions for surveys in the different countries participating in the project may conceal nuances of meaning. Responses to household income questions may be conditioned by factors such as traditions which value privacy from other family members or from the intrusions of officialdom. In any case, opinions may be an imperfect guide to behaviour, including voting behaviour. The relationship between what is said in interview to the choices actually made may vary from country to country, so that the views expressed in the survey do not correspond to the pressures on policy-making. One important factor here is the differences in institutional structure discussed in chapter 7 which mediate the link between interests and policy. Opinion survey cannot be an exact science, but does offer concise indications of the pattern of opinion across a population in a way that no other approach can. When there are substantial differences between the pattern of answers in different countries in surveys carried out by reputable agencies, it is a good indication that differences exist which theory should recognize and seek to explain.

Our analysis comprises three stages. First, we look at the development of opinion over time, in order to establish whether attitudes have moved against the principle of state welfare in the way that is commonly assumed by politicians who fear tax revolt. Secondly, we use cross-sectional data to examine the views of different groups, to see whether the influences on attitudes correspond to the divisions between social groups highlighted in the second and third theories considered earlier or to the general shifts in values across the population as a whole described in the first. Thirdly, the analysis considers attitudes to taxation and particularly willingness to pay for different welfare services among various social groups. State services are only sustainable if the costs are accepted. However, those who are most enthusiastic for extra provision may also want tax cuts at the same time, trapping governments in a policy dilemma.

## *Attitude change since the mid-1980s: what should the government provide?*

The material available from the surveys includes questions on the services for which those interviewed think government should assume responsibility, and, by implication, those areas for which they think the government is under no obligation to provide. These allow us to focus on issues of principle in relation to welfare. A full range of data over the whole period is available only for former West Germany and the UK, among major EU member states, with data for Italy up to 1992. Former East Germany joined the survey in 1990 and Sweden in 1992. In our analysis of trends over time we have retained the distinction between the Western and Eastern sections of united Germany in order to draw attention to the considerable attitudinal differences that exist between these two regions. We have also included the most prominent liberal welfare regime – the USA – for purposes of comparison. It is here that Galbraith originally developed his thesis and it represents a different national context with distinctive welfare policies.

First we will examine two core areas of welfare state policy during the period – whether government should provide jobs for everyone who needs one (in other words, the Keynesian assumption of a full-employment policy, which forms the basis of the traditional welfare state and which has been increasingly threatened by labour market change in recent years) and whether government should reduce income differences between better- and worse-off people (in other words the commitment to redistribution that underlies much welfare provision and is threatened by policies designed to cut direct taxes). The graphs in figures 4.1 and 4.2 show net support for each policy, measured by subtracting the percentage who did not endorse state responsibility from those who did, and ignoring the small percentage who expressed no opinion. This is a convenient way of simplifying the material available in order to give a clear summary of attitudes in the countries.

The data displayed in the graphs lead to four main conclusions about attitudes to welfare in the various countries:

- There is a strong measure of consistency over time. The gradients on the graphs are not steep, there is little cross-over in the trajectory of attitudes in the different countries and those which are relatively low or high at the beginning of the decade retain roughly the same position at the end.
- There are clear differences between the liberal USA, where the balance of opinion is against government responsibility for much of the period studied, and the European nations, which have stronger welfare traditions. Attitudes in the UK are stable and

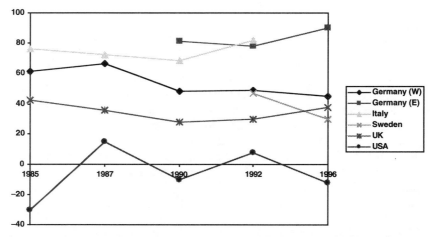

**Figure 4.1** Government responsibility for full employment, 1985–96 (%)

*Source*: International Social Survey Project.

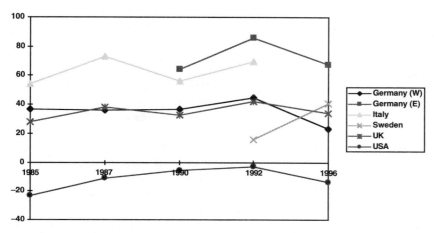

**Figure 4.2**  Government responsibility for income redistribution, 1985–96 (%)

*Source*: International Social Survey Project.

tend to be rather less enthusiastic for state intervention than else-where in Europe.

- Within the European countries, East Germany and Italy have the strongest support for full employment and redistributive welfare, while there is less enthusiasm in the other countries. The com-paratively moderate level of support for strongly interventionist policies in Sweden is surprising in view of the strong reputation enjoyed by that country for social democratic welfarism.

- The data give little support to the claim that public opinion is moving away from endorsement of welfare and towards retrench-ment. What variation there is in attitudes may best be explained by details of survey technique or by political circumstances. Thus the questions asked in 1987 and 1992 surveys were set in the context of other questions about inequality that might have pro-voked more interventionist answers compared with the 1985, 1990 and 1996 surveys, which focused on the more neutral topic of the role of government. The decline in net support for employment policy between 1992 and 1996 in Sweden may be related to aware-ness of the impact of international competition on that country's competitive position, brought home by the late 1992 financial crisis and the package of cuts which followed. These circumstances may also go some way to explain the increased enthusiasm for redis-tribution to the poor.

This brief analysis of the way attitudes develop over time contradicts theoretical assumptions about retrenchment and cultural shifts. The public mood is not moving against an interventionist welfare state. Other analyses point to similar conclusions. Evans concludes that the pattern of attitudes in East and West Europe, the USA and Australasia suggests 'the existence of stable and distinct types of redistributive cultures, with the clearest divisions between America and Australia . . . and European countries . . . There is also some generally trendless fluctuation' (Evans, 1996, p. 194). The European Science Foundation's Beliefs in Government project discussed theories of tax revolt and welfare backlash, government overload, legitimation crisis and rational choice, which have all been seen to imply a diminution of support for state intervention, particularly in the sphere of welfare. Its conclusion is similar: 'changes in mass attitudes have been slow and limited . . . there have been shifts in public priorities, but these have not resulted in a widespread rejection of the old attitudes and agendas . . . the result has been stability, continuity and adaptation, rather than fundamental or wholesale change' (Kaase and Newton, 1996, p. 96). The European Union's Eurobarometer survey shows that: 'citizens' attachment to the fundamental tenets of the European welfare tradition does not appear to be in doubt: thus indicating that the necessary adaptive reforms may be able to rest on a precious layer of normative continuity' (Ferrera, 1993, p. 4). General overviews of attitude data show 'broad public support, consistently revealed in polls' (for example, Pierson, 1998, p. 552).

Recent analysis, based on comparison of Eurobarometer and national surveys, however, shows some evidence of a tax backlash in Italy (Ferrera, 1997b, p. 245). This may be due to the very heavy pressures on Italy to reduce its public debt (123.8 per cent of GDP in 1995) as a condition of EMU membership and to dissatisfaction with the inefficiencies and inequities of the system. Concern about the current welfare arrangements does not appear to undermine support for the principle of state welfare in the country.

If there is little evidence to supports claims of a secular shift in attitudes against state welfarism since the 1980s, despite the theories discussed earlier, what of the structure of attitudes in the 1990s? We will examine the answers to questions about particular services among members of different social groups to determine whether attitudes divide along plausible lines of social interest.

## *Attitudes in the 1990s: divisions in support for different services*

The material discussed so far is concerned with attitudes to retrenchment or expansion measured through trends in attitudes to welfare interventionism over time. We now consider the structure of current attitudes. Previous analysis (see, for example, Ferrera, 1993, p. 3; Kaase and Newton, 1996, p. 83; Coughlin, 1980, pp. 153–4; Svallfors, 1997, p. 296) shows that the strongest cleavage in answers to these questions lies between those concerned with the core needs and risks which most people either experience or anticipate experiencing during their lives (for example, needs for health care or old age pensions) as against those catering for needs which tend to be confined to lower-income minorities (such as unemployment benefits or social housing). Provision for other needs which are discussed in the surveys (support for students, full employment, redistribution between better- and worse-off) fits somewhere between these favoured and less favoured services.

This division in attitudes has been explained in terms of a moralistic notion of desert (for example, Leiserung and Leibfried, 1998, ch. 4) or in terms of mass versus minority interest (for example, Alt, 1983). Here, we can use this division to summarize the main points from the data. Each country is represented by two lines in the graph. One represents support for the view that the two 'favoured' services should definitely be provided by the government, the other for the view that the 'less favoured' services should definitely be the state's responsibility. Clearly the patterns of provision and of social need in different countries will influence national patterns of answers. However, the difference in popular attitudes between favoured and less favoured provision produces a clear overall picture, despite such variations.

Figure 4.3 reinforces some of the points made earlier.

- In general, support for the view that the state should be responsible for provision declines somewhat as income rises, from left to right across the graphs, with some minor variation in the middle of the income range. This is true for both favoured and less favoured services.
- Support is more vigorous in every country for those services which provide for the needs of large groups in the population and are not targeted on those who declare themselves poor and needy and run the risk of being seen as undeserving.
- There is very little 'cross-over' in the graphs. The lines of the graph cutting across each other would imply different patterns of support by different income groups in different countries. The trend to a decline in support as income rises is relatively uniform across the two groups of services and across the countries considered.
- Support for both favoured and less favoured services is lowest in the USA followed by Germany and then the UK and Sweden close together. Support for state responsibility for the provision of

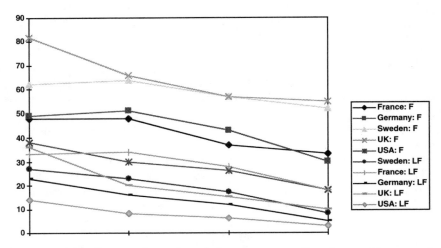

**Figure 4.3**   Proportion of each income quartile who see favoured and less favoured services as definitely the government's responsibility, 1996 (%)

F = Favoured services ('It is definitely the government's responsibility to provide: health care for the sick; a decent standard of living for the old').
LF = Less favoured services ('It is definitely the government's responsibility to provide: a decent standard of living for the unemployed; decent housing for those who can't afford it').
*Source*: International Social Survey Project.

less favoured services is the strongest in France (in fact stronger than US support for favoured services) but French attitudes to more favoured services are relatively less enthusiastic and are close to those in Germany.

The evidence of a division between the mass 'more favoured' and the minority 'less favoured' services lends support to Pierson's analysis. It indicates that the real division lies not between particular groups, but between services and countries. The favoured services (health care and pensions) are the most expensive aspects of state welfare. The strength of support for provision in these areas creates real dilemmas for governments that feel they can no longer sustain the cost of traditional welfare services in all welfare states. These points do not support the theoretical claims about the way in which shifts in overall values or the self-interest of comfortable majorities undermines support for state welfare. The change in attitudes across income groups is a general tendency, hardly sufficiently significant to explain the shift towards retrenchment discussed in chapter 2. Even in the USA it is not sufficiently emphatic to bear the weight of explanation that Galbraith places on it. Interestingly, there is no division in support for more or less favoured services between income groups, although it is the provisions specifically directed at poor minorities which one might expect a comfortable majority to reject most strongly, as irrelevant to their own interests. Similarly, the other theories which point to the success of welfare, the influence of exogenous factors or ideological change as the motor behind a disenchantment with state welfare, do not fit the evidence.

So far we have considered the level of principle – what should the state provide as a matter of the obligations of government to its citizens? We move on to consider the key question in current political debate: practical preferences between different welfare services and the willingness to pay the taxes and social contributions necessary to finance them. The material here covers social democratic Sweden, liberal USA and liberal-leaning Britain, and France and Germany, which represent different varieties of social insurance, corporatist welfare systems. It includes the main European economies containing more than half the EU population and producing substantially over half the EU GDP, and nations representing the different types of welfare state discussed in chapter 1.

## Paying for welfare: tax versus services

Figure 4.4 presents the responses of members of different income groups to a general question which asked whether the respondent would prefer lower taxes or more spending on social services. The graph shows major differences between the views expressed in the different countries, both overall and by income group. Three points stand out:

- There are strong variations between countries which show some relation to current levels of spending. Thus, the USA and the UK have the highest levels of support for greater spending, while social spending in these countries is relatively low. France, a relatively high spender, has the lowest level of support, but Sweden, the highest welfare spender of all, falls towards the middle of the graph. While factors other than current spending levels clearly affect enthusiasm for higher state spending on welfare, there is an association between low spending and support for more tax.
- There is a general tendency for support for increased spending to decline somewhat as one moves to the right across the graph, towards higher income groups. The exceptions to this are in the

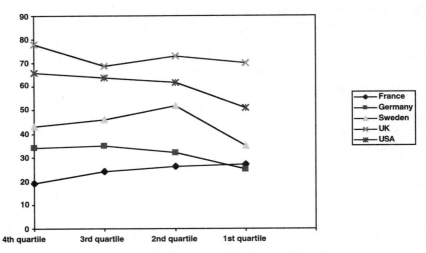

**Figure 4.4** Willingness to pay more tax for better social services by income quartile, 1996 (%)
*Source*: International Social Service Project.

case of France, where the lowest income group is least keen on more spending and in the case of Sweden and the UK where the tendency to reduced enthusiasm is reversed towards the middle of the income distribution, but declines sufficiently at the top end to compensate for this shift.

- The sharpest gaps between the attitudes of income groups appear in different places in the income order. In the case of France and the UK, the biggest divisions are between the low-income group and the rest, although, in the case of France, this group is the least and, in the case of the UK, the most supportive of more spending. In the case of Germany, the USA and, to a lesser extent, Sweden it is the highest income group who are most clearly distinct in their opposition to higher taxes and spending.

The theoretical arguments about the obsolescence of state welfare discussed earlier developed in two directions: the value-shift approach assumed a secular decline in support for welfare resulting from experience of the shortcomings of state welfare. Galbraith and others suggest that higher-income groups who see themselves as advantaged by tax cuts will tend to support retrenchment more than lower-income groups do, but will be able to use their greater political influence to impose their interests on policy. In addition, the third perspective claims that there are real electoral obstacles to reform and that these are provided mainly by those who gain most from the existing system. The comments made here are also reinforced by a more detailed multivariate analysis carried out on the same data (Taylor-Gooby, 1998c) and can therefore be advanced with some confidence.

The surveys lend only limited support to the contention that support for welfare has declined among all groups. There are rather different patterns in different countries, but it is clear that in the lower-spending countries (the UK and the USA), support in all income groups for more tax and spending is substantial. However, attitudes in the other countries, and particularly in the highest social spender with the strongest established welfare regime – Sweden – are not uniformly opposed to increased social spending. The same point applies to the 'risk society' variant of this approach which argues that the perceived shortcomings of modernity lead to disenchantment with welfare among all social groups, or to Etzioni's argument that it is the desire for a simpler life that turns individuals against modern state interventionism.

The pattern of attitudes to tax and social spending does not support the thesis that it is the opposition of a comfortable majority of the electorate which is the motor of welfare state retrenchment. In most of the major European countries (and indeed in the USA) the variation in support for higher taxes and welfare between the top quartile (or any combination of higher quartiles) and the bottom or lower quartiles of the income distribution is simply not great enough to sustain such an explanation.

## Paying for welfare: who should pay the taxes?

Evidence that people say they are willing to pay more tax for better welfare provokes the question of where the tax is actually going to come from. Table 4.1 examines the views of those on high and low incomes on whether taxes and social contributions for high, middle and low income tax payers are too high or too low. The pattern of attitudes is complex. Here we draw attention to three points:

- First, the most striking pattern in the whole table is the high level of support across all income groups and in all the countries covered for the view that tax for those on low incomes is too high, shown in the bottom third of the table. Very few indeed think that tax on this groups is too low, although there is a slight tendency for those in the top quartile themselves to be less enthusiastic in endorsing the view that tax on low-income

**Table 4.1** Views on whether tax levels on members of different income groups are too low or too high by those in the bottom and top income quartiles, 1996 (%)

| | France | | Germany | | Sweden | | UK | | US | |
|---|---|---|---|---|---|---|---|---|---|---|
| | Bottom | Top | Bottom | Top | Bottom | Top | Bottom | Top | Bottom | Top |
| **Tax on high income** | | | | | | | | | | |
| Too high | 35 | 39 | 12 | 16 | 12 | 36 | 23 | 20 | 31 | 44 |
| Too low | 45 | 39 | 64 | 58 | 67 | 46 | 46 | 41 | 44 | 33 |
| N | 195 | 364 | 784 | 647 | 236 | 293 | 169 | 203 | 256 | 336 |
| **Tax on middle income** | | | | | | | | | | |
| Too high | 82 | 80 | 49 | 50 | 40 | 53 | 36 | 31 | 60 | 69 |
| Too low | 2 | 1 | 5 | 3 | 6 | 1 | 11 | 9 | 3 | 2 |
| N | 206 | 377 | 799 | 667 | 234 | 296 | 176 | 207 | 262 | 339 |
| **Tax on low income** | | | | | | | | | | |
| Too high | 86 | 58 | 88 | 79 | 84 | 70 | 85 | 63 | 75 | 52 |
| Too low | 3 | 11 | 0 | 1 | 2 | 1 | 2 | 1 | 3 | 5 |
| N | 201 | 365 | 830 | 665 | 239 | 290 | 176 | 206 | 267 | 322 |

For simplicity of presentation, the table gives data only on extreme positions. Those who answered that tax was 'about right' for each of the three income groups or fall into the second and third income quartiles for each country are omitted.
*Source*: International Social Survey Project.

people is too high, rather more noticeable in France, the UK and the USA.

- Secondly, there is a similarly low level of agreement with the view that tax for middle income people is too low, displayed in the middle third. Here the main division lies between those who think tax is about right (a view more strongly held in the UK and Sweden) and those who think it too high (particularly evident in France).
- Thirdly, there is a considerable body of agreement that tax on high-income people is too low, rather lower among high-income people themselves and rather stronger in Germany and Sweden.

This evidence indicates that there is little enthusiasm among the mass of the population for higher taxation on those with low or middle incomes, although there is clearly strong support for more welfare spending. Indeed, it may well be that relatively few of those interviewed would see themselves as especially high earners, so that the significance of the view that extra revenue should be raised by soaking the rich may be mis-leading. The table uses objective evidence on income distribution, since no questions about where people thought they stood in the income dis-tribution were asked.

These findings indicate that the enthusiasm for extra spending on welfare, found in answer to the questions reviewed earlier, should be viewed with caution. While many people support extra spending in prin-ciple, it may well be that they think that the tax rises involved should fall on others whom they see as better off than themselves. If this is the case, the evidence of enthusiasm for higher spending may mean little in con-crete terms and the concerns of politicians about tax revolt may be justified.

This issue directs attention to the detail of support for welfare. We went on to examine the nature of support for the various welfare ser-vices among different groups in the population in order to find out which groups were most likely to be eager to retain particular services and to form the strongest constituency opposing retrenchment in those areas.

## *Paying for welfare: ambivalent attitudes and the politics of retrenchment*

We analysed a series of questions which asked whether individuals would like to see extra spending on particular social services, bearing in mind this would imply tax increases, or lower spending, which would imply tax cuts. We broke down the pattern of answers between social groups which might be expected to have different interests in relation to the various areas of provision. Labour market status is plausibly related to interests in relation to benefits for unemployed people and pensions; age relates closely to interest in retirement pensions and health care, and also to education, since families are typically involved in this service at a particular stage in the life cycle. Gender also relates to welfare interests since women make up a greater proportion of pensioners and of health care users.

These patterns might be expected to differ between different countries. In general, corporatist countries might be expected to display a stronger division of interest between labour market 'insiders' and 'outsiders' than social democratic or liberal countries, since labour market status is more closely linked to welfare in these regimes. Social democratic regimes, which set greater store by social cohesiveness, might be expected to produce a lower level of variation between different social groups. The liberal nations which rely on market allocations to a greater extent might produce stronger divisions between social groups. This might apply particularly to gender, since women do not have equal access with men to either security in paid work or private welfare.

There is a high level of support for more social spending with rather lower enthusiasm for provision for unemployed people in the UK, USA and France and for higher pensions spending in France. Most of those who do not want more spending endorse the status quo in all countries. Relatively few actually opt for cuts in services. As might be expected, the detail of the pattern of attitudes is complex, since so many factors affect ideas about the role of government in welfare. As is the case in other attitude material, national differences outweigh differences between social groups. In general, younger people are more supportive of educational spending and older people are keener on pensions. Women favour health and pensions spending more strongly and also spending on unemployed people. However, these associations are not particularly strong. Some of the strongest associations (table 4.2) are with labour market position. Those of working age who are not in employment are more likely to favour spending on unemployed people than those in work or retired, while retired people prefer spending on pensions rather than education. None of these associations is particularly striking, but they do give an indication of the way in which the interests of particular groups may furnish an obstacle to welfare cuts, even when there is no enthusiasm among any social group for actually paying more tax.

The pattern of answers in response to a general question on public spending and taxation was discussed earlier. This question sought to tap preferences between reductions in tax and contributions as against increases in social spending. The question was carefully designed to ensure that the phrasing included the various forms of social

**Table 4.2** Support for higher spending on particular services and labour market position, 1996 (%)

| Govt. should spend more on: | France | | | Germany | | | Sweden | | | UK | | | US | | |
|---|---|---|---|---|---|---|---|---|---|---|---|---|---|---|---|
| | In | Out | Old | In | Out | Old | In | Out | Old | In | Out | Old | In | Out | Old |
| Health | 52 | 54 | 49 | 55 | 62 | 67 | 73 | 80 | 83 | 90 | 92 | 93 | 68 | 70 | 59 |
| Education | 65 | 68 | 54 | 53 | 57 | 52 | 62 | 61 | 52 | 84 | 85 | 83 | 79 | 82 | 59 |
| Pensions | 30 | 38 | 47 | 43 | 52 | 62 | 48 | 58 | 72 | 74 | 76 | 87 | 51 | 52 | 45 |
| Unemployed people | 21 | 32 | 23 | 32 | 42 | 44 | 36 | 51 | 44 | 27 | 41 | 42 | 26 | 33 | 25 |

Labour market positions are defined as follows: 'In' means in full-time employment; 'Out' means of working age and not in full-time employment – part-time or unwaged employment, student, housewife; 'Old' means retired or permanently disabled. These categorizations are a simplification of the reality of labour market experience, but reflect the coding of the survey.
*Source*: International Social Survey Project.

contribution (which are typically thought of as an entirely separate form of revenue in corporatist countries) as well as state taxation, and to stress the link between tax reduction and service cuts, or conversely between service improvements and tax rises.

As the graph in figure 4.4 shows, majorities are in favour of tax cuts in all the countries reviewed except the liberal-leaning UK and the liberal USA. Enthusiasm for cuts is not directly associated with level of spending, since support is lower in Sweden than in the more corporatist countries. The particularly high level of support in France may be associated with recent political debates about the high level of social contributions and the impact of this form of finance for social provision on labour costs and competitiveness. Further analysis showed that there is, however, little association between preference for tax cuts and social factors plausibly related to interest, such as gender, age or labour market position.

The next stage in the research considered the relation between support for tax cuts and the endorsement of social spending discussed earlier (table 4.3). A high percentage of those in favour of more spending also supported cuts in taxes and social contributions in France, Germany and Sweden, but not in the more liberal countries which have lower levels of social spending in any case. The table shows a real conflict, especially among the citizens of the corporatist and social democratic countries that spend the most on welfare. The same people who want more spent on particular services also want cuts in taxation and contributions. This reinforces the view that governments face demands for a contraction of the welfare state but must balance this against demands for the improvement or at least the maintenance of particular services from particular constituencies. It is this that leads to the dilemma of 'Squaring the Welfare Circle' that we discuss in chapter 6 and makes the

**Table 4.3**  Contradictory attitudes: percentage of those who state that they want more spending on particular services who also state a preference for reductions in tax and social contributions to more social spending, 1996

|  | France | Germany | Sweden | UK | USA |
|---|---|---|---|---|---|
| Health | 70 | 53 | 51 | 27 | 25 |
| Education | 71 | 54 | 52 | 25 | 32 |
| Pensions | 72 | 54 | 51 | 25 | 25 |
| Unemployed people | 61 | 45 | 45 | 15 | 21 |

*Source*: International Social Survey Project.

political process of retrenchment so difficult. In the liberal and liberal-leaning countries the conflict is less marked. Here spending and taxation levels are lower and demands for better services are linked to a willingness to pay for the improvements in the mind of most people.

## Conclusion: Values and Welfare Politics

The review of attitude survey data in this chapter shows that the level of enthusiasm for increased state spending and of commitment to the idea of state responsibility for services fluctuates to a moderate extent over time and varies between countries and policy areas. The pattern of attitudes does not fit the idea that cultural values have shifted sharply against state welfare. Nor does it support the notion of a clear division between a comfortable majority, who want lower taxation above all, and a welfare-friendly minority in either Europe or the USA. There is some evidence that enthusiasm for increased state spending is rather stronger in the lower-spending Anglo-Saxon countries. In all countries, the division in support between more or less favoured services is more striking than any division between income groups in enthusiasm for state welfare. The first two theoretical approaches which have been influential in academic discussion, and have also contributed to the legitimation of retrenchment policies, seem to be at variance with the facts about what people say they want.

When we consider ideas about who will pay for welfare, a different picture emerges: there is no obvious group willing to finance public services. There is general support for more spending, but at the same time many people prefer tax cuts to increased spending, especially in higher-spending countries. In the corporatist and social democratic regimes many of those who want more spending in particular service areas which meet their own interests also confront government with demands to have their tax and social contributions reduced.

The claim that the politics of welfare cut-backs involves peculiar difficulties for governments is thus endorsed. As we shall see, this contributes to the pressures on welfare states and emphasizes the importance of national political and institutional frameworks in determining how policy develops in different contexts.

# 5
# The Neo-liberal Argument for Welfare Retrenchment

The basic premise of the neo-liberal account of welfare retrenchment is that generous state welfare provision is inimical to the economic, social and political well-being of a country, particularly in today's increasingly globalized world system. Reducing the role of government in welfare states is a necessary, if not a sufficient, prerequisite to the improvement of the situation of a country. Without such reduction, the situation will continue to deteriorate until it reaches a stage when there is no political option but to retrench. Welfare retrenchment is, in the long run, an inevitable course of action forced on government by the realities of economics and human nature.

This view stands in stark contrast to the human capital view which holds that government expenditure is a necessary prerequisite to the improvement of a nation's welfare. These two contrasting views of government activity have always competed with each other for ideological and political supremacy. From the end of the last world war to the late 1970s, the human capital view dominated government policy but during the 1980s the neo-liberal or New Right view gained ascendancy. Welfare programmes, argued Milton and Rose Friedman in 1980, have a pervasive ill-effect on all aspects of society: 'They weaken the family; reduce the incentive to work, save and innovate; reduce the accumulation of capital; and limit our freedom' (Friedman and Friedman, 1980, p. 158).

The economic aspects of this claim gradually came to be accepted in varying degrees by many governments, to be used as the major explanation of their economic difficulties and to justify welfare retrenchment policies. It was first expressed most crisply in a government white paper in the UK in 1979: 'Public expenditure is at the heart of Britain's present economic difficulties' (HM Treasury, 1979, p. 1). It was also cited as the major cause of the economic crisis in Sweden as late as in 1994 by a major official Report (Ministry of Finance, Stockholm, 1994, pp. 15–17, quoted in Olsen, 1996, p. 11); while the authors of the European Union's paper *Growth and Employment* concluded that in the coming years 'the agenda should be to make the welfare state leaner and more efficient' (Dreze and Malinvaud, 1994, p. 82).

The social claims of the neo-liberal position, that generous welfare provision undermines the social fabric of society by creating a 'dependency culture' and an 'underclass', have received a good deal of attention by academics but not by governments outside the USA. The political claims of this approach, that generous welfare provision undermines political stability or is the 'road to serfdom', have commanded even less support from academics and none from governments.

## The Economic Costs of the Welfare State

High levels of public and particularly social expenditure are said to be harmful to economic progress because they undermine incentives to work, to save and to invest in a country. This view of welfare stems from the basic ideological belief that human beings are rational actors motivated primarily by self-interest. Only in exceptional circumstances, such as war or natural catastrophes, does self-interest give way to the common good. This view of human nature means that 'the profit motive is the only spontaneous and reliable spur to efficiency. Public production of goods and services which is not profit-driven has been viewed with suspicion as harbouring a chronic tendency to slackness and waste' (Flemming and Oppenheimer, 1996, p. 61).

### Benefits for the unemployed and the willingness to work

What evidence is there to substantiate this claim of the disincentive effects of benefits for the unemployed in the UK? The evidence is presented in the form of answers to four questions that are part of the claim regarding the destructive effects of social security benefits on the willingness to work. The evidence presented spans the last two decades, during which time benefits for the unemployed declined in generosity.

*Do benefits for the unemployed sap the willingness to work?* The evidence from British studies during the 1970s, when benefits for the unemployed were relatively higher than today, generally agreed that benefits were barely sufficient for even basic needs. A national study of 1,604 two-parent families for 1978 and 1979 concluded that 'the evidence suggests that the living standards of the long-term unemployed are lower than those in short-term unemployment and the living standards of both are below those of the poorer families at work' (Bradshaw et al., 1983, p. 450).

The same picture emerges from studies in the 1980s and 1990s, when benefits for the unemployed were made less generous. A government longitudinal study of thirty unemployed two-parent families for the four years 1984–8 confirmed the low living standards of the unemployed and also showed that their situation deteriorates over time. At the beginning of their unemployment 'two thirds of the families were "managing" and one third were not. By the end of the reference period of unemployment, over half of the managing families had continued to "make ends meet" on a regular basis. The rest had found it more difficult to manage in the longer term and had accrued debts and arrears' (Ritchie, 1990, p. vi).

Perhaps a more accurate indicator of the adequacy of benefits is the incidence of debts among the unemployed. A recent government study of people of working age drawing income support during 1992–4 found that debts were very common, particularly for those families with children – 71 per cent of those with children and 45 per cent of those without children had debts. Moreover, in-depth interviews indicated that 'going into debt is one of the biggest fears of those on income support' (Shaw et al., 1996, p. 51).

On a European basis, the European Commission's survey of benefit levels for the unemployed concludes that 'they do not seem overly generous in terms of ensuring that those out of work can avoid living in poverty' (CEC, 1995, p. 104).

*Are the unemployed better off on benefit than in employment?*   There have been several government studies on this issue during the post-war period. The most comprehensive study in the 1970s was published in the final *Report* of the Supplementary Benefits Commission (SBC) in 1979. It summarized the findings of a national study on work incentives for the unemployed as follows:

> (a) The proportion of the unemployed who actually get more money in benefit than in work is very small.
> (b) A section of these are low-paid men with large families and many of these 'are in poor health and have other personal problems'. (SBC, 1980, p. 39)

Bearing in mind the decline in the real value of benefits and the tightening up of the qualifying regulations, subsequent studies have understandably confirmed the findings of the SBC study. The longitudinal qualitative study by Ritchie cited above concluded that: 'Almost without exception, the families felt that the standard of living they had in unemployment was lower than when they had been employed' (Ritchie, 1990, p. v). Another government study involving interviews with a national sample of 3,000 unemployed men and women in 1987 showed that overall only 2 per cent of men and none of the women in full-time employment were financially better off on benefits than on wages; the corresponding proportions for part-time work were 4 and 9 per cent respectively. The vast majority were low-paid workers with large families (Garman et al., 1992, table 3.18, p. 29).

In brief, a high replacement ratio of benefits to wages in the UK is rather rare and it applies to only the low-paid with three or more children, who are fairly uncommon in the British social structure – they 'make up only 4 per cent of supplementary benefit claims for unemployment' (Morris and Llewellyn, 1991, p. 127).

*Does benefit fraud undermine work incentives?* Successive governments in the UK have always feared that, despite the absence of reliable evidence, benefit fraud among the unemployed is so high that it blunts their willingness to look for and obtain jobs. These fears 'seem to grow as unemployment itself is rising' (Morris and Llewellyn, 1991, p. 90).

The Fisher Committee on Benefit Fraud in the UK in 1973 concluded that: 'Although the percentage of claims which are known to be fraudulent is not great, substantial sums of money are misappropriated each year' (DHSS, 1973, p. 224). Eight years later another government committee on benefit fraud, the Rayner Committee, came to similar conclusions: It found it impossible to document the exact extent of fraud but it nevertheless concluded that the existing fragmentary evidence indicated that 7 per cent to 8 per cent of all claims by the unemployed were fraudulent (DE/DHSS, 1981, pp. 61–3).

A more recent government examination of a large number of benefit cases of all beneficiary groups in 1994 showed that in 77 per cent of cases the correct payment had been made; in 5 per cent of cases an error was committed by the staff; in 9 per cent of cases an error was committed by the claimants that did not constitute fraud; in 5 per cent of cases fraud was strongly suspected though not proven; and in 5 per cent of cases fraud had been established (Rowlingson et al., 1997, table 3.4, p. 23). The methods used in government studies to estimate the extent of fraud have been criticized by many including the government's own National Audit report on fraud, which pointed out that the methods used to estimate it 'may artificially inflate the levels of fraud detected and may compromise a true understanding of underlying fraud levels' (National Audit Office, 1997, p. 47).

A number of qualitative studies support the existence of fraud but they also show that most of it is occasional fraud committed in order to meet specific needs. Only a small minority of fraud offences are of the organized and chronic type involving substantial amounts of money. MacDonald's work on the unemployed in Tyneside found that some were involved in 'fiddly jobs' but this was not a widespread activity covering all and sundry. Rather 'fiddly work tends to be restricted to certain social groups' – young white working-class males with particular skills and social contacts (MacDonald, 1994, p. 528).

The research by Jordan and his associates found fraud among both the unemployed and the employed more prevalent but again episodic involving small amounts of money. They found that 'two-thirds of the households described times when they did undeclared work for cash while claiming benefits, or supplemented low wages by doing cash jobs that were not declared to the Inland Revenue' (Jordan et al., 1992, p. 2).

The government study by Rowlingson and others of forty-five people who were either receiving or had received benefits found that two-thirds of them had committed fraud at some time. Again, most of it was episodic of small amounts and the main reason given by respondents 'was that they needed the money and the social security system made it difficult and sometimes economically irrational for them to declare income' (Rowlingson et al., 1997, p. 128).

A study of a small group of unemployed people in the Netherlands found that the extent of fraud 'appears to be neither extensive nor expensive' though it may be 'more prevalent in the Netherlands than in Britain or America' (Hessing et al., 1993, pp. 226 and 227).

To summarize: the exact incidence of fraud is not and cannot be known; most benefit fraud involves small amounts of money; it is committed by a small proportion of both those on benefits and those at work; it is usually used to supplement either low wages or even lower benefits; it is often prompted by the low earnings disregard rules of the benefit system; and, in recent years, it is encouraged or at least made more possible by government policies on labour flexibility (Evason and Woods, 1995).

While the government sees fraud as both illegal and immoral, others feel that many of those who commit fraud 'have little *real* choice. They could be described as caught in a pincer movement, as the demands of an increasingly flexible labour market and those of an increasingly strict benefit system squeeze their lives' (Cook, 1998, p. 15). Whether one views people who commit fraud as dashing enterpreneurs or immoral fiddlers, the evidence does not justify the attempt to elevate benefit fraud to either a major or a minor cause of the country's economic problems.

*Do the unemployed want to work?*    Most research evidence does not support the claim that the unemployed lose their willingness to work.

A government cohort study of a large number of employed and unemployed persons during 1978–80, when benefits were far more generous than today, concluded that the unemployed were more than prepared to look for work, In fact, 'few of the unemployed expected an increase in their net pay and even fewer required an increase. By contrast probably at least one half were willing to accept a drop in their real pay' (Moylan and Davies, 1981, p. 32).

Recent qualitative and quantitative studies confirm this overall finding. McLaughlin's study of 110 long-term unemployed in 1986/7 found that they were not only willing to work but also they were not making claims for 'unrealistic or inflexible wage levels' (McLaughlin, 1991, p. 495). The national government study in 1994 of people of working age who received income support for all or part of the period 1992–4 found that most claimants 'want to work and take a flexible approach towards the type of job and wage levels which they are prepared to accept'; and 'most of the small minority (12 per cent) who do not want a regular paid job are either sick, disabled or injured or have responsibilities for dependants' (Shaw et al., 1996, p. 5). Another government study of a representative sample of 5,000 unemployed during 1995–6 found that job search was high; 'there was no evidence of widespread indolence or people becoming enamoured with life on benefit'; and 'most were reasonably flexible in the work that they would take' (Mckay et al., 1997, pp. 4 and 6).

The findings of British studies are supported by those of studies in other advanced industrial societies. Cebrian and his associates summarize their findings from a longitudinal study of unemployment benefit recipients in Spain during 1987–93 as follows: 'On the whole, our analysis tends to suggest that unemployment benefits do not exert a clear negative influence on the job search behaviour of the unemployed' (Cebrian et al., 1996, p. 265).

Ulrich and Zika conclude from their comparative study of EU countries with particular emphasis on Germany that there was no correlation between benefit levels on the one hand and employment and economic growth rates on the other during 1983–95. They do, however, make the significant point that what is important is the way in which the social protection system 'is organized – and thus ultimately how much it costs – and by the way it is funded, i.e. who picks up the bill for social security' that can have implications for employment (Ulrich and Zika, 1997, p. 7).

Despite all the evidence, social protection measures for the unemployed not only in terms of level of benefits but also in terms of qualifying conditions, duration of benefit payments and state surveillance of benefit recipients have always been less generous than those found in the benefit systems for other needy groups (Van Langendonck, 1997).

*Benefits for lone parents and the willingness to work*

Many of the claims made about the benefit system and the unemployed are also made in relation to lone parents. Much of the empirical evidence relating to these claims is also very similar. It is, therefore, not necessary to go through these in the same detail. The claim that benefits to lone parents are a heavy burden on the government budget is only relevant in countries, such as the UK, where the proportion of lone parents in the community is high and where a large proportion of lone parents rely on benefits.

*Benefits and the creation of lone parenthood*   There is substantial evidence that the living standards of lone parents, two-thirds of whom are on benefit in the UK, are far lower than those of two-parent families even after taking into account social class factors. A recent government study involving interviews with a national sample of 880 lone parents in 1994 found that lone parents' incomes 'were typically less than half those of two-parent families' and that two-thirds had either mild or severe problems in paying their debts (Marsh et al., 1997, p. xiv). There is also equally substantial evidence which shows that the risk of poverty is much higher among lone-parent than two-parent families.

Bradshaw's and Millar's study of 1,276 lone-parent families headed by women in 1990 found that 38 per cent of them said that they were financially a lot worse off than they were before they became one-parent families; a further 16 per cent said that they were a bit worse off; and only 27 per cent said they were either a lot or a bit better off, mainly because they felt independent to manage their own finances (Bradshaw and Millar, 1991, p. 31).

*Benefits and work incentives for lone parents*   For many lone parents going out to work will not bring short-term financial rewards bearing in mind their skills, low wages and high child-care costs. Added to this is the belief among lone parents that being on benefit is the best option for their children. The qualitative study by Evason and Robinson involving group discussions with thirty-eight lone mothers found that they

> did not consider income support sufficient to meet their needs. They simply thought that this was their best option in their current circumstances. This conclusion was grounded, first, in the priority these lone mothers gave to meeting the needs of their children mixed in with concern over the strain of combining employment with home care and child-care. (Evason and Robinson, 1998, p. 18)

Most lone mothers want to go out to work when their child-care duties are less heavy and demanding. Bradshaw's and Millar's study cited above found that only 9 per cent of lone mothers did not ever want to go out to work. The remainder were keen to take up paid employment as soon their child-care duties eased (Bradshaw and Millar, 1991, p. 42). Similarly, the study by Marsh, Ford and Finlayson concluded that the first two predictive factors for lone parents ability to obtain employment were 'having older children, especially older than five years; having fewer children, especially fewer than three' (Marsh et al., 1997, p. 54).

The main conclusion that can be drawn from the research evidence on the unemployed and lone parents in relation to benefits and incentives is that benefits constitute only a very minor influence on the prevalence of unemployment or lone parenthood either in their creation or in their prolongation. This is also the main conclusion drawn by Rawlingson and Berthoud in relation to disability benefits and employment:

> There is no direct evidence that financial disincentives are the main reason why disabled people remain so much longer out of work, and on benefit, than unemployed people. It is clear that for most of them, the main problem is being disabled: the dispute is whether this is because they cannot work or because employers will not hire them. (Rowlingson and Berthoud, 1996, p. 213)

## Taxation and work incentives

The essence of the neo-liberal claim is that high direct taxes encourage workers to reduce their work effort, with the result that the economy of the country suffers. Workers are discouraged from working overtime, from working harder when paid on piece rates and from accepting offers or opportunities for any other work apart from the one they are employed in. High taxes also undermine the willingness of business people to take risks, with the result that the whole economy suffers.

Sir Geoffrey Howe, as chancellor of the exchequer in the first Thatcher government, expressed this view most vividly as follows in 1979: 'Excessive rates of income tax bear a heavy responsibility for the lack lustre performance of the British economy' (Howe, 1979). It was this belief that led to the substantial reductions in the rates of direct taxation in the UK during the 1980s and 1990s. The maximum rate was reduced from 83 per cent to 40 per cent and the lower rate from 33 per cent to 10 per cent. At the same time, however, national insurance contributions and indirect taxes were increased to make up for the ensuing loss in government revenues.

At the common-sense level, however, it could be argued that the effect of taxation on work incentives depends on the economic and family circumstances of the individual. Thus workers with low or average wages and with family responsibilities may be forced by high taxes to work longer hours in order to receive the net wages that they need for the maintenance of their families. The opposite may be the case for employees with high salaries and low family responsibilities. Many workers, of course, have little opportunity to vary their working hours or work effort, irrespective of the level of direct taxation.

It is important to examine the taxation issue at a time when direct taxes in the UK were high rather than today when they are historically and comparatively very low. All the evidence produced in the 1970s, when direct taxes were at their highest levels in the UK, showed that direct taxes had negligible effects, either positive or negative, on the national work effort and hence on the economy. A national study of industrial workers' attitudes involving a sample of 2,000 weekly paid workers in the early 1970s concluded as follows: 'The evidence clearly suggests, therefore, that the aggregate effect of tax on overtime is small; it may perhaps add about 1 per cent to the total hours worked, since, on balance, tax has made people work more rather than less' (Brown and Levin, 1974, p. 834).

Opinion studies may not reflect actual behaviour (Brown, 1980). Econometric studies, however, that trace the effects of taxation on actual behaviour arrive at similar results. A national study in 1971 of male married workers who could vary their work effort found that higher rates of taxation tended to increase rather than decrease the number of hours worked (Brown et al., 1976). Reviewing the situation after all the reductions in taxation rates during the 1980s, Brown concluded: 'there is little evidence to suggest that there will be any significant increase in short-run labour supply as a result of the increase in allowances or the cut in the basic rate of tax. The evidence from both sides of the Atlantic is about as firm as any empirical evidence in economics' (Brown, 1988, p. 106).

Godfrey's review of the relevant literature for a number of OECD countries in the early 1970s reached a similar conclusion, that 'taxation does not have a large and significant effect in the total supply of work effort and that, in particular, the net effect on the labour supply of male family heads is likely to be very small' (Godfrey, 1975, p. 126). Another study by the OECD ten years later reached a very similar conclusion: taxation has no significant effects on labour supply (Saunders and Klau, 1985).

It may well be, however, that high direct taxes do have a negative effect on the work effort of the small minority of highly paid professionals, managers or artists with low family responsibilities. This hardly constitutes a threat to the economy of a country even though it is a highly publicized issue. The view sometimes expressed that this can lead to the 'brain drain' is not substantiated by evidence. Professionals, according to an early government report, move to other countries for work because of higher salaries or better working conditions rather than because of taxation levels (Committee on Manpower Resources for Science and Technology, 1967).

We examine the issue of taxation in relation to employers in the following section for it is part of the overall debate concerning labour costs to employers and their willingness to invest.

Similar comments apply to the claim that taxation levels affect people's willingness or ability to save. While it can be argued that high taxes make it difficult for people to save, it can also be argued that individuals have to save less to reach a given target of savings when taxes are low. The general conclusion from the available evidence within the OECD countries is that: 'There is no clear evidence that taxation does affect the volume of household saving' (Owens and Robson, 1995, p. 27). As table 5.2 shows, there is no relationship between levels of taxation and saving ratios of private households.

*Labour costs and capital investment*

One of the central strands of the neo-liberal, as well as of the globalization, thesis is that the increasing mobility of capital in search of the most profitable national locations has significant implications for the welfare state. Labour costs and labour regulations, it is argued, are a major determinant of this process, with the result that countries with generous welfare states will be avoided in preference to those with modest levels of welfare provision. The available evidence can be used to both support and refute this claim, as a recent ILO report shows. The report lists several studies that refute the claim that generous welfare provision is a barrier to investment.

1  It refers to a study which showed that within the USA 'locational choice seems to be little affected by differences in state tax regimes' despite the tax concessions offered by state governments in an effort to attract investments by big companies (ILO, 1997, pp. 70–1).

2  There has been no massive relocation of firms within the European Union away from those countries with high tax and regulatory policies to other member countries.

3  Europe with its high labour costs has not lost out to other countries in recent years in terms of new investment.

4  Using Germany with its high labour costs as an example, the inflow of the total volume of foreign capital for investment has not declined all that much. During the period 1980–94, Germany slipped from second to third place within the European Union in terms of total foreign capital

investment. Its place, however, was taken not by member countries with low labour costs but by France. Similarly, the rate of German capital outflow was exceeded by the outflow of capital from such countries with low labour costs as the USA, the UK and Japan. Indeed, the outflow of German capital as a proportion of its GDP 'is about average, less than one would expect from a country of its size and wealth' (ILO, 1997, p. 71).

5    The evidence does not seem to support the claim that high taxes on capital have an adverse effect on investment and savings rates. Indeed, savings rates in Europe 'are far higher than those in the United States' while investment rates compare favourably despite the fact that such taxes are higher in Europe than in the USA (ILO, 1997, p. 71).

6    Finally, it is not so much labour costs that are the important factor but productivity rates. As Kaletsky points out, though hourly wage rates in Germany and the UK grew at about the same pace during the period 1990–7, unit labour costs rose in the UK but fell in Germany. The reason being that in Germany, 'companies have squeezed more than enough productivity out of each working hour to pay higher wages and still lower their costs' (Kaletsky, 1998, p. 33).

The evidence supporting the neo-liberal claim, however, is equally strong. Using the ILO report, it can be summarized as follows:

First, several studies have shown that investment within the USA is affected by the taxation rates and unionization rates prevailing in different states. There are more studies suggesting this possibility than the one mentioned earlier whereby state tax and welfare policies are not important.

Secondly, though there has been no major relocation of firms within the European Union, it is clear that 'Spain and the United Kingdom are relatively attractive to investors' with the result that Spain climbed from seventh to fourth place in terms of foreign direct investment while the UK has climbed to first place (ILO, 1997, p. 72).

Thirdly, one study of the investment behaviour of US and Japanese multinational enterprises in Europe found that they were sensitive to both tax rates and labour regulation regimes (ILO, 1997, p. 72).

Though the empirical evidence is ambivalent, the view that labour costs and labour regulation measures are a major impediment to economic growth has gained the ascendancy among governments. This is shown not only by pronouncements but by the actions of governments. First, corporation taxes have been reduced in the majority of OECD countries since 1990 (ILO, 1997, figure 4.1, p. 73); and, secondly, there are plenty of examples where governments are quite prepared not only to offer tax concessions to multinationals but to enter into competitive tenders with other governments in order to secure investments by multinationals.

In brief, it is not so much the actual but the perceived reality that affects government decisions in this area. In these circumstances, governments feel that the prudent course of action is to try and contain their labour costs and ease their labour regulations.

## *Historical and comparative evidence on benefits, taxation and economic growth*

The experience of the UK during the 1980s provides no support for the neo-liberal thesis concerning the beneficial effects of benefit cuts on economic growth. Despite the fact that the level of benefits for the unemployed *vis-à-vis* wages declined, the qualifying conditions tightened and the duration for which the benefit was paid shortened, unemployment did not decline. In fact it rose continually so that, by the end of the 1980s, it was higher than at any time during the post-war era. Neither did rates of economic growth rise as a result.

Comparative statistical evidence at the aggregate level by itself cannot provide firm evidence on the relationship between, on the one hand, public expenditure or social expenditure and economic growth on the other, as table 5.1 indicates. From the mid-1980s to the mid-1990s, Japan had the lowest rates of expenditure and the highest rates of economic growth, which might suggest a negative relationship. The USA and Germany, however, had almost identical rates of economic growth despite their very different rates of public and social expenditure. Denmark with its very high rates of public and social expenditure had very similar rates of economic growth to those of the UK despite the latter's low and declining rates of public and social expenditure. Greece's social expenditure was almost as low as that of Japan's but its rates of economic growth were far lower. In brief, the comparative evidence on public expenditure and economic growth provides no clear and unequivocal support for the neo-liberal thesis.

This conclusion is similar to that reached by Pfaller and associates concerning level of welfare expenditure and national competitiveness. Though there seemed to exist some support for the neo-liberal thesis, 'our findings do not *prove* that welfare statism is – in the economic context of the 1980s – a competitive handicap' (Pfaller et al., 1991, p. 41). The main finding of their detailed examination of the fortunes of five advanced capitalist societies – France, Germany, Sweden, the UK and USA – was that the constraint on welfare provision in the 1980s in four out of the five countries 'was not sheer economic necessity which demanded this sacrifice. It was rather the way the issue was projected into the political arena which let the welfare state extension appear to

**Table 5.1**   Public expenditure and economic growth, 1984–1994

|  | *Public expenditure*[a] *(% of GDP)* | *Social expenditure*[b] *(% of GDP)* | *GDP growth rates*[c] *(%)* |
|---|---|---|---|
| Denmark | 60 | 29.1 | 2.2 |
| France | 52 | 26.8 | 2.0 |
| Germany | 47 | 25.7 | 2.8 |
| Greece | 45 | 16.8 | 1.7 |
| Italy | 52 | 22.7 | 2.2 |
| Netherlands | 56 | 29.1 | 2.5 |
| Norway | 47 | 25.3 | 2.7 |
| Spain | 42 | 15.6 | 2.7 |
| Sweden | 63 | 33.3 | 1.3 |
| UK | 42 | 20.9 | 2.3 |
| USA | 34 | 13.9 | 2.9 |
| Japan | 32 | 12.4 | 3.1 |

[a] Public expenditure refers to annual average rate for 1984–94.
[b] Social expenditure refers to all expenditure on cash benefits and health care services, annual average rate 1984–93.
[c] GDP growth rates refers to the annual average growth, 1984–94.
*Sources*: OECD, 1994d, Annexe, table 27; OECD, 1996, table 1.1, p. 19; OECD, 1994d, Annexe, table 1.

be in conflict with economic imperatives in a competitive world' (1991, p. 290).

Atkinson's assessment of the available evidence on this issue reached a very similar conclusion. Of the nine studies that he reviewed, two found an insignificant effect of the welfare state on growth rates, four found a negative effect, and three studies found a positive effect. His overall conclusion is that such studies are 'unlikely to yield conclusive evidence' (Atkinson, 1995, p. 45). Apart from the methodological problems – definition of public or social expenditure, the period under review, the countries that are included and so on – there is the more fundamental problem that the same level of public or social expenditure may involve different benefit regimes in terms of benefit levels and methods of delivery or inspection all of which can influence work behaviour in different ways.

All the comparative studies refer to state expenditure on welfare. They do not include private or charitable expenditure, which often changes the whole picture of total welfare expenditure in a country. Mediterranean countries, for example, may rank low in state welfare expenditure but they may be high in voluntary and charitable expenditure. The United States was one of the lowest state spenders on health among advanced industrial countries in 1991 but it was the highest spender when private expenditure on health was included (OECD, 1994a, table 2, pp. 70–4).

Discussion on the effect of taxes on growth rates faces very similar problems and reaches similar conclusions. The reduction of direct tax rates, particularly for the high income earners, during the 1980s in the UK did not result in any upward surge in productivity or rates of economic growth though it did help create wider inequalities and higher levels of poverty.

Comparative evidence on taxation rates and economic growth does not suggest any negative or positive relationship between them, as table 5.2 shows. In general, Scandinavian countries are the most heavily taxed countries both in total and in terms of the taxes paid by households even though they exhibit different rates of economic growth. France appears to levy direct taxes on households which are as low as those of Japan but

**Table 5.2**  Taxation rates and economic growth rates, 1984–1994

|  | Total taxes[a] (% of GDP) | Direct taxes on households[b] (% of GDP) | GDP growth rate (%) | Net savings ratio[c] of households (%) |
|---|---|---|---|---|
| Denmark | 52.0 | 27.7 | 2.2 | −4.4 |
| France | 44.1 | 6.1 | 2.0 | 10.5 |
| Germany | 41.0 | 10.2 | 2.8 | 11.6 |
| Greece | 36.0 | 4.0 | 1.7 | 17.2 |
| Italy | 38.3 | 11.3 | 2.2 | 14.5 |
| Netherlands | 46.8 | 11.1 | 2.5 | 11.9 |
| Norway | 44.9 | 20.0 | 2.7 | 5.6 |
| Spain | 34.2 | 10.9 | 2.7 | 8.2 |
| Sweden | 54.1 | 20.7 | 1.3 | 6.9 |
| UK | 36.4 | 10.4 | 2.3 | 8.0 |
| USA | 29.2 | 10.5 | 2.9 | 5.7 |
| Japan | 29.4 | 7.2 | 3.1 | 13.1 |

[a] Total taxes refers to all direct taxes on households and corporations, on social security contributions, taxes on capital and indirect taxes.
[b] Direct taxes on households does not include social security contributions paid by members of households; they are included in the overall figure of total taxes.
[c] Net savings ratio refers to net savings of households as a percentage of disposable income for 1995.
*Sources*: Richards and Madden, 1996, table 1, p. 23, table 4, pp. 25–8, table 3.2; OECD, 1998, pp. 218–22.

it raises considerably more than Japan from social security contributions paid by both employers and employees. The evidence concerning taxes and savings is very similar. The USA with low taxes has a savings ratio that is lower than that of Germany whose taxes are heavier; Italy has a savings ratio that is higher than that of the UK and almost as high as that of Japan even though it has higher rates of taxation. It is also worth pointing out that Japan's high rates of economic growth declined substantially during the late 1990s and unemployment rose despite the continuing low rates of taxation.

In recent years, neo-liberal writers have argued that it is not only benefits and taxes but the whole range of labour market protective legislation that affects the economy of a country. A recent study of this claim found no supportive evidence. Teague and Grahl constructed a 'synthetic index' of the intensity of labour market legislation in sixteen European countries and related this to the countries' economic performance for the period 1985–95. They found that, first, 'the UK employment growth rate is not particularly better than in other countries even though its labour market is the least regulated' (Teague and Grahl, 1998, p. 10). Secondly, in relation to 'competitive performance – unit labour costs and investment rates – . . . there is no discernible difference between flexibility oriented and regulated economies' (p. 11). In conclusion, 'the claim that flexibility and deregulation are the route to better economic performance is not borne out by the evidence' (p. 11).

## The Social Costs of the Welfare State

The view that state cash benefits demoralize or deprave the very people they are supposed to assist is not new – it was part and parcel of the Poor Law system. In the post-war years, however, it is the American literature that has given primacy to this view of welfare. It has appeared under different guises, the most recent of which are the twin related theses of welfare dependency and the underclass.

Murray's work on welfare dependency and the underclass has been most influential on both sides of the Atlantic. People come to realize, argues Murray, that it is better or just as good to rely on benefits than to work. This general perception of life on benefits has grad ually spread, with the result that a large underclass has been created in the USA and the UK. It is not the absence of work or the lack of child-care facilities or any other such structural reason that accounts for the large number of able-bodied people on welfare but the belief backed up by experience that life on welfare *vis à vis* work is rather cosy. This view of state cash benefits is encapsulated in what he calls the Law of Unintended Rewards: 'Any social transfer increases the net value of being in the condition that prompted the transfer' (Murray, 1984, p. 212).

In the long run cash benefits to the unemployed and lone parents create a moral hazard – they not only increase the possibilities that the recipients of the benefits will continue in that situation but others, too, will get themselves into the same messy situation. Inevitably, an underclass develops whose values and practices are a threat to the rest of society. Writing about the situation in the UK, Murray claimed, that like the USA, Britain 'has a growing population of working aged, healthy people who live in a different world from other Britons, who are raising their children to live in it, and whose values are now contaminating the life of entire neighbourhoods' (Murray, 1990, p. 4). It is a most serious problem requiring an equally drastic solution: 'scrapping the entire federal welfare and income support structure for working-age persons' (Murray, 1984, pp. 228–9).

If Murray's thesis is correct one would expect (a) that the more relatively generous the benefit system, the greater the incidence of unemployment, lone parenthood and disability, and (b) those on benefits have a different value system from the rest of society – they place far less value on the work ethic and the family. We will examine each of these two propositions.

*Generosity of benefits and the incidence of unemployment and lone parenthood*

Comparative evidence on the relative generosity of benefits within the European Union and the prevailing unemployment rates in 1993 shows no correlation between the two. There are countries with generous benefit systems which have both high and low rates of unemployment. Vice versa, countries with modest benefit systems can have both high and low rates of unemployment. This applies to both short- and long-term unemployment as well as to both youth and adult unemployment (CEC, 1994a, pp. 38–42 and CEC, 1995, figures 36 and 37, pp. 90 and 91). In the mid-1990s, Greece with its very low level of benefit for the young unemployed had a youth unemployment rate that was higher than that of Denmark with its generous system. The Netherlands with its very generous unemployment benefit schemes had a less serious unemployment problem than the UK with its modest benefit system.

In an effort to go beyond this simple comparative method and to deal with cyclical issues of unemployment, Piachaud looked at unemployment rates for a number of European countries during the five years 1989–93 and related these to benefit levels through regression analysis. Comparing these results with those of the simple comparative method, he concluded: 'They remained very similar and, again, there was no significant relationship between the rate of unemployment and the benefit level' (Piachaud, 1997, pp. 44–5).

Turning to lone parenthood, the picture is very much the same. Ellwood's study of lone parenthood in the various states of the USA in the mid-1980s attempted to find out whether Murray's thesis had any empirical support. It showed that: 'the highest percentages of children living in female-headed families in 1980 are often in the states with the *lowest* benefits' and not with the highest as one would expect from the dependency thesis (Ellwood, 1988, p. 61). Moreover, the number of children in female-headed families increased considerably during 1972–84 despite the fact that during this period the value of benefits declined and the number of children in such families receiving benefits also declined. Clearly, the rise in the number of lone-parent families must be attributed to factors other than the benefit system.

Piachaud's study found no relationship between the level of benefits for lone parents and the incidence of lone parenthood. A similar finding comes out of Whiteford's and Bradshaw's study. The three countries with the highest rates of lone parenthood have very different types of benefit in terms of generosity. The USA has by far the highest incidence of lone parenthood but it also has 'very low levels of benefits after housing costs' (Whiteford and Bradshaw, 1994, p. 84); Sweden has the second highest rate of lone parenthood and one of the most generous benefit systems; and the UK has the third highest rate of lone parenthood and a rather modest benefit system. Generosity of the benefit was also found to be unconnected with the size of lone-parent families. They found that lone-parent families 'are largest in Ireland, France and the United States' but these countries have benefit systems that vary considerably in generosity (1994, p. 85).

There were in both studies several countries where a low-level benefit system corresponded with low incidence of lone parenthood. Greece, Portugal and Spain were the most obvious examples but it would be unconvincing to suggest that the benefit system was the cause of this. Apart from the obvious cultural and religious reasons, it might well be, as Whiteford and Bradshaw point out, that the causal relationship may be the exact opposite of what the New Right argues – since 'there are relatively few lone parents and their problems are not perceived to be pressing' (1994, p. 85).

Lone parenthood is a complex issue that cannot be attributed to one single cause. It may well be that the benefit system plays a minor role in all this but it is extremely difficult, if not impossible, to separate and quantify its direct influence. The available evidence suggests, however, that structural factors such as the economic independence of women and the more liberal attitudes towards sex and marriage are the major causes behind the growth of lone parenthood in contemporary industrial societies.

## The dysfunctional values of the underclass

A central theme of the underclass thesis is that members of the underclass have a value system that is both different from that of the rest of society and dysfunctional in the sense that it encourages them to break the established norms of society. It is a claim similar to the culture of poverty thesis put forward by Lewis in the late 1960s in the USA and Joseph in the UK as well as other similar concepts previously enunciated (Macnicol, 1987).

At the general level, it is inconceivable that all the unemployed and lone parents have values that are different from those of the rest of society, especially bearing in mind the constant flows in and out of unemployment and lone parenthood. As Dean and Taylor-Gooby (1992, p. 78) conclude in relation to the dependency culture: 'Large scale national surveys detect little evidence of such a culture among unemployed people or single parents on benefit.'

Similarly, the evidence provided earlier in this chapter showed that the majority of the unemployed are anxious to return to work on very flexible financial and labour market terms. The conclusion by one of the recent government national studies of the unemployed that 'the vast majority of claimants are not malingerers or workshy' (McKay et al., 1997, p. 191) is shared by most such studies. MacDonald found 'no evidence that a taste for work had been displaced by a taste for dependence upon benefits' (MacDonald, 1996, p. 445). What neo-liberals call dependency culture, he calls the survival culture of people on low incomes working hard under very difficult circumstances. Similarly, Dean and Taylor-Gooby found in their study of a small group of unemployed, disabled and lone parents on benefits that they 'are by and large highly motivated to work' (1992, p. 78). The study by Hessing and associates showed that the group of the unemployed involved in fraud had a 'higher score on the Protestant Work Ethic scale' than the group of the unemployed who had not been involved in fraud (Hessing et al., 1993, p. 28).

Historically, it is also not possible to explain the ups and downs of the unemployment rate in the UK during the 1980s and 1990s through the underclass dysfunctional value system. Why should the unemployment rate rise from 6 per cent in 1979 to 12 per cent in 1985, decline to its 1979 level by 1990, rise again to 10 per cent in 1992 and decline after that again?

A great deal of the neo-liberal writing on lone parents states or implies that benefits have fostered both dependency and promiscuity. Yet government data show that among lone parents in the UK 'Multiple serial partnerships are not common' and 'Eight out of ten never-married lone parents and nine out of ten of the formerly married had all their children by one partner only. Fewer than three in every 100 had more than two partners' (Marsh et al., 1997, p. xiii).

Recent research by Edwards and Duncan provides interesting evidence concerning the validity of the twin theses of dependency and the underclass. Using evidence from both micro and macro studies, they show first that the very group of lone mothers which is supposed to be steeped in dependency culture – black lone mothers living in inner-city public housing – 'are more likely to take up paid work and to work full-time' than other groups of lone mothers even though they hold views on mothering that fall outside the dominant value system. Secondly, white lone mothers, irrespective of class or residential location, hold traditional values concerning the role of women as carers and workers but 'are less likely to seek employment, especially full-time' (Edwards and Duncan, 1997, p. 45). The implication is that it is the dominant traditional rather than the new values on motherhood that may discourage paid employment and hence reliance on benefits.

A recent study of lone parents in the USA reached similar results. The vast majority 'were making plans to leave welfare for work as soon as their health, skills, and/or child care arrangements were sufficient to allow them to make ends meet on their earnings' (Edin, 1995, p. 6). Only 14 per cent of the mothers had no such plans and many of these were either disabled themselves or were looking after disabled children.

Murray's emphasis on cultural factors as the sole basis of dependency does not reflect reality. Of more interest and relevance is the approach by Bane and Ellwood, who identify three different models of dependency – the rational choice model, the expectancy model and the cultural model – each of which has different implications for the issues discussed in this chapter.

According to the rational choice models 'individuals examine the options they face, evaluate them according to their tastes and preferences, and then select the option that brings them the greatest utility or satisfaction' (Bane and Ellwood, 1994, p. 69). Murray's dependency thesis falls broadly within this paradigm even though he acknowledges that people's decision-making is less direct and purposeful than the model implies. The evidence produced in this chapter suggests that only a very small minority of benefit claimants fall into this category.

Expectancy models emphasize not rational thinking but 'the individuals' sense of control over a desired outcome' (Bane and Ellwood, 1994, p. 74). Long-term unemployed may come to believe that they are not wanted in the labour market; beneficiaries may have resigned themselves to the situation against their wishes because of lack of information about their prospects in the labour market; and so on. Again, our evidence suggests that only a small proportion of the long-term benefit recipients fit into this category – those of the long-term unemployed who feel resigned to their situation after repeated rejections for jobs; and those of the lone mothers who do not realize that their low wages can be supplemented by state cash benefits.

Cultural models 'typically emphasize that groups differ widely in values, orientations and expectations' (Bane and Ellwood, 1994, p. 78). The result is that members of this 'underclass' reject the values of work, self-support, stable family life and other such central values of their society. It is not, therefore, surprising that they are long-term clients of state benefit systems with no desire to live by the values of their society. All the evidence presented in this chapter refutes this thesis for the vast majority of benefit claimants.

Bane and Ellwood's more complex thesis is a welcome correction to Murray's thesis but it still underestimates the significance of structural factors at both the national and the international level for the economic and social condition of a country.

## The Political Costs of the Welfare State

The early liberal fears that the welfare state was the slippery 'road to serfdom' (Hayek, 1944) never commanded much support outside the inner liberal circle and it is not being voiced now. Similarly, the view that the political cost of continuous expansion of state welfare as politicians try to out-promise each other is not voiced any longer since welfare retrenchment rather than expansion is the general rule.

The current neo-liberal political critique of the welfare state is that state universal services, by their near monopolistic nature, constrain individual choice in welfare and hence individual freedom. The necessity to levy taxes that are sufficient to finance such services is another related aspect of the same critique – welfare state taxation policies reduce the freedom of individuals to spend their income as they think fit.

As chapter 4 showed, public support of welfare state provision has been robust over the years in all EU countries. However, public willingness to pay the necessary taxes in order to finance such services has not been equally strong. On the other hand, public support for private provision has been rather limited over the years. What all this adds up to is that the public does not feel that their private freedom is undermined by public provision in welfare. It is true that the small minority of high income earners may dissent from this general picture but this should be seen for what it is – sectional interests and not the public interest.

The new neo-liberal view that state services undermine and constrain individual freedom raises the question of whether private services nourish and expand it for all citizens. Clearly this cannot be the case for those who cannot afford to buy these services in the private market. The issue then becomes of how large this group of citizens is and the evidence here is not very helpful, for the size of the group depends on a number of assumptions – what the cost of these services will actually be, what the effect of abolishing state services will be on levels of taxation and wages, and so on.

The problem is acknowledged by many neo-liberals and hence their proposals for welfare vouchers, even though the idea is supported by others. It is accepted that total private welfare provision is impossible and that the state has to provide the finance through vouchers even though the services will be provided by non-state bodies. Assuming that the value of vouchers is equivalent to the cost of privately provided services, the question immediately arises of whether the cost to the nation will be any different from that of state-provided services in education, health, social welfare and social security.

Flemming and Oppenheimer point out that a fully privatized welfare state funded through vouchers for all 'would probably result in a higher public expenditure ratio . . . than obtains today (Flemming and Oppenheimer, 1996, p. 63) for several reasons. First, it will necessitate more expenditure on inspection in order to ensure government-set standards; secondly, those who opt out of state services today will also receive vouchers if the scheme is universal; thirdly, consumer choice will probably result in demands for both more quantity and better quality of services; and fourthly, there is the possibility that a plethora of bodies providing services might make it easier for trade unions to extract higher wages than under a monopolistic system. They could also have added that truly privately provided services involve some profit-making which raises costs.

It could, of course, be counter-argued that privately provided services will be more efficient than state services and hence costs will decline. There is no reliable evidence to support or refute this claim in the field of welfare services. Transferring evidence from business to welfare provision is misguided, for the two are not comparable. Social services are intrinsically different for both the individual and society from consumer goods.

In brief, the neo-liberal claim that state-provided services constrain while private services expand individual choice and freedom for all in society is a false dichotomy of what is a more complex situation. Pub-

licly provided services can liberate people though they have to be provided in user-friendly ways.

## An Assessment

The neo-liberal thesis underestimates the positive effects of public
expenditure and does not give sufficient recognition to the structural
factors that affect the economy of a country.

A balanced assessment of the impact of public expenditure on economic growth needs to look at the claims for both the positive as well as
the negative influences. A substantial body of literature, most under the
human capital theory, makes the case for the positive effects, which can
be summarized under five headings.

1   There is substantial evidence showing that several public services,
particularly education, improve the quality of labour and hence assist in
the improvement of productivity rates and economic growth (George
and Wilding, 1984; ISSA, 1996).

2   Government training and retraining programmes, regional policies
and other active labour market policies are necessary to provide more
jobs, to bring about a better match between the demand for and the
supply of labour at both the local and the regional level.

3   Social security benefits assist consumption and thus reduce the
possibilities of a deepening recession. As the International Social Security Association put it: Cash benefits 'have become increasingly important as a means of sustaining consumer demand, particularly during
periods of economic recession when consumption tends to fall in the
active population' (ISSA, 1996, p. 8).

4   In a rapidly changing technological world, the support of the
workers is most crucial in the use of new technology that often leads to
more unemployment in the short term. Cash benefits encourage workers
to accept industrial change without excessive rates of industrial conflict
that can have adverse effects on economic progress.

5   Adequate social provision for all sections of the population can
increase social stability in society, particularly if it is accompanied by a
full employment society.

The overall conclusion of this chapter is that the neo-liberal claim that
welfare retrenchment is an inevitable and a necessary prerequisite to
economic regeneration is primarily ideological. Since most of the micro-
evidence reviewed in the chapter refers to the UK, it is not safe to extend
this conclusion to other countries. It may well be that the situation is different in those countries with relatively high levels of social security

benefits, paid for longer periods and provided under more generous qualifying conditions.

The comparative statistical macro-evidence reviewed in the chapter, however, suggests that it is most unlikely that the economic problems experienced by advanced industrial societies – unemployment and low rates of economic growth – are primarily the result of current levels of public expenditure or of the existing social protection measures, as the neo-liberal thesis claims.

Public expenditure has both positive and negative effects on society. It is the balance between the two sets of effects that is the issue and this depends on a complex web of factors – the quality of the educational system, the relative generosity of benefit systems, the method of their administration, the range of employment supportive services, the extent of training and retraining, the generosity and the cultural tradition surrounding the benefit system of the country, and so on.

Despite the complexity of the issue and the evidence provided here, the neo-liberal approach has received substantial support among many governments and several international bodies, with the result that its effects on welfare retrenchment may have been far greater than they should have been had the research evidence been used as a guide to policy. Here, as in other areas, it is the political interpretation of the evidence, rather than the evidence itself, that is the crucial factor in influencing government policy.

# 6
# Squaring the Welfare Circle

## Introduction

The phrase 'squaring the welfare circle' describes the situation in which most welfare states are currently finding themselves. It refers to the dilemma of managing two conflicting pressures which threaten the viability of social programmes: on the one hand, the demand for social protection is on an upward trend, because of population ageing, changes in the structure of production, rising public expectations, and so forth. On the other hand, the ability of industrial countries to finance increased levels of social expenditure is being undermined by lower rates of economic growth, reduced capacity of governments to increase tax rates and a general reluctance to use deficit spending as a means to finance an expanding welfare state.

The result is an increasingly worrying mismatch between social expenditure, which because of mechanisms built into most social programmes tends to follow the expansion in demand for social protection, and the amount of resources that governments can make available to finance their welfare states. While in theory the welfare circle could be squared in two different ways, by reducing expenditure or by increasing the amount of available resources, in practice the second option is not feasible for most industrial countries. Partly, this is a result of the trends in the international economy reviewed in chapter 3 (globalization), which are reducing the room for manoeuvre that governments have for increasing tax revenues; partly, it might be related to the political difficulty involved in requiring a bigger contribution from the middle classes, a key constituency in electoral terms. In addition, given the spread of neoliberal ideas in most Western countries, it is difficult to imagine governments increasing taxation in order to restore the equilibrium between social expenditure and receipts. In this context, the squaring the welfare circle view of current social policy change explains welfare retrenchment as a possible solution to the mismatch between the demand for social protection and the ability of industrial countries to finance it. Obviously, this is likely to have an impact on the extent to which social needs are met. If retrenchment is pursued consistently and radically, the social risks and needs which were more or less successfully covered by the welfare state might re-emerge.

This thesis is found in various strands of social policy analysis. George and Miller (1994) and George and Taylor-Gooby (1996) use this understanding as a starting point for examining current social policy change in Britain and in Western Europe respectively. Basically, the reform of the British welfare state which took place in the 1980s, and the current process of adaptation under way in most continental European countries, are understood as responses to the twin pressures of rising demand and declining ability to finance it mentioned above. As George and Miller put it:

> Governments in all advanced industrial societies have to preserve an equilibrium between (a) meeting the constantly rising need and demand for welfare provision and (b) meeting simultaneous demands for limiting public expenditure while maintaining electoral acceptability. A complex web of interacting economic, political, social and demographic factors determine the ways in which governments attempt to bridge the gap between public revenues and public policy provision. (George and Miller, 1994, pp. 1–2)

A similar understanding is also found in the official views expressed by international agencies, such as the OECD and the European Commission. Sometimes the squaring the welfare circle view acquires a normative dimension and is used as a basis for arguing in favour of a reduction in social expenditure (Oxley and Martin, 1991). More recently, however, both the OECD and the European Commission have tended to adopt a more optimistic understanding of current pressures on the welfare state which values the investment component of social policies (see, for example, OECD, 1994a, or CEC, 1994b). Social policies are not regarded only as responses to people's needs and demands, but also as elements of a harmonious and productive economic environment.

More in general, the squaring the welfare circle view refers to an understanding of current social policy change in terms of an adaptation process. Most social programmes were introduced some decades ago, in a radically different socio-economic context. To a large extent, they are still based on old assumptions with regard to employment, social and demographic structures which are no longer true (Ferrera, 1998). The end of full employment, the decline of the family and the increase in the proportion of older people are all trends which contribute to make traditional welfare arrangements inadequate. This chapter attempts to assess the validity of this view on the basis of the available evidence. First, we review some of the literature which makes reference to such an understanding; in the second and third parts, we examine the pressures of increasing demands for services and the capacity of government to finance them; and, finally, we assess the accuracy of the thesis in its various versions.

## Perspectives on Welfare State Adaptation

In the literature on current social policy change, one can find at least two different views on welfare state adaptation: pessimistic analyses, which regard the adaptation process as a zero-sum game; and more optimistic views, which believe that, by channelling expenditure towards the most productive areas of the welfare state, governments can actually find a way out of the squaring the welfare circle dilemma.

The first group comprises mainly authors who have studied retrenchment in English-speaking countries and have tended to understand welfare state adaptation as a zero-sum game (George and Taylor-Gooby, 1996; George and Miller, 1994; Mishra, 1990; Pierson, 1994). In their view, the reductions in the level of social expenditure that have been adopted in order to restore the correspondence between welfare spending and available resources will result in a lower coverage of people's needs. George and Miller make reference to the concept of 'affordable welfare state', which implies that 'resources rather than needs are the overriding determinant of public expenditure' (1994, p. 17). By implication, reductions in available resources will result in an expansion of unmet needs.

It is probably not accidental that this view is found predominantly among scholars who have examined welfare state developments in English-speaking countries. Both in the USA and in the UK governments have tended to deal with the squaring the welfare circle dilemma by reducing expenditure. Since in most social programmes there is limited scope for efficiency savings, reductions in expenditure have meant a general decline of the generosity, the coverage and the quality of welfare programmes and services. In these two countries the Reagan and the Thatcher governments, to a large extent inspired by the neo-liberal ideas discussed in chapter 5, have adopted cuts in social programmes up to the limit of what they regarded as politically feasible.

Their understanding of the imbalance between welfare state resources and expenditure resembled very much a zero-sum game: to restore the financial viability of welfare states the level of provision had to be cut or the level of taxation needed to be increased. Given their ideological orientation and the general political climate in which these governments where operating, there was in fact little scope for the second option. The result was that both in the United States and the UK governments have adopted a fairly unilateral approach to squaring the welfare circle, based on the reduction of expenditure. This strategy, although successful in restoring balanced government budgets, has resulted in an increase in unmet needs, which, in the late 1990s, has put governments in these countries under pressure to correct some of the measures adopted by their predecessors.

In sum, this first perspective on welfare state adaptation regards the range of basic options available to governments willing to square the welfare circle as limited to two: governments can either increase taxation or cut provision (or a combination of both). Decisions as to what is the most appropriate mix of these two strategies will depend on various factors, among which the political orientation of the government in power may be crucial.

A second view on welfare state adaptation can be found in some of the reports produced by international agencies such as the European Commission and, more recently, the OECD. This understanding of the imbalance between welfare resources and expenditure does not accept the zero-sum game character of any attempt to restore the viability of welfare states. In contrast, it believes that at least some forms of welfare expenditure are conducive to stronger economic growth and thus to more resources available for redistribution. This view tends to emphasize the 'investment' dimension of social policy, and makes reference to areas such as education, labour market policy and family policy. Its basic claim is that if social programmes in these areas are designed appropriately, then the resources spent on them are likely to enhance the competitive position of the country in the international economy and thus contribute to the welfare of the whole nation. The relationship between social welfare and economic competitiveness is seen here as one of mutual reinforcement (Gough, 1996).

This view features in recent OECD and EU documents. For instance, the European Commission's white paper *European Social Policy* argues that 'competitiveness and social progress are two sides of the same coin' (CEC, 1994b, p. 12). In a similar vein, a recent OECD report points out that 'non-inflationary growth of output and jobs, and political and social stability are enhanced by the role of social expenditures as investments in society' (1994a, p. 12). This view acknowledges the potentially favourable impact of social policy on economic competitiveness, and, as a result, on the general well-being of the population. It denies the existence of the squaring the welfare circle dilemma in so far as productive social expenditure is seen as leading to stronger and more sustainable economic growth, which in turn allows governments to spend more on social policy. Social protection and economic growth are seen as elements in a virtuous circle: the exact opposite of New Right's view on the welfare state discussed in chapter 5.

Not all social expenditure, though, can be expected to be equally conducive to growth. Two features seem to be crucial in the design of social programmes. First, it is important that social protection schemes do not significantly interfere with market incentives. This is particularly the case with unemployment benefits which, in order not to undermine work incentives, need to be co-ordinated with in-work benefits, the tax system and minimum wages where applicable (CEC, 1993b, p. 95). The objective is to avoid marginal rates of taxation close to or higher than 100 per cent, when every extra pound earned is matched by a reduction in benefits and increases in taxation of the same amount. It is a strategy which is known as 'making work pay', or making sure that someone will always be better off in work than out of work, and which can be pursued with instruments such as tax-credits, in-work benefits and a minimum wage.

General social expenditure should not be allowed to grow indiscriminately, as this would require too high levels of taxation which would also have a detrimental impact on economic incentives. As a matter of fact, international agencies, even when generally supportive of social protection, tend to oppose increases in taxation as a means of restoring the financial balance of the welfare state. For instance, according to the OECD, 'Increasing the flow of resources to social protection remains an option, but often neither attractive nor feasible' (OECD, 1994a, p. 13).

Secondly, expenditure should be channelled to those services which have a strong 'investment' component. These include education, training and active labour market policies. In this respect, the language used by the European Commission is revealing: 'investment in education and training is now recognized as one of the essential requirements for the competitiveness of the [European] Union as well as for the cohesion of our societies' (CEC, 1994b, p. 23). EU member states have also seen an expansion of active labour market policies in their attempt to deal with the unemployment problem (Abrahamson, 1993). The shift from passive unemployment compensation to active labour market policies illustrates well the new emphasis given to the investment dimension of social protection.

This optimistic view of welfare state adaptation has been adopted by a number of continental European governments, and might reflect the difficulty that these governments have encountered when they attempted to apply Thatcherite recipes in reforming their welfare states. Countries like France and Germany have had more problems in retrenching their welfare states than was the case for their Anglo-Saxon counterparts. This might explain the emphasis on the non-zero-sum game character of welfare state adaptation. It can be seen as a more optimistic view than the one which characterized the debates in Britain and in the USA in the 1980s, but it can also be seen as some sort of smokescreen designed to reduce the visibility of cuts in social programmes. More recently, the British Labour government elected in 1997 has also insisted on reconciling social protection with economic competitiveness through strengthening the investment dimension of social policy (DSS, 1998).

After this brief review of some of the main theoretical perspectives on the squaring the welfare circle explanation of welfare retrenchment, the next two sections turn to empirical considerations. First, we will look at the factors that have affected the demand for social protection over the last few decades: most of these are likely to continue to exert an upward pressure on social expenditure over the next few years. Secondly, we will focus on the financing side of the welfare state, by looking at the factors that have affected the ability to pay for welfare in industrial countries over the last few decades, and which are likely to continue influencing their financial capacity in the near future. Because most measurements of welfare demand and of state financial capacity are sensitive to economic cycles, the tables reported below provide average measurements for ten-year periods which include both recessionary and expansionary economic cycles. This should enable us to highlight the existence of underlying structural trends. These developments are analysed in relation to a sample of six countries which are representative of the various models of social policy found in the European Union: Sweden as an exemplar of the Social Democratic model; France and Germany as conservative-Bismarckian welfare states; Britain as a representative of the liberal family; and Italy and Spain, as exemplars of the Southern European model.

## Increasing Demand

As table 6.1 shows, social expenditure, if measured as a proportion of GDP as is usually the case, has increased constantly throughout the period under consideration, although the data for the early 1990s may be misleading since almost all countries were in recession at that time. In the period between 1960 and 1979, increased expenditure on welfare was due primarily to the expansion of social protection systems. In many countries new programmes were introduced, while existing ones were made more generous and comprehensive. The 1980s, however, witnessed a change of direction in social policy-making in most countries: with a few exceptions levels of welfare provision have entered into a phase of consolidation, characterized by a mix of improvements and cuts. Despite the shift from expansion to consolidation in social policy-making, social

**Table 6.1** Public expenditure on social protection as a percentage of GDP

|  | *1960–9* | *1970–9* | *1980–9* | *1990–3* |
|---|---|---|---|---|
| France | 16.1 | 21.1 | 27.5 | 27.5 |
| Germany | 19.1 | 22.5 | 25.3 | 27.2 |
| Italy | 15.0 | 19.7 | 22.4 | 24.3 |
| Spain | na | na | 18.3 | na |
| Sweden | 13.2 | 21.1 | 33.3 | 36.6 |
| UK | 11.5 | 14.9 | 22.8 | 23.4 |

*Source*: OECD, 1994a, table 1a and 1b, pp. 57–61.

expenditure has continued rising even after 1980. This suggests that factors other than programme expansion account for this development.

It is widely accepted that the main trends responsible for the increase in social expenditure are those in the labour market and in the population structure. For instance, in a survey of elite opinion on current social policy issues, we found a relatively strong level of agreement among those we interviewed on the fact that the two most important factors affecting the demand for social protection were lack of work and population ageing (George et al., 1995). These two factors are central to virtually any debate on welfare state adaptation, and are generally portrayed as being the main sources of strain for social protection systems. In this section, we look at the evidence available on each of them. Other factors, like changes in family structures or rising public expectation, might also be playing a role, but they are generally more difficult to measure, are likely to have a smaller impact on aggregate expenditures and, perhaps most importantly, have a less clear-cut impact on expenditure levels. They are briefly discussed at the end of this section.

## Lack of employment

Unemployment rates have increased in most industrial countries in recent years. In most cases, the end of full employment coincided with the oil shock of the mid-1970s, though some countries, like Sweden and Switzerland, managed to retain extremely low unemployment rates until the early 1990s. Unemployment is currently high in the whole of Europe, with the exception of the UK, which has seen a reduction in the last few years.

**Table 6.2**   Total employment as a percentage of population aged fifteen to sixty-four

|         | 1960–7 | 1968–79 | 1980–90 | 1991–6 |
|---------|--------|---------|---------|--------|
| France  | 67.2   | 65.5    | 60.4    | 55.8   |
| Germany | 69.8   | 67.4    | 63.7    | 61.0   |
| Italy   | 60.2   | 55.8    | 54.5    | 48.2   |
| Spain   | 59.8   | 58.5    | 47.3    | 46.9   |
| Sweden  | 72.3   | 75.2    | 79.8    | 71.3   |
| UK      | 71.4   | 70.7    | 67.6    | 66.9   |
| USA     | na     | 64.6[a] | 69.1    | 72.6   |

[a]  1970–9.
*Sources*:  OECD, 1992, table 2.14, p. 42; OECD, 1997a, table 19, p. A22 and table 21, p. A24.

Unemployment rates, however, are not the most suitable indicator for cross-national and longitudinal comparisons of the availability of work for those who want it, as the proportion of the population seeking paid employment tends to change over time. For this reason, we decided to use employment rates as a better measurement of the trends in employment availability.

Table 6.2 shows the existence of substantial differences in the levels of employment achieved by different countries. Southern European countries tend to have lower rates, which might be explained by the lower degree of involvement of women in the labour market, by the big unemployment problem and by the existence of a larger informal economy sector. Nordic countries, in contrast, tend to have higher levels of employment because of the stronger participation of women in the labour market. The big increase in Swedish employment between 1960 and 1990 is to a large extent explained by an expansion in female employment.

With the exception of the USA, the countries above share a long-term downward trend in levels of employment. This is particularly strong in Southern and in continental European countries, which have experienced a constant and steady decline in employment levels. This trend seems to confirm the view that there is a structural tendency towards a reduction in the availability of work in these societies. This can be seen as an irreversible trend due to increased substitution of human beings by machines in the productive sector (Rifkin, 1995), or as an idiosyncratic feature of these economies and, in particular, of the operation of their labour markets (Esping-Andersen, 1996).

Sweden, Britain and the USA lend some support to the second interpretation, as all these countries have, in different ways, been able to escape from the constant downward trend in employment experienced by their continental and Southern European counterparts.

In Sweden employment continued to grow until the early 1990s, but it has dropped dramatically since then. As mentioned above, the expansion was to a large extent due to the entry of women in the labour market, which was actively encouraged by the various Social Democratic governments. By expanding social services, the Swedish labour market was able to absorb large numbers of women over the last few decades, without generating unemployment. The massive entry of women in the labour market, by increasing demand for services such as child-care and domestic services, resulted in further expansion of employment. This virtuous circle, however, depended essentially on government funds being available to finance the expansion of public social services. In the early 1990s, however, the strategy became unsustainable because too costly for the public purse. As a result, the unemployment rate was allowed to rise for the first time in Swedish post-war history (Esping-Andersen, 1994b).

Britain, in contrast, although it has experienced a decline in levels of employment, seems to have been able to moderate and possibly stopped the downward trend. The loss of employment experienced between the 1980s and the first half of the 1990s was of 0.8 percentage points, while the same figures for France and Germany were 4.6 and 2.7 respectively. The better performance of Britain in terms of job creation is generally explained with reference to its more flexible labour market, which allows job creation in the public sector to be more substantial (Esping-Andersen, 1994b). Much of the expansion here has been in part-time employment.

The US case is even more impressive in job creation, and even though not part of the focus of this book, it is worth looking at a bit more closely. Of the advanced capitalist countries covered by table 6.2, the USA is the only country which has witnessed a constant expansion of employment throughout the 1970–late 1990s period. American employment, however, has not only expanded over the years; it has also changed in composition.

The USA, like most other advanced economies, has been losing jobs in manufacturing industry since the 1970s. While in 1970 some 16 per cent of the working-age population was still employed in manufacturing, this figure had dropped to 11.8 per cent by 1996. However, unlike other countries, the USA was able to more than compensate for this decline by an expansion in the service sector. Critics of the US performance have pointed out that job creation there consists mainly in the so-called 'junk jobs', that is, the low-skill, low-paid often part-time jobs at the bottom end of the labour market in the service sector (Albert, 1991). In reality, job creation has taken place at both extremes of the service economy: the low-paid insecure jobs in the trade, catering, and personal services industry; but also the highly paid, highly skilled jobs in the financial and business services.

If we compare the USA with Europe in terms of performance at creating jobs, however, we find that the gap between the two areas is mainly due to the poorer performance in Europe in expanding low-paid, low-skill employment. European countries have seen an expansion in high-skill service jobs. Between 1980 and 1995, the proportion of working-age population employed in the sectors of finance, insurance, real estate and business services has increased from 3.8 to 5.7 per cent in Germany, from 5.1 to 9.4 in the UK, from 5.3 to 8.1 in Sweden. These developments, are not qualitatively different from what has been happening in the USA: there the same period saw an increase from 5.5 to 8.1 per cent of the working-age population being employed in this sector of the economy. In contrast, the employment creation gap is substantial at the bottom end of the labour market. Employment in the sectors of wholesale and retail trade, restaurants and hotels has increased in the USA, from 14.2 to 16.1 per cent between 1980 and 1995. During the same period, the same figure for Germany and Sweden stagnated at around 10 per cent; for Britain it moved slightly up from 13.4 to 13.7 per cent (OECD, 1997c).

The comparison of the employment creation performances of the USA and Europe suggests that the American strategy based on flexible labour markets is more successful in numerical terms, but what distinguishes it from the European approach is mainly its stronger capacity for creating jobs in the low-skill sectors of the service economy. These tend to be poorly paid and insecure. From the point of view of the welfare state, these jobs are a mixed blessing. On the one hand they do take people off unemployment benefit, but on the other they are often not sufficient to afford a decent standard of living. Many of those in low-pay employment remain recipients of welfare state programmes, such as tax credits or housing benefit. Besides, given the low pay rates, these jobs are unlikely to make a substantial contribution to the financing of the welfare state.

In sum, while it is difficult to assess whether or not the trend towards a reduction in employment levels is an inevitable development in modern societies, it seems clear that over the last forty years work has become more scarce in each of the European countries covered. Their welfare states, which were to a large extent based on the existence of full employment, have been put under considerable strain by this development. Lower levels of employment mean that a higher proportion of the population is dependent on the welfare state for its livelihood. Whether this is through unemployment benefits, social assistance, early retirement, or state-sponsored sheltered employment, the demand for social expenditure has certainly been pushed up by this trend. The North American approach, based on flexible and deregulated labour markets, can improve employment prospects for the low-skilled, but is unlikely, if adopted in Europe, to make a substantial contribution to the sustainability of its welfare states.

## Population ageing

The second important trend which is often mentioned as being responsible for increasing demand for social protection is population ageing. In the whole OECD area, the proportion of the population aged sixty-five and over increased from 7.8 per cent in 1950 to 11.5 per cent in 1980 (OECD, 1988b, p. 78). This trend can be observed also in our six countries which, although with some variation, have all experienced a similar increase in the proportion of older people. This development has affected expenditure in three main age-related areas of social protection: old age pensions, health care and social care. With regard to pensions, it has been estimated that between 1960 and 1985, in OECD countries, some 23.7 per cent of the increase in pension expenditure is attributable to population ageing. The main factors explaining increases in pension expenditure over the period, however, are extension of eligibility, which accounts for 45.6 per cent of the increase, and increases in benefits, which explains 24.7 per cent of the change (OECD, 1988a, p. 26). In this respect, it seems that population ageing has played a role as a factor affecting the demand for social expenditure, but this role was less important than that of other factors which were the result of political decisions.

As table 6.3 shows, however, the increase in the proportion of older people in western societies is expected to continue throughout the first decades of the twenty-first century. According to many commentators this trend, unless governments take action, is going to result in an unsus-

**Table 6.3**  Percentage of the population aged sixty-five and over

|  | 1950 | 1980 | 1990 | 2000 | 2010 | 2020 |
|---|---|---|---|---|---|---|
| France | 11.3 | 14.0 | 13.7 | 15.5 | 16.3 | 20.2 |
| Germany | 9.3 | 15.5 | 14.9 | 16.2 | 20.2 | 22.5 |
| Italy | 8.0 | 13.4 | 14.8 | 17.9 | 20.6 | 23.6 |
| Spain | 7.3 | 10.9 | 13.2 | 16.2 | 17.6 | 20.1 |
| Sweden | 10.2 | 16.3 | 17.8 | 16.5 | 18.4 | 20.4 |
| UK | 10.7 | 14.9 | 15.7 | 19.9 | 17.0 | 19.7 |

*Sources*: OECD, 1988b, p. 80, table A2; and World Bank, 1994.

tainable demographic situation, in which the older population will appropriate increasingly large shares of national income at the expense of younger generations (Thurow, 1996; Longman, 1987). In reality, there is much uncertainty as to what the relative proportions of working age and of older people after 2015–2010 will be. This is because projections are highly sensitive to variations in fertility rates, which are extremely difficult to predict. As a result, population structure projections are reliable up to a twenty-year horizon, when those who are going to make up the labour force have already been born (Johnson and Falkingham, 1992). Moreover, the effect of ageing on social expenditure will be mediated by a series of factors that cannot be predicted, like rates of productivity and of employment. These developments could actually override the impact of ageing. As an EU report put it:

> If job availability . . . could be expanded over the next 30 years to reduce unemployment . . . and to accommodate a continuing increase in the participation of women in the work force, as well as perhaps a reversal of the trend towards early retirement, this would more than offset the effect on the dependency ratio of the ageing of the population. (CEC, 1995, p. 13)

However, despite the uncertainty involved in assessing the size of the ageing problem in relation to social expenditure, there is a widespread agreement among policy-makers on the fact that demographic change constitutes a crucial pressure on the welfare state, and that action is needed in order to anticipate its potentially disastrous consequences. To some extent this is related to the fact that the impact of ageing has been exacerbated by the employment crisis of the 1990s. The result has been a sharp worsening of social insurance budgets in most European countries, which was only partly due to changes in the demographic structure of the population. On the other hand, the ageing problem provides a powerful argument for a government wishing to redefine distributional equilibria by reducing the redistributive role of the state. This latter observation refers mainly to the British case under Thatcher, when according to many commentators the gravity of the ageing problem was intentionally exaggerated in order to justify cuts in social programmes. As Walker put it: 'Concern about the ageing of the population in Britain has been amplified artificially as economic and demographic imperative in order to legitimate ideologically driven policies aimed at reducing the state's role in welfare' (Walker, 1991, p. 31).

Finally, it should also be said that the gloomy predictions of a demographic 'time bomb', generally refer to a hypothetical future in which current pension legislation is still applied. They are generally based on the 'if nothing is done' scenario. Now, while there is much uncertainty about the future evolution of demographic and, even more so, economic variables, the 'if nothing is done' scenario seems most unlikely. In fact, as we showed in chapter 2, a majority of industrial countries have started a process of pension reform, intended also to prepare for the demographic shift. This has mainly taken the form of retrenchment of pay-as-you-go state pensions, accompanied by the expansion of funded provision (Myles and Quadagno, 1997). The impact of ageing, thus, might be somewhat moderated by these and future reforms.

Pensions, however, are not the only area of age-related social expenditure. Spending on health care and social care is also going to be subjected to an upward pressure as a result of population ageing. Demographic change will probably not lead to the catastrophic scenarios depicted by some, but it is likely to have an impact on social expenditure. In sum, while population ageing has not been the primary factor influencing increasing welfare expenditure in the past, it did play a role and, more importantly, it is likely to constitute a significant upward pressure on social expenditure over the next twenty years or so, a period of time for which demographic projections are relatively reliable.

Other factors besides ageing and lack of employment are also likely to increase the demand for social protection. Among the most frequently cited are rising public expectations, changes in family structures, technological advances in the area of health care, migration, and so forth. To assess the impact of these factors on welfare expenditure, however, is a less straightforward exercise than in the case of population ageing and lack of employment. First, it is difficult to find reliable information on the whole period we cover on these variables, as it is to pinpoint specific indicators to measure at least some of them. Secondly, these developments have a less clear-cut impact on social expenditure than ageing and lack of employment.

For instance, rising public expectations could result in pressure for increased state spending on welfare as well as in larger numbers willing to pay privately for their own services, which in contrast relieves pressure on state welfare. For instance, in Britain, there is evidence that increasing numbers are turning to private medical insurance (Burchardt, 1997). Similarly, technological advances in medicine make available new expensive drugs and treatments, but at the same time they allow shorter hospital stays for given pathologies. As a result it is unclear what the overall impact on expenditure will be. Changes in family structures are likely to increase demand for services like child-care and parental leave. As most societies move from a male breadwinner family model to one characterized by a dual earner couple, the unpaid care-work which used to be performed by women needs to be taken over by the state. However, the entry of women in the labour market has other positive effects, like an expansion of the labour force which might help in dealing with the demographic transition. In sum, while it is difficult to make accurate predictions concerning the evolution of the variables which affect levels of social expenditure, it seems likely that the trends observed in the 1980s and early 1990s will continue for a few years at least. This suggests that the two most important socio-economic factors in explaining changes in social expenditure, lack of employment and population ageing, are going to continue putting pressure on welfare states. The demand side of the squaring the welfare circle thesis seems to be fairly strongly supported by empirical evidence.

## Declining Ability to Finance

During the post-war boom, the expansion of welfare states was to a large extent financed by high and sustained rates of economic growth. In practice, because most OECD countries had annual GDP growth rates of around 4 per cent, governments saw corresponding yearly increases in their tax revenues, which were used to finance expanding welfare states. Growth-financed increases of social expenditure had the big advantage of being politically easy to bring about. In theory, every redistributive policy, like most social programmes, is a zero-sum game: benefits for some must be financed by payments made by others. However, in the post-war context of rapid economic growth, those who were financing the expansion of welfare states (workers) saw their post-tax incomes increase, in spite of the expansion of social transfers. In this respect, the visibility of the zero-sum game character of the redistributive policy was not particularly high. Beneficiaries were obviously aware of improvements in their conditions, and payers were also experiencing increases in real incomes. This made the expansion of welfare states a politically attractive enterprise (Pierson, 1994).

### Declining rates of economic growth

As table 6.4 shows, however, rates of economic growth have declined constantly throughout the period covered, and they are now around half of what they used to be in the 1960s. With the exception of Britain, which has traditionally known lower rates of economic growth, most countries have experienced a decline in economic growth from above 4 per cent per year in the 1960s to between 1 and 2 per cent in the first half of the 1990s. There is no generally agreed explanation for this trend. One account, provided by neo-liberals, would hold the welfare state responsible for the reduced ability of welfare societies to expand their employment. However, as seen in chapter 5, there is little evidence of a negative effect of social protection on economic growth.

**Table 6.4** Real GDP growth, 1960–1996

|         | *1960–9* | *1970–9* | *1980–9* | *1990–6* |
|---------|----------|----------|----------|----------|
| France  | 5.6      | 4.1      | 2.2      | 1.4      |
| Germany | 4.5      | 3.2      | 1.9      | 2.5[a]   |
| Italy   | 5.7      | 3.3      | 2.3      | 1.2      |
| Spain   | 7.6      | 4.0      | 2.8      | 1.8      |
| Sweden  | 4.4      | 2.5      | 2.0      | 0.7      |
| UK      | 2.9      | 2.3      | 2.2      | 1.3      |

[a] Unified Germany beginning in 1991.
*Sources*: OECD, 1983, table 3.1, p. 44; OECD, 1997a, table 1, p. A4.

More sensibly, the reduction in rates of GDP growth can be explained in terms of market saturation. It is typical for countries with relatively low levels of economic development to experience higher rates of economic growth. However, when an economy reaches maturity, with much of its population having managed to acquire a standard range of commodities, then the potential for expansion is bound to decline. In addition, changes in the rate of increase of labour and capital productivity are also responsible for lower economic growth. While in OECD countries between 1960 and 1973 the annual increase of the combined labour–capital productivity rate was 3.0 per cent, the same figure for the 1973–9 period was 0.6 per cent and for 1979–92 it was 0.9 per cent (OECD, 1994b, p. A63). Lower increases in productivity, combined with a stagnation of the workforce, means a reduced potential for economic growth.

## Reduced scope for tax increases

The result of this trend in rates of GDP growth is that the sort of politically painless expansion of social expenditure that we saw in the years of the post-war boom is no longer possible. In the current context, increases in government revenues must be financed by increases in the rates of taxation. If a welfare state needs to be expanded, for example in order to meet the increase in demand reviewed in the previous section, then a larger proportion of a country's GDP will have to be consumed by the government.

This is partly reflected in the evolution of tax revenues as a percentage of GDP (table 6.5). Tax revenues have increased constantly in all countries throughout the period covered, with the exception of Britain, where between the 1980s and the 1990s there has been a reduction of

**Table 6.5**    Total tax revenue as a percentage of GDP

|           | *1965–9* | *1970–9* | *1980–9* | *1990–4* |
|-----------|----------|----------|----------|----------|
| France    | 34.8     | 37.6     | 43.2     | 43.8     |
| Germany   | 32.4     | 36.0     | 37.8     | 38.4     |
| Italy     | 26.0     | 26.5     | 34.7     | 41.3     |
| Spain     | 15.5     | 19.5     | 29.0     | 35.1     |
| Sweden    | 37.2     | 44.6     | 51.5     | 52.3     |
| UK        | 33.1     | 34.2     | 37.2     | 34.9     |

*Source*: OECD, 1997b, table 3, p. 75.

just over 2 percentage points. Interestingly, in countries like France, Italy and Britain, the proportion of GDP assigned to taxation did not increase substantially during the first fifteen years of the period covered. This in spite of it being one of welfare state expansion. In contrast, the 1980s have seen a dramatic increase in the fiscal requirements of most governments. Ironically, this has been a decade of welfare stagnation and retrenchment. Finally, the 1990s have not seen a substantial increase in tax revenues, with the exception of Southern European countries, arguably still involved in a catching-up process.

The overall stabilization in the proportion of GDP consumed by governments, after three decades of increase, suggests that the expansion of government intervention in the economy might have reached some sort of limit. These limits, however, seem to be country-specific, as in the 1990s there are still huge variations in tax revenues among OECD countries, and might be related to changes in the international context, rather than to the internal capacity of a market economy to sustain a large public sector. Economic globalization (see chapter 3) has reduced the exit cost for capital, which means that revenues can more easily than in the past be shifted to countries which offer a more favourable tax treatment. The result of this trend is a loss in the fiscal capacity of Western governments, but also an increased competition among countries which are struggling to attract revenues. Governments have had to renounce punitive rates of taxation, and lower rates of income or corporate taxation are generally used to attract economic activity in a country.

*Deficit spending*

An alternative way to finance increases in social expenditure is by deficit spending. This strategy, in fact, has been used by most Western governments throughout the 1980s and the 1990s, often in combination with

**Table 6.6**   General government debt (gross)
as a percentage of GDP

|         | *1981* | *1990* | *1998* |
|---------|--------|--------|--------|
| France  | 30     | 40     | 67     |
| Germany | 35     | 46     | 63     |
| Italy   | 60     | 104    | 120    |
| Spain   | 24     | 50     | 73     |
| Sweden  | 52     | 44     | 70     |
| UK      | 55     | 39     | 57     |

*Source*: OECD, 1999, table 34, p. 258.

increases in rates of taxation. As table 6.6 shows, the size of the debt has
increased sharply over the period in all countries except Britain, where
the increase has been modest. However, there are various reasons to
believe that such a strategy will not be available in the future. First, like
rates of taxation, high levels of public borrowing are regarded with suspicion by private investors. In the case of Italy, for example, as government debt reached 100 per cent of GDP in the early 1990s, two American
rating agencies (Moody's and Standard and Poor) reduced their credit
rating of the Italian public debt. This constituted a serious blow for the
government, and a clear indication that private investors were not prepared to continue to finance government spending through borrowing.
As capital becomes more international, heavily indebted governments
will find it increasingly difficult to raise funds on capital markets.

Secondly, the criteria established by the Maastricht Treaty on monetary union include limits on government deficit and debt for member
states, which must not exceed 3 per cent and 60 per cent of GDP respectively. Although the European Council has shown that these requirements can be interpreted with some leniency, it seems clear that
large-scale deficit financing of social policies will not be tolerated in the
future.

This brief review of the main options available to increase revenues
shows that governments seem to have little room for manoeuvre if they
wish to increase their expenditure. Within the overall context of lower
rates of economic growth, increased spending needs to be financed
by increases in levels of taxation or by borrowing. As we have seen,
however, neither of these two options seems practical, largely because of
changes in the international context (globalization and economic integration in Europe). In this respect, the adaptation process of welfare
states is likely to emphasize reduction in expenditure, in line with the

first interpretation of squaring the welfare circle, as there is little scope for increasing revenues.

## Paths to Welfare State Adaptation

Given the limited room for manoeuvre available to governments wishing to increase their revenues, it seems likely that, in order to solve the imbalance between the demand for social protection and the availability of resources, governments will increasingly be turning towards retrenchment. This, at least, is the main development in social policy-making observed in the 1980s in Britain and in the United States, and in the 1990s in continental Europe and in the Nordic countries. While adaptation can arguably take various forms, elements of retrenchment are likely to be included in any restructuring of a social protection system. In some countries, however, the restructuring of welfare states seems to combine retrenchment in some sectors with expansion in other ones. From the point of view of expenditure, however, it is retrenchment that tends to dominate the picture. This is the case mainly in the Southern European welfare states, where traditionally social expenditure has focused primarily on old age, and on benefits for the core of the workforce (unemployment, sickness and disability benefits).

Countries like Italy or Greece have some of the most generous pension systems in the world; however, they are very weak when it comes to provision for families and for the 'outsiders', people who have never been involved in the labour market, and have thus been unable to gain entitlement to the generous social insurance system (Ferrera, 1996). Italy is a case in point. Reductions in pension benefits, and a tightening of eligibility criteria for disability benefits, has been accompanied by a new minimum income for families, which although low by European standards, constitutes a first step towards establishing a last-resort safety net.

A second form of welfare state adaptation has consisted in combining retrenchment in some areas with measures designed to meet emerging new needs of modern societies. Germany, for instance, introduced a new insurance scheme to pay for long-term care (*Pflegeversicherung*) in the first half of the 1990s (Ruppel and King, 1995), a time when other programmes (pensions, health care, unemployment insurance) were being cut back. Similarly, in France cuts in pensions, unemployment benefits and increases in user charges in health care have been accompanied by an important expansion in active labour market policies. To some extent, it seems that in continental European countries the adaptation process is less unilateral than was the case in Britain and in the United States, where adaptation has meant almost exclusively retrenchment. In the case of Southern European countries the high levels of inefficiency which characterized their post-war welfare settlement provide some additional room for efficiency savings, and thus for the introduction of elements of expansion. More generally, the strength of the labour movement and the existence of veto points in their political systems have forced continental European governments to take into account a wider range of demands in the restructuring of their welfare states.

An alternative path to welfare state adaptation, based on an optimistic view of the problems currently facing social protection, favours a shift from a largely passive welfare state, intended to meet people's needs when these were not met through the market, to an active welfare state, which enhances the competitive position of the country. This approach, which is supported by the European Commission and seems to have been adopted by the British Labour government, puts much emphasis on spending on education and on active labour market policies, which constitute investment, as opposed to mere compensation (DSS, 1998). The active welfare state is supposed to constitute a way out from the squaring the welfare circle dilemma, in so far as it is expected to have a positive feedback on revenues through improvements in national competitiveness. Although this view makes sense theoretically, it is difficult at this stage to assess its accuracy. The expected returns on investment in skills and social cohesion are not likely to materialize in a few years. Moreover, it may also be difficult to measure them, as they are likely to impact on disparate areas such as health, crime, and so forth.

What seems likely, however, is that to be effective, such investment policies need to be well resourced. This, for instance, is what emerges from the evaluation of active labour market policies, which are found to be more effective when provided with significant financial means (Abrahamson, 1993; McLaughlin, 1997). Similarly, if education is to provide highly skilled workers to make the economy more competitive, it can be expected that the financial requirements of this operation will be substantial. In sum, it seems that the investment option is unlikely to constitute an easy panacea to the problems of welfare states. Though it might be something desirable in its own right, it seems unlikely that such an approach will generate savings (unless in the very long term) and it requires the commitment of substantial resources from the outset.

## Conclusion

Given the lack of empirical data on the success of the investment approach to welfare state adaptation, it is difficult at this stage to make a claim in relation to its validity. Nevertheless, the amount of empirical evidence presented in this chapter which supports the alternative view is rather substantial. The long-term trends in the areas of employment, population ageing, economic growth and government revenues explored above indicate that the current equilibrium is precarious. Further adjustment of current arrangements will most likely be needed. As the option to increase revenues seems increasingly difficult to adopt, most governments are *de facto* forced to embrace welfare retrenchment. An investment strategy in social policy is certainly a positive development, but whether it can spare governments the politically difficult task of containing growing social expenditures remains to be seen.

The socio-economic pressures reviewed in this chapter pose serious constraints to the direction of government policy in the area of welfare. However, within these constraints governments do have some limited room for manoeuvre. While it is clear that limits and constraints exist, it is extremely difficult to set an objective and quantifiable level of expenditure which is unbearable for a country's economy. Governments have the capacity to influence the interpretation that will be made of economic conditions, and to shape their policy accordingly. Depending on the government's perception of the constraints it faces, retrenchment could be more or less thorough.

Moreover, retrenchment can be combined with other measures of improvement or investment, which can mitigate the impact of cuts on the welfare of recipients. Whether this more humane approach to welfare state adaptation will be adopted, however, depends on a number of factors, which are more of a political or an institutional nature. Given the constraints, the outcome of the adaptation process must be an 'affordable welfare state' (George and Miller, 1994), but there is more than one possible type of affordable welfare state, and more than one route to the balancing of available demand and provision. We go on in the next chapter to review the various factors that influence government response in welfare states to the dilemma of squaring the welfare circle.

# 7
# The Impact of Institutional Frameworks

The accounts of welfare retrenchment reviewed in the previous chapters have focused on different sources of socio-economic pressures on modern welfare states. They refer to developments in societies, economies and international relations which have combined to undermine the basis of the post-war model of welfare capitalism. These developments are common to virtually all advanced capitalist societies, with, of course, differences of degree, but not of substance. The problems of the constraints posed by the international economy (chapter 3), political limits to people's willingness to finance redistribution (chapter 4), concerns about economic incentives and dependency (chapter 5) and of imbalances between available resources and social expenditures (chapter 6), are common themes in welfare developments throughout Western Europe. There are differences of degree. Ageing and une ploy-ment seem to pose more serious problems in some countries than in others; the impact of globalization depends on the structural features of the national economy; and there are cross-national differences in people's support for the welfare state. Overall, however, in the late 1990s modern welfare states are subject to strong, and broadly similar, socio-economic pressures.

The commonality of socio-economic pressures constitutes a push for convergence in social policy across Western countries. Similar problems can be expected to attract similar responses from government. Yet, as seen in chapter 2, there is little evidence that recent policy changes are bringing European welfare states closer in terms of their structures. What the reforms reviewed in chapter 2 have in common is the fact that they include elements of retrenchment. If we look at the details of reform, however, we still find an impressive degree of cross-national variation and little evidence of convergence.

The lack of convergence in social and economic policy, in spite of common pressures, has been a key concern of New Institutionalists over the last few years (North, 1990). Their explanation of the persistence of national specificity in social and economic policy is based on the role of institutions, broadly understood in terms of rules that shape economic and political interactions. Institutions are seen as an important intermediary variable, which mediates between socio-economic pressures and policy outcomes. Similar pressures can translate into different problems in welfare states with different structures, and result in different solutions. Institutional factors need to be taken into account if we want to assess the impact of the socio-economic factors which provide the bases for our accounts of welfare retrenchment.

Students of welfare state expansion have long recognized the impact that national institutions have had on the shape of welfare states. As seen in chapter 1, institutional explanations have provided a useful tool for understanding many observed developments of European welfare states. The literature on welfare state expansion has highlighted two distinct institutional effects on social policy-making: first the impact of welfare state institutions, which refers to how the initial choices in social policy often affect developments over several decades (pp. 11–12); and secondly, the role of political institutions, which constitute the toolbox of policy-makers and can affect their capacity to transform policy (pp. 24–7). These two institutional effects can be expected to be at work in the current phase of welfare retrenchment as well.

In this chapter, we consider the possible impact on retrenchment of both institutional effects. We first look at the way in which welfare systems themselves are organized and the implications this has for responses to demands for retrenchment, and secondly at the broader level of political and government structures which provide the context in which welfare policy is made. Different institutional arrangements on each of these levels can have a substantial impact on the vulnerability of welfare states to pressure for retrenchment. In the discussion that follows, we look at the theoretical argument behind each institutional effect, and provide some illustrative examples.

## The Institutions of Welfare Provision

The impact of welfare state institutions on current policy-making has been the focus of much recent work on retrenchment. Pierson, for instance, has argued that welfare retrenchment takes place in a political context which is shaped by welfare institutions. Patterns of mobilization in defence of existing arrangements are likely to be significantly affected by the structure of existing social programmes (Pierson, 1994).

The institutional structure of welfare systems is likely to have an impact on retrenchment as a result of the opportunities for resistance to policies designed to restrict spending that it allows, and conversely in relation to the extent to which it permits governments' direct control over those aspects of the system that entail expenditure. Two aspects are of great importance:

- Whether welfare is financed mainly through social contributions or through general taxation. This determines the extent to which welfare budgets are seen as committed to that purpose and hence difficult for governments to cut or redirect.
- The organizational details of the systems, and in particular the extent to which consumers are represented on the bodies that run schemes and are therefore well placed to resist change.

The key distinction in welfare finance is between the continental social insurance or 'Bismarckian' model, which relies on contributions, and the 'Nordic' model financed through government taxation. Sweden, Finland and Norway have to some extent departed from the pure form of the Nordic model as they have established substantial contributory schemes especially for pensions. The UK and Japan occupy middle positions, with a substantial element from both kinds of revenue source. The US system relies heavily on tax-finance, but this is in the context of an overall low level of state spending.

**Table 7.1**   Sources of state revenue: taxes and social security contributions as a percentage of GDP, 1995

|  | Taxes on income and profits | Social security contributions | Taxes on goods and services | Total tax revenue |
|---|---|---|---|---|
| France | 7.8 | 19.3 | 12.2 | 44.5 |
| Germany | 11.8 | 15.4 | 10.9 | 39.2 |
| Italy | 14.5 | 13.1 | 11.3 | 41.3 |
| Spain | 10.0 | 12.3 | 9.7 | 34.0 |
| Sweden | 20.6 | 14.5 | 12.1 | 49.7 |
| UK | 13.0 | 6.3 | 12.3 | 35.3 |
| EU15 | 14.4 | 12.3 | 12.8 | 41.8 |
| Japan | 10.4 | 10.4 | 4.3 | 28.5 |
| US | 12.8 | 7.0 | 5.0 | 27.9 |

*Source*:  OECD, 1997b, tables 1 and 6.

Insurance contributions are divided differently between employers and employees in different countries (OECD, 1997b). The Netherlands stands out as a country in which contributions fall on employees, although there is also a substantial employee burden in Greece, Germany, the USA and Japan. Employers pay a particularly large cost contribution in France, and interestingly in Sweden, as a result of the ATP second-tier pension schemes, despite the Nordic model, and Spain, which often sees itself as leaning toward the Beveridgean system. There is also a noticeable employer contribution in Finland, Belgium, Germany and Italy.

This evidence helps to explain the concerns about the link between welfare spending and labour costs in France, and also some of the concerns in Germany and the core Christian Democrat European countries. It is, however, interesting that countries which have a highly visible individual tax burden, such as Denmark, Sweden and Ireland, do not produce a strong citizen backlash against welfare taxes. Such a response is evident in recent political debate in the UK, reflected in the election commitment of both major political parties not to raise direct taxation and contributions, despite the fact that taxes are relatively low in the UK by European standards.

The administrative systems of European welfare states can be ranged between two poles, represented by France (where there are self-governing funds, administered by committees which include representatives of employees, employers and the government for sickness, family benefits, pensions and unemployment benefits) and the UK (where central government manages the assistance and the National Insurance schemes as well as the National Health Service with very little involvement from either side of industry). In the French model there is both a high degree of possible resistance to retrenchment from employees' organizations and also a strong motive for trade unionists to involve themselves in general welfare considerations, at least in so far as these affect their members, in addition to their traditional industrial role. The capacity of government to effect radical changes in the system on paper is much stronger in the UK system, but there is also a more overt politicization of welfare benefit issues. According to the Pierson model, where a central consideration in retrenchment is 'blame avoidance', the French system may, surprisingly, allow better opportunities for successful retrenchment than that of the UK, since the government can hold retrenchment at arm's length. However, successful blame avoidance requires that overt conflict, in which the government might be seen to be pursuing particular cut-backs against resistance from trade unions, does not take place. Government may therefore make major concessions to trade union interests, as, for example, in the 1993 pension reforms.

Other systems fall between these two poles. Close to the French system are the core Bismarckian countries: Germany, where the funds are also self-governing but rather more closely supervised by the state in practice and also limited by a legal framework derived from case law and from Articles 20 and 28 of the German Basic Law; Austria, where twenty-eight self-governing insurance funds provide pension and health insurance, but the state runs unemployment insurance and family benefits (*MISSOC*, 1996, p. 82); Belgium where 'administrative responsibility lies with semi-public agencies and public institutions of social security, which have administrative autonomy' (Hantrais, 1995, p. 220); the Netherlands, where the unemployment benefit scheme is 'run by industrial councils composed of representatives of employees and employers who are also represented in the Social Insurance Bank' which administers the other insurance benefits (Hantrais, 1995, p. 223); and Italy where the administration is through boards of 'governors' where the employers are by law in the majority.

Closer to the UK in the role played by central government in administration are Denmark and Ireland, where government ministries control all schemes, although implementation is decentralized to local government; Sweden, where there is strong central control through the National Social Insurance Board; and Finland, where the Central Pension Security Institute is responsible for both the state-run basic scheme and the co-ordination of additional schemes run by private pension organizations, employees have considerable influence on unemployment and sick pay insurance and local government runs health insurance. Perhaps the clearest hybrid is Spain, where the state runs social and health insurance schemes, but there is provision for employers' and employees' organizations to participate in the supervision of these schemes through participation in the National Council. There is also a multiplicity of private schemes, and a complex programme of decentralization to the regions is under way. In Portugal the three insurance schemes are legally autonomous, but in practice under the control of government ministries (*MISSOC*, 1996, p. 84). In Greece there is a basic state scheme of social insurance and a large number of different private schemes with slightly different legal arrangements. These schemes are supervised by boards which include state, employers' and employees' representatives.

Thus the pattern of organization of social welfare in Europe is complex but broadly speaking reflects the distinction drawn above between Bismarckian and Nordic models of finance. One strategy used to maintain social cover while reducing state obligations is to encourage the growth of private schemes, through subsidy and the withdrawal or dilution of state alternatives. This process, which is under way to a varying degree in most European countries, passes administration to the private sector and permits government to withdraw from obligations in this area, and to avoid responsibility for retrenchment, although there are conflicts about the success of the state regulation of the private sector. However, privatization is too recent a development to have a marked effect.

How does the organizational structure relate to changes in welfare policy? In theory, state-run largely tax-financed systems such as pre-dominate in the UK and in most Scandinavian countries permit the swiftest changes, while the Bismarckian insurance systems appear most likely to resist such changes, particularly where there is a high degree of employee involvement. If governments control finance directly they are in a strong position to retrench, whereas employees have interests opposed to such policies and a structural position within the management of welfare entrenches those interests to resist change. However, experience indicates that the reality of welfare spending constraint is not so simple.

Differences in organizational structure do not correspond directly to the pattern of change reviewed in chapter 2. Scandinavia and the UK (the most reluctant and the most enthusiastic retrenchers) fall into the same category when it comes to the broad features of organization of welfare although their policy directions are so divergent. Governments may find it difficult to avoid criticism when retrenching schemes for which they are clearly directly responsible, as in the Nordic model, so that in these cases the political strength of the government may well relate to its success in pushing through reform. Conversely, social insurance schemes may be slower to change, but changes here may be less politicized when they occur. We cannot explain the response to pressure for cuts solely in terms of differences in the organizational structure of welfare systems and must look at the broader political and institutional context within which welfare policy-making is located.

## Political Institutions and Welfare Policy-making

The nature of policy-making institutions (both formal institutions and well-established practices of policy-making) exerts a strong influence on the way in which welfare states have developed in the past (Immergut, 1992; Huber et al., 1993). Institutional arrangements which allow well-organized minorities greater access to policy-making and in which the power of the central government can be effectively challenged tend to be associated with lower levels of state provision. Groups who fear they are going to be worse off because they will foot the bill for welfare for the poor are able to block or limit new programmes. The USA and Switzerland are the two most obvious examples of this process. In the former, the independence of Congress in relation to the presidency allows groups who believe their interests are damaged by social legislation to lobby parliament to prevent the adoption of redistributive measures. Similarly, in Switzerland, minorities can challenge legislation put forward by the government by calling for a referendum. These two countries are the only nations at a comparable level of economic development which have neither public health insurance nor an NHS, since interested minorities have succeeded in blocking such schemes.

The fragmentation of political power has acted as a brake on the development of welfare systems. How does it influence policy in a climate of retrenchment? The concentration of power in the hands of the executive is often assumed to favour the adoption of such policies. Once retrenchment measures are decided at the top, there are few opportunities for groups not involved in policy-making to challenge them. However, in practice, such concentration of authority does not always seem to operate as an advantage. In general, political institutions that concentrate power tend, by the same token, to concentrate accountability (Pierson, 1994; Pierson and Weaver, 1993). In other words, a government that enjoys full control over policy will be better able to enforce unpopular measures such as retrenchment, but on the other hand it will find it difficult to avoid blame for that. For those who lose out in welfare reforms, it will be easy to identify who is responsible for retrenchment. In contrast, in political systems characterized by power fragmentation, it will be more difficult for citizens-voters to ascertain who was behind cuts in social programmes. From this perspective, political institutions have an undetermined effect on retrenchment. Power concentration is not inherently more nor less conducive to retrenchment than power fragmentation (Pierson, 1994).

Political institutions have a more clear-cut impact on the political strategies adopted by governments to reform their welfare states, and hence on the path that will be followed to reform a welfare state. In political systems characterized by power fragmentation, governments will be more inclined to negotiate with external interests, such as the labour movement and opposition parties. Because they have less control over policy-making, negotiation is a precondition for success in adopting policy. In contrast, governments operating in political systems with strong power concentration will be less inclined to negotiate. These different political strategies for adopting welfare reforms are likely to lead to different patterns of welfare state adaptation. In the first case, unilateral retrenchment will arguably not be an available option, as the external groups from which governments need to obtain support will demand some sort of quid pro quo for their approval. In these countries welfare state adaptation is likely to combine retrenchment with moderate improvements. In countries with strong power concentration, in contrast, governments will be under less pressure to negotiate, and more free to fulfil their objectives. These can include radical and unilateral retrenchment.

There are three principal areas of difference between the main EU member countries in the impact of institutional and procedural factors on policy-making. First, the structure of formal institutions, including the relationship between the different branches of the state apparatus, provides the basic framework in which the law-making process takes place (Lijphart, 1984). Secondly, the existence of well-established corporatist practices, typically associated with a strong and integrated labour movement, is a powerful factor which can compel governments to seek agreement from external interests (Schmitter and Lembruch, 1979). Finally, contingent factors (the balance of electoral support for particular parties, the proximity of the next election, the individual authority of leading political figures, the role of the mass media and so on) can also play an important role in the way governments decide to go about implementing cuts in welfare. A powerful electoral mandate can strengthen the position of the government in relation to external interests and thus make it more capable of adopting far-reaching reform (Pierson, 1994). A focus on these three areas can inform our understanding of the pressures for negotiation that will be at work on retrenchment-minded governments, and thus of the constraints that will define the limits of political feasibility.

*Formal institutions*

Perhaps the most crucial institutional feature influencing the degree of autonomy that a government enjoys in implementing legislation is the electoral system. It indirectly affects a number of other variables which are of considerable importance. First, it has been well documented that first-past-the-post electoral systems encourage bipartisanism and the creation of manufactured parliamentary majorities, since a party can secure a parliamentary majority even though it does not have a majority of all votes cast (Duverger, 1963; Lijphart, 1984). In these electoral systems a single party is often able to rule alone. Conversely, proportional representation encourages the development of a multi-party system, which usually means that governments are constituted of a coalition of different parties. Coalition governments are more unstable than one-party executives particularly when unpopular measures, such as retrenchment policies, are on the agenda. Coalition members have an incentive to defect from the pro-retrenchment camp, in order to gain support as defenders of popular social programmes.

Electoral systems in the main EU member states vary considerably. The UK, where general elections are fought on a simple first-past-the-post basis, stands at one extreme. France has a similar system, but with two rounds. Unless a candidate has an absolute majority on the first round, a second poll is held some two weeks later, where a simple majority is sufficient to win the seat. Typically, between the first and the second round the weaker candidates are withdrawn, and their parties support one of the two stronger ones. Italy reformed its electoral system in 1994. Elections were previously fought on a pure proportional representation (PR) basis, which came to be regarded as one of the main causes of the country's political instability. Since 1994 a mixed system has been put in place, in which 25 per cent of seats are still elected through proportional representation while the remaining 75 per cent are chosen on a first-past-the-post basis. The main result of the change was the formation of two large and relatively stable coalitions, representing the left-of-centre and right-of-centre parties. Germany also has a mixed system, but one that is closer to pure PR. However, since only parties with at least 5 per cent of the national vote can enter parliament, the effects of proportionality are constrained. Finally, Sweden and Spain both elect their parliaments on a pure PR basis.

A second important institutional feature concerns the relationship between the executive and the legislative powers. Five of the six countries mentioned above (all except France) can be characterized as parliamentary systems. This means that the government receives its legitimacy from parliament, and depends on it for its durability. Conversely the government can expect parliament to comply with its legislative proposals. The relationship between the government and parliament is dependent on other factors as well, such as type of government (coalition or one-party government). Typically, one-party governments are better able to control parliament. France, in contrast, has a semi-presidential system, in which the president is elected by voters. However, because the French president does not carry out an executive function himself but selects a prime minister among the parliamentary majority, the French system shares some features of the parliamentary model. As will be seen below, however, there are substantial differences according to whether or not president and prime minister belong to the same party.

The nature of parliament, whether it has one or two chambers, and in the second case whether the two have equal powers (symmetrical bicameralism), can also affect the course of policy. The impact of a second chamber is particularly relevant when the two branches of parliament are dominated by different majorities. This can happen in countries where the two chambers are elected on a different basis (incongruent bicameralism). In Germany, for instance, where the upper chamber is composed of individuals designated by the regional governments (*Länder*), it has often been found in recent years that while the lower

chamber has had a right-wing majority, the upper one has been dominated by the Social Democrats. The result is that a Christian Democrat-
led government is under considerable pressure to produce policy
proposals which are acceptable to the opposition. In contrast, in countries like France, the UK, Spain or Sweden, which either do not have a
second chamber or have one in which decisions can be easily overruled
by the main branch of parliament, the position of the government is
significantly stronger.

Formal institutions, however, seldom affect the course of policy *per se*.
More often it is a matter of a combination of institutional and political
factors that has an impact on policy-making. Bicameralism alone, for
instance, does not reduce the degree of control a government has on
legislation. Instead, it is the combination of bicameralism and different
majorities that can force a government to be more responsive to external pressures. Institutions make a given outcome more likely, but
whether or not it will occur must depend on political contingencies. For
this reason, formal institutions should not be looked at as a constant
factor, exerting an invariable pressure over time. Their impact must be
reassessed in relation to changes in the political context. Moreover
formal institutions provide only the basic framework within which the
law-making process takes place. Most countries have also developed particular patterns of informal policy-making in addition to those established by law which influence the involvement in decisions of other social
interests not directly represented in the formal political institutions. The
most important aspect here is the role played by employers' organizations and trade unions (the 'social partners') in policy-making, a key
concern of the debate on corporatism.

## Corporatism and the power of the labour movement

It has been argued that while the labour movement has been a key force
behind the construction of modern welfare states, its role in the present
phase of retrenchment and restructuring tends to be marginal (Pierson,
1994, p. 29). This may be correct for the USA and the UK. However,
recent events in some continental European countries have shown that
organized labour does have the capacity to force governments to modify
and sometimes to withdraw plans for welfare retrenchment. In France in
November 1995, for example, a massive wave of strikes compelled the
government to renounce plans to reform public sector pensions. A
similar event had taken place only a year earlier in Italy.

Organized labour does have an impact on current social policy reform
depending on two related factors: its own strength which can be
measured in terms of union 'density' (the proportion of the employed

population that are members of trade unions), and the degree to which trade unions have been traditionally included in policy-making, often referred to as 'corporatism'. Union density has declined in all European countries. While union density can be measured uncontroversially, estimates of the degree of corporatism require judgements of union influence. Sweden and to a lesser extent Germany are generally viewed as typical cases of strong corporatism. Co-operation or 'concertation' between different and often conflicting interests is a key feature of policy-making in these countries (Lehmbruch, 1984). In the late 1970s in Italy and in the UK attempts were made to introduce some form of concertation between organized labour, employers and the state, in the 'Social Contract'. This, however, proved impossible to sustain (Regini, 1984). Similarly in Spain the government tried throughout the 1980s to encourage a system of co-operation between the social partners. This met with relatively little success owing to the lack of centralization in the labour movement (Crouch, 1992). In France economic policy is generally enforced by the government without being significantly affected by external interests. However, in the case of social policy organized labour has acquired a special influence as a result of the institutional structure of the social security funds which are managed jointly by representatives of employers and employees.

The existence of a well-established corporatist tradition is relevant to the debate on welfare retrenchment. Countries that are used to dealing with legislative change through tripartite negotiations are more inclined to follow the same route in the case of current reform in the area of social policy and are more likely to succeed as well. That has been the case in recent German and Swedish reforms. Italy, despite the lack of a well-established corporatist tradition, has managed to implement cut-backs in the areas of pensions, health care and other benefits with the support of the main trade unions. The exigencies of the country's financial problems (public debt is higher than GDP) and of the unprecedented political crisis prompted by an immense corruption scandal have forced policy-makers to act consensually. France is arguably the most intriguing case, since its labour movement is poorly integrated (there are four union federations with different ideological orientations) and weak in terms of measures of density (only 14 per cent of the workforce are paid-up members). However, in recent years French trade unions have been among the most successful in Europe in preventing the adoption of measures designed to retrench welfare spending. Their success can be explained in terms of their extraordinary capacity to mobilize public opinion in defence of existing programmes in a context where attempts at wholesale and highly visible reform served to energize and unify opposition. Their role in the management of the welfare system gives them a peculiar legitimacy in speaking on behalf of public interests in relation to welfare.

## Contingent factors

The impact that formal institutions and procedural variables have on the shape of social policy change depends largely on several contingent factors. The timing of reform is an obvious one. Governments are generally more inclined to take necessary but unpopular measures at the beginning of their mandate while leaving widely approved policies for the run-up to the next election. The connection between political cycle and policy-making is fairly straightforward in the case of stable political systems (for example, the UK) where elections are held at relatively regular intervals. In the case of France, however, the presence of two parallel but not co-ordinated political cycles adds some complexity to the relationship. The French parliament is renewed every five years, unless the president calls an early election. In contrast, presidential elections are held every seven years. This means that French policy-makers have a shorter time in which to enact unpopular measures than their British counterparts if they wish to avoid the risk of controversy in the run-up to either a presidential or a parliamentary election.

In addition, because of the fact that president and parliament are elected independently, it is possible to have a situation in which president and prime minister belong to different parties (cohabitation). This has occurred twice since the establishment of a semi-presidential system. Between 1986 and 1988 and between 1993 and 1995 France had a Socialist president and a Gaullist prime minister (since 1997 France has again been in a situation of cohabitation). The result was a lack of unity in the executive branch of the state, and therefore a weakening in the ability of the government to control policy. Especially between 1993 and 1995, the result of cohabitation was to moderate substantially the direction of government policy, which was more responsive to external interests than is usual for France.

Contingent political factors are likely to play an even bigger role in the case of unstable political systems, particularly where a clear parliamentary majority is lacking. This has been the case in Italy since 1992. There the 1995 pension reform has been adopted by a government composed of non-politicians (*tecnici*) who had no direct support in parliament. In that situation it would have been unthinkable to impose a pension reform without being responsive to external demands. The result was a reform package that had been successfully negotiated with the trade unions and other interested parties and therefore offers the promise of providing a stable settlement, but in the face of a generally accepted severe debt crisis.

The impact of contingent factors on policy is perhaps the most elusive element of the institutional variable. Political change is fast and the way it affects the relationship between institutions and policy is often difficult to capture *ex ante*. In general, contingent factors that strengthen the position of the government in relation to the opposition and to outside interests are likely to make the government less responsive to demands made by external groups. What matters, however, is not so much contingent factors *per se*, but the way in which they interact with the other two sets of factors reviewed above, formal institutions and policy-making patterns.

In the light of the discussion presented above, European countries can be divided into three groups according to the degree of autonomy that a pro-retrenchment government can enjoy in reforming welfare. The first group includes countries in which interests that are not represented in or connected to the government have little opportunity to influence the course of policy. This is the case in the UK and in France, provided that president and prime minister belong to the same party. The second group comprises cases whose formal institutions allow government substantial room for manoeuvre in the definition of policy, but which, because of contingent reasons (lack of a strong majority in parliament, proximity of an important election), are unable to impose controversial measures. This group includes France, when president and prime minister belong to different parties, Italy and Spain, both ruled by relatively unstable coalitions. Retrenchment in these countries can take a consensual form or be imposed by the government, but, in the second case, the risk of defeat for imposed policies is substantial. The third group includes countries such as Germany and Sweden where the strength and integration of the labour movement and its traditional inclusion in policy-making make the imposition of controversial measures a particularly difficult and risky task. As a result, retrenchment-minded governments in these countries are more likely to attempt negotiated solutions with the trade unions. On the basis of a focus on political institutions, we can expect countries with strong power concentration and without a tradition of corporatist policy-making to adopt the more radical departures from existing arrangements. However, it is impossible to make predictions on likely outcomes on the basis of the observation of one institutional effect only, as it most likely interacts with other institutional and non-institutional factors in affecting the course of policy.

## Conclusion

The discussion presented in this chapter suggests a strong case for the inclusion of institutional effects in a theory of welfare retrenchment.

While these effects still need to be investigated in a systematic way, the examples given here confirm what has already been argued by New Institutionalists – that institutions are an important intermediary variable of policy-making, and their inclusion in explanatory models of welfare retrenchment can help account for the overall lack of convergence among European welfare states. Institutional effects, however, tend to be extremely complex and are generally the result of multiple interactions (both between different institutional effects, and with other, non-institutional, factors). In this respect, it is difficult to integrate institutions in an *ex ante* explanatory model of social policy-making. Rather, a focus on institutions can help us understand *ex post* why a certain course of action has been adopted. This leads to two conclusions. First, any centrally planned project for the future development of welfare policy in European countries is likely to be upset by unpredicted events stemming from institutional factors. Secondly, the question of institutional convergence is central to any discussion of convergence in welfare policy. We take these issues further in the next chapter in relation to the member countries of the European Union.

# 8
# European Welfare Futures

A defining feature of the European approach to expansion during the past half-century has been the centrality of state welfare. At the close of the century, the keynote in welfare policy is retrenchment. Welfare retrenchment is primarily a political issue. Trends in the economy, the population structure and the family are important factors in welfare retrenchment but their influence is heightened or lessened by the way they are perceived, presented and accepted as arguments for retrenchment in the political process. Countries with very similar trends in their economies have adopted retrenchment policies which differ in their depth, range and nature during the 1990s. Similarly, a cursory examination of changes in retirement pensions or policies on child support shows that it is not so much demography but politics that has shaped the nature of recent reforms. Recent changes in the family have been dealt with differently in various European countries: they have been ignored by some or dealt with through different policies by different governments. In brief, objective data in the economic, demographic and social spheres have greater or lesser impact as forces for welfare retrenchment according to the way they are politically interpreted and accepted in the country's policy-making process.

There are no certainties, let alone inevitabilities, in politics and in policy-making, only probabilities. Governments cannot ignore totally the pressures for welfare retrenchment, and certain courses of action are more probable than others under certain circumstances. Current developments in the labour market, population structures and family life, in the growing importance of transnational competition and in European economic rapprochement seem likely to lead to the trends in welfare policy that we describe below. However, pressures in these directions operate in complex political and institutional contexts, so that outcomes must remain uncertain.

## Trends in Welfare Policy

We are able to identify nine trends affecting policy in the future:

1    It is likely that both the need and the demand for state welfare will continue to increase in the foreseeable future. Rates of unemployment may rise and fall but employment prospects are unlikely to return to the halcyon decades of the 1950s, 1960s and 1970s. Demand for welfare stemming from demographic changes is unlikely to abate and may rise in the near future. The implications of new family forms, including serial relationships, gay partnering and single-parent child-rearing, for welfare policy must depend partly on the access of all parents to adequate paid employment and partly on ideologies about family life that shape welfare support. The standard of services expected by the public will continue to rise in line with increased economic affluence and higher living standards. Changes in technology and in labour markets will require more spending on education and training. All these demand factors are likely to continue the pressures for welfare expansion.

2    The ability and perhaps the willingness of governments to finance the expanding demand for state welfare are unlikely to improve. Rates of economic growth are likely to remain modest in the near future; public unwillingness to vote for political parties committed to increases in personal taxation is unlikely to change; pressures from the business community to reduce labour costs will continue and may intensify with the increased geographic mobility of capital and expanding cross-national investment and trade; and the dominance of neo-liberal ideology in relation to work, welfare and incentives is unlikely to change very much in the near future. We analyse the simultaneous but contrary trends to welfare expansion and contraction as the dilemma of squaring the welfare circle in chapter 6.

3    The most likely outcome of these conflicting trends in demand and supply is that retrenchment in state welfare provision will continue in the near future. Even governments that are anxious to maintain the status quo in state welfare are likely to rely less on personal taxation and to make more use of other forms of revenue. The past approach of financing expanding welfare through increased personal taxation and government borrowing is no longer an option for members of the European Union's single currency, since Maastricht Treaty obligations impose strict limits on public debt. European governments will resolve the

dilemma of squaring the welfare circle through retrenchment policies pursued in different ways within differing national contexts.

4   The gap between a rising demand for services and the mainte-nance of the status quo or a real decline in state welfare will probably be filled by an increase in private provision. Non-state welfare can be provided through a variety of mechanisms. Mandatory provision involves legislation requiring employers or others to provide certain benefits or services. Voluntary non-state provision can be promoted through fiscal or other subsidies. The ratio of private to state provision rose during the 1980s and early 1990s in most countries and this trend is likely to accel-erate (Adema and Einerhand, 1998, table A1.2, p. 51; see also chapter 2). The vertical overall distributional effects of private provision are likely to be disadvantageous to lower socio-economic groups.

5   The current debate over labour market policy will intensify as pressures from economic globalization become stronger and more obvious. The proponents of increased labour market freedom and flexi-bility as practised in the USA and the UK will continue to point to the advantages of the policy for the creation of jobs. Opponents will con-tinue to doubt the validity of these claims and will stress the rise in poverty and inequality and the destructive effects of such policies on family life and on social cohesion. The resolution of this conflict is uncer-tain. However, a shift away from increased flexibility seems unlikely as pressures from globalization and multinational enterprises exert a growing influence on governments. These struggles are currently being played out in the conflicts surrounding attempts by the World Trade Organization to challenge policies which limit the openness of markets, for example in the case of banana imports to Europe or genetically modified foodstuffs in the late 1990s.

6   As chapter 7 demonstrates, the nature of these trends will vary from one country to another depending on institutional structure. Private provision, for example, will continue to play a greater role in the UK than in Germany because of historical factors and the stronger influence of neo-liberal ideas about welfare provision; state provision for lone parents will continue to be less substantial in the Mediterranean than in other countries because of the greater role of the family in welfare provision; labour market flexibility is likely to make slower progress in countries where unions have an established position in the institutional structure.

7   Despite the importance of institutional factors on welfare retrenchment, it is likely that inequality and relative poverty will increase in all countries in the near future. The expansion in low-paid, part-time employment, changes in taxation, the growth of private provision and the retrenchment of state welfare are the main reasons for this trend. Again, the pace of change will vary from one country to another but it

is difficult to see how current trends can lead to a reduction in inequality and relative poverty.

8   Real progress in relation to equal opportunities in access to education, training and employment is being achieved in most European countries for women and to a limited extent for disabled people. For ethnic minorities, and particularly for black minorities, progress is more limited. Problems of discrimination are likely to be exacerbated in the context of stricter immigration controls which will particularly affect those from the East and the South. However, formal welfare citizenship may achieve real gains, as rights are more strictly formulated and opportunities to pursue them through a legal process expand.

9   We may go beyond the evidence presented in this book and speculate that real economic growth will continue as markets expand and technical innovation progresses, and that the mechanisms of liberal democracy will distribute some of the gains to the mass of the population. The European continent will avoid major wars. Average living standards will probably rise both in the field of consumer goods and in human welfare. It is likely that recent trends in lower mortality and higher life expectancy will continue in the future alongside a greater use of consumer goods, old and new. Human welfare results as much from the operations of the economy as from state welfare interventions. Work is the primary source of welfare for most people directly and indirectly during both their working life and their retirement. However, inequalities will increase and it is those excluded from the labour market who are most likely to suffer. It is in relation to this group that future trends in welfare policy are of greatest importance.

The current direction of welfare policy seems likely to lead to provision that is more closely linked to employability and to economic competitiveness. While this may be good news for groups who are able to use arguments based on equal opportunities in the labour market to make progress, it is certain to widen the gap between a poorer minority and a comfortable majority. This shift will take place with different policy detail and at a varying pace according to national political and institutional context.

## The Impact of the European Union

Most European countries are now members of the European Union and further expansion to the East and South will take place in the near future. EU membership has certain implications for the development of state welfare. The long-term vision of the founders of the European Union was the creation of a Europe that was united in the economic, political and social field. So far, however, progress has been made only in the economic field. Firms can invest freely in any part of the Union that they may choose; barriers to trade within the Union are being removed; legislation guaranteeing free movement of labour has been achieved; common standards for the recognition of professional and trade qualifications are being established; equal minimum conditions in employment, workplace standards, worker representation and health and safety are required by law; and in a few years a common currency and monetary policy will prevail in most member countries. A great deal has been achieved on this front. Economic unity in the European Union is fast becoming a reality. Progress to unification in this field, however, bears a close resemblance to the growing integration of the world economic system under the pressures of globalization. It differs primarily in the area of legally enforceable labour market standards which exist in the European Union but not in the world labour market and in the traditions of state welfare that are entrenched in the European political economy.

As in the world globalization process, it is the movement of goods, services and capital that has been most marked. The movement of labour is still very restricted despite the virtual abolition of legal barriers within the EU. In the case of health care, for example, 'where action has been taken to promote ... free movement of professionals, the impact has been very limited' (McKee, 1996, p. 283).

Political integration has lagged far behind economic integration. The European Parliament and the European Commission are largely debating chambers with mainly advisory powers at present. National governments retain their traditional powers, diminished only by globalization trends. Under the subsidiarity principle, they are free to accept or reject most legislation or regulations passed at the European level. In fact, the principle of subsidiarity seems sometimes to function 'virtually as a synonym for national sovereignty' (Spicker, 1991, p. 3). The current system of voting within the EU militates strongly against harmonization of services and provisions. Not unexpectedly, EC legislation 'is mainly procedural and not substantive' (Leibfried, 1993, p. 143) in most areas. It can have an incremental and modest impact on national legislative systems but it can rarely make radical changes quickly. Whether this will change under the pressures of economic unity and the common currency remains to be seen.

The Social Protocol annexed to the Maastricht Treaty requires 'unanimity rather than qualified majority voting' in a wide range of areas which include social protection. Agreements in these areas 'are likely to be difficult to achieve and will be slow to materialize' (Begg and Nectoux, 1995, p. 300). In any case, the European Commission's green paper *European Social Policy* stated explicitly in 1993 that the aim of the EU was not to harmonize national social policy systems but to encourage them to adopt similar broad policy objectives:

> The aim is not the harmonisation of national systems, but a framework for efforts to strengthen social protection systems and enable Community legislation on social policy to fit into a dynamic framework based on common objectives. (CEC, 1993a, p. 44)

The white paper which followed (CEC, 1994b), constrained by attempts to reconcile different national and sectional interests, failed to provide any clear lead on the future direction of social policy within the EU. Its position was 'even more problematic' than that of the green paper (Vobruda, 1996, p. 308).

Taxation regimes have a strong bearing on the means available to achieve social policy goals. At present there is great divergence between EU member countries in the way they raise revenue. Systems of taxation and social contributions play very different roles in relation to social protection and impinge in different ways on economic competitiveness. Attempts towards harmonization have been resisted, exacerbating the risk of social dumping, although there is little sign of such a development on a large scale so far (Adnett, 1995). Whether progress towards convergence will be achieved is at present unclear.

Social integration is even more remote than political integration. The welfare states of EU member countries are different in the way they are financed, in the level or generosity of their services and benefits, and in the institutional arrangements that they make to provide services and benefits. The classification of European welfare states into various regimes (see chapter 1) simplifies complexities which makes social policy harmonization a distant dream. It is doubtful whether social integration has ever been high on the agenda of the EU. For example, labour mobility is encouraged through legislation, but there is no corresponding support for the movement of non-workers and the possibility of 'welfare tourism' is viewed with concern.

Kleinman and Piachaud correctly pointed out some time ago that the kind of social policy that can prevail in the EU depends very much on the nature of the Union itself – whether it is merely a customs union, whether it extends to cover economic integration or whether it is a fully-fledged economic and political union (1993, p. 8). At the time of writing, the first level of integration seems likely to be achieved in the near future and considerable progress has been made towards the second. Moves towards the third level are tentative. Any attempt by the European Commission to legislate directly from above for social integration in the field of welfare, beyond the vague minimum standards contained in the Social Chapter of the Maastricht Treaty or the spill-over of European Commission competence from areas such as equal opportunities or equal rights in the workplace, would be firmly resisted. Indeed, in the absence of political union, it is inconceivable that such a move can be made, for the political reality is that national interests remain supreme. The fact is that 'the European Union is capable of effective action only in areas in which the major interests affected are either convergent or complementary. Such areas do exist . . . but social policy and the welfare state are not among them' (Scharpf, 1997, p. 25).

## Conclusion: EU Futures

Economic integration has had as many adverse as positive effects on the welfare states of all EU member countries. The positive effects have been largely in relation to employment and the labour market and in social provision that is directly linked to success in these areas, which includes measures to ensure that women's contribution to the competitive market is fully utilized. The negative effects stem from government competition to reduce labour costs in order to attract and retain capital investment. Furthermore, the Maastricht criteria for monetary union – balanced budgets, low inflation and low debts – have forced several countries to introduce policies designed to control public expenditure, particularly in the social field. Such changes are of course driven by the hope that a more competitive Europe will achieve a greater prosperity for all its citizens. However, for the reasons given above, the prospect for the medium term at least is that inequalities will grow stronger within the various contexts of national institutional structure.

In conclusion, and despite all the uncertainties, state welfare provision in European countries is unlikely to expand to cover a greater range of needs in more generous terms. It may even contract in a variety of ways depending on the political institutions of the country. The rising trend in social expenditure may well persist in some countries as a result of continued growth in the demand for established services rather than improvements in provision.

Early predictions that the Common Market would bring about convergence in social policy during the 1990s have not been borne out. For example, one influential writer argued: 'the 1990s are likely to see far-reaching changes in the social policy agendas of the countries of the European Community, as a result, first and foremost, of the Single Market and the integration of the economies of the twelve member states' (Room, 1991, p. 2). On the evidence currently available the influence of the European Union on the development of welfare is likely to be limited for the foreseeable future. Some regulatory measures may lead to the advance of state welfare in defined fields in countries which lag behind in provision, or to the imposition of equal employment standards across different social groups. However, the emphasis on low inflation, low debts and balanced budgets is likely to have a restrictive effect that will far outweigh any pressures for growth. In this context, non-state welfare, provided commercially, by employers or by the family, is likely to expand. Social inequalities, especially between those whose security derives from their position in the labour market and those who are outside paid employment, will grow more marked. Moves towards equal opportunities may lead to greater autonomy for women – especially as workers – but to more uncertain futures for members of most ethnic minorities. Welfare outcomes will depend on contribution to the world of paid work. Globalization will ensure that welfare objectives take second place to economic competitiveness in Europe.

Divergence within convergence is the most likely outcome in the sphere of welfare. The pressures of globalization, EU regulations and voluntary agreements between EU member countries may well make for some convergence in social protection. This, however, will be mediated through the differing national institutions so that current differences in patterns of provision continue into the future. The drive towards commonality in employment standards and opportunities, labour market flexibility and spending constraint will remain. The European Welfare State of the medium-term future will be less generous, more employment-oriented – and just as national.

# References

Abrahamson, P. (1993) 'Labour Market Insertion: Some International Experiences', in M. Ferrera (ed.), *The Evaluation of Social Policies: Experiences and Perspectives*, Milan, Giuffrè, pp. 123–37.

Adema, W. and Einerhand, M. (1998) *The Growing Role of Private Social Benefits*, Labour Market and Social Policy Occasional Paper 32, Paris, OECD.

Adnett, N. (1995) 'Social Dumping and European Economic Integration', *Journal of European Social Policy*, 5/1, pp. 1–13.

Albert, M. (1991) *Capitalisme contre capitalisme*, Paris, Seuil.

Almond, G. and Verba, S. (1965) *The Civic Culture*, Boston, Little, Brown.

Alt, J. (1983) 'The Evolution of Tax Structures', *Public Choice*, 41/1, pp. 181–222.

Arthuis, J. (1993) *Délocalisations et l'emploi: mieux comprendre les mécanismes des délocations industrielles et des services*, Paris, Editions d'Organisation.

Artoni, R. and Zanardi, A. (1996) 'The Evolution of the Italian Pension System', paper presented at the conference 'Comparing Welfare States in Southern Europe', Florence, European University Institute, 22–4 February.

Aspinwall, M. (1996) 'The Unholy Social Trinity: Modelling Social Dumping under Conditions of Capital Mobility and Free Trade', *West European Politics*, 19/1, January, pp. 125–50.

Atkinson, A. B. (1994) *State Pensions for Today and Tomorrow*, Welfare State Programme Discussion Paper 104, London, STICERD, LSE.

—— (1995) *The Welfare State and Economic Performance*, Welfare State Programme Discussion Paper 109, London, STICERD, LSE.

Atkinson, A. B. and Micklewright, J. (1989) 'Turning the Screw: Benefits for the Unemployed 1979–1988, in A. Dilnot and I. Walker (eds), *The Economics of Social Security*, Oxford, Oxford University Press, pp. 17–51.

Baldwin, P. (1990) *The Politics of Social Solidarity*, Cambridge, Cambridge University Press.

Bane, M. and Ellwood, D. (1994) *Welfare Realities: From Rhetoric to Reform*, Cambridge, Mass., Harvard University Press.

Bauman, Z. (1987) *Legislators and Interpreters*, Cambridge, Polity Press.

Beck, U. (1986) *Risk Society*, Cambridge, Polity Press.

Beck, U., Giddens, A. and Lash, S. (1994) *Reflexive Modernization*, Cambridge, Polity Press.

Begg, I. and Nectoux, F. (1995) 'Social Protection and Economic Union', *Journal of European Social Policy*, 5/4, pp. 285–302.

Benoist, A. (1996) 'Confronting Globalization', *Telos*, 108, summer, pp. 117–37.

Bonoli, G. (1997) 'Pension Politics in France: Patterns of Co-operation and Conflict in Two Recent Reforms, *West European Politics*, 20/4, 160–81.

Bonoli, G. and Palier, B. (1996) 'Reclaiming Welfare: The Politics of Social Protection Reform in France', in M. Rhodes (ed.), *Southern European Welfare States: Between Crisis and Reform*, London, Francis Cass.

——(1998) 'Patterns of Welfare State Restructuring in Britain and France', paper presented at the 14th World Congress of Sociology, Montreal, 26 July–1 August.

Bonturi, M. and Fukasaka, K. (1993) *Globalisation and Intra-Firm Trade: An Empirical Note*, OECD Economic Studies 2, spring, pp. 145–59.

Bradshaw, J. and Millar, J. (1991) *Lone Parents in the UK*, London, HMSO.

Bradshaw, J., Cooke, K. and Godfrey, C. (1983) 'The Impact of Unemployment on the Living Standards of Families', *Journal of Social Policy*, 12/4, pp. 433–52.

Brown, C. V. (1980) *Taxation and the Incentive to Work*, Oxford, Oxford University Press.

——(1988) 'Will the Tax Cuts either Increase Incentives or Raise more Revenue?' *Fiscal Studies*, 9/4, pp. 93–107.

Brown, C. and Levin, E. (1974) 'The Effect of Taxation on Overtime: The Results of a National Survey', *Economic Journal*, 84, December, pp. 833–49.

Brown, C. V., Levin, E. and Ulph, D. T. (1976) 'Estimates of Labour Hours Supplied by Married Male Workers in Great Britain', *Scottish Journal of Political Economy*, 23, November.

Burchardt, T. (1997) *Boundaries between Public and Private Welfare: A Typology and Map of Services*, CASE paper 2.

Bureau of Industry and Economics (1993) *Multinationals and Governments: Issues and Implications for Australia*, Research Report 49, Canberra, Australian Government Publishing Service.

Burton, J. (1972) *World Society*, Cambridge, Cambridge University Press.

Bussemaker, J. and Voet, R. (1998) 'Citizenship and Gender: Theoretical Approaches and Historical Legacies', *Critical Social Policy*, 18/3, pp. 277–307.

Cable, V. (1995) 'The Diminished Nation State: A Study in the Loss of Economic Power', *Daedalus*, 124/2, spring, pp. 23–54.

Callinicos, A. (1989) *Against Postmodernism: A Marxist Critique*, Cambridge, Polity Press.

Cass, B. (1990) 'Gender and Social Citizenship', paper presented at the 24th Annual Social Policy Association Conference, University of Bath, July.

Castles, F. and McKinlay, R. (1979a) 'Does Politics Matter? An Analysis of the Public Welfare Commitment in Advanced Democratic States', *European Journal of Political Research*, 7, pp. 169–86.

——(1979b) 'Public Welfare Provision, Scandinavia, and the Sheer Futility of a Sociological Approach to Politics', *British Journal of Political Science*, 9, pp. 157–71.

Castles, F. and Mitchell, D. (1990) *Three Worlds of Welfare Capitalism or Four?*, Public Policy Programme Discussion Paper 21, Australian National University.

Cebrian, I., Garcia, C., Munro, J., Toharia, L. and Villagomez, E. (1996) 'The Influence of Unemployment Benefits on Unemployment Duration: Evidence from Spain', *Labour*, 10/2, summer, pp. 239–69.

Clasen, J. (1997) 'Social Insurance in Germany: Dismantling or Reconstruction?', in J. Clasen (ed.), *Social Insurance in Europe*, Bristol, Policy Press, pp. 60–83.

Commission of the European Communities (CEC) (1993a) *European Social Policy: Options for the Union* (EU Social Policy green paper), Com. (93) 551, Brussels, CEC.

—— (1993b) *Growth, Competitiveness and Employment* (EU Employment white paper), *CEC Bulletin*, supplement 6/93, Brussels, CEC.

—— (1994a) *Social Protection in Europe – 1993*, Brussels, CEC.

—— (1994b) *European Social Policy: A Way Forward for the Union* (white paper), Brussels.

—— (1994c) *Employment in Europe*, Brussels.

—— (1995) *Social Protection in Europe*, Brussels, CEC.

—— (1996) *Social Protection in Europe – 1995*, Brussels, CEC.

Committee on Manpower Resources for Science and Technology (1967) *The Brain Drain: Report of the Working Group on Migration*, Cmnd 3417, London, HMSO.

Convery, P. (1997) 'The New Deal Gets Real', *Working Brief*, 88, pp. 7–14.

Cook, D. (1998) 'Between a Rock and a Hard Place: The Realities of Working on the Side', *Benefits*, 21, January, pp. 14–16.

Coughlin, R. (1980) *Ideology, Public Opinion and Welfare Policy*, Berkeley, Institute of International Studies, University of California.

Crouch, C. (1992) 'The Fate of Articulated Industrial Relations Systems: A Stock-taking after the Neo-liberal Decade', in M. Regini (ed.), *The Future of Labour Movements*, London, Sage, 169–87.

Daly, M. (1993) 'Comparing Welfare States: Towards a Gender-friendly Approach', presented at the ECPR Workshop on 'Welfare States and Gender', University of Leiden, April.

Deacon, B. (1997) *Global Social Policy*, London, Sage.

Dean, H. and Taylor-Gooby, P. (1992) *Dependency Culture*, Hemel Hempstead, Harvester Wheatsheaf.

Department of Employment (DE) (1988) *Employment in the 1990s*, Cm 540, London, HMSO.

Department of Employment/Department of Health and Social Security (1981) *Payment of Benefits to Unemployed People*, London, HMSO (the Rayner Report).

Department of Health and Social Security (DHSS) (1973) *Report of the Committee on Abuse of Social Security Benefits*, Cmnd 5228, London, HMSO (the Fisher Report).

Department of Social Security (DSS) (1998) *A New Contract for Welfare*, Cm 3805 (green paper), London, HMSO.

Department of Trade and Industry (1995) *Trade and Industry 1995*, Cm 2804, London, HMSO.

Doyal, L. and Gough, I. (1991) *A Theory of Human Need*, London, Macmillan.

Dreze, J. H. and Malinvaud, E. (1994) 'Growth and Employment: The Scope for a European Initiative', *European Economy*, 1, pp. 77–106.

Druffus, G. and Gooding, P. (1997) 'Globalisation: Scope, Issues and Statistics', *Economic Trends*, 358, November, pp. 28–46.

Dunn, J. (1994) 'Introduction: Crisis of the Nation State?' *Political Studies*, 42, special issue, pp. 3–15.

Dunning, J. (1992) 'Governments, Markets and Multinational Companies: Some Emerging Issues', *International Trade Journal*, fall, pp. 1–14.

——(1993) *Multinational Enterprises and the Global Economy*, Wokingham, Berks., Addison-Wesley.

Duverger, M. (1963) *Political Parties: Their Organization and Activity in the Modern State*, New York, Wiley.

Edin, K. (1995) 'The Myths of Dependence and Self-sufficiency: Women, Welfare and Low-wage Work', *Focus*, 17/2, pp. 1–10.

Edwards, R. and Duncan, S. (1997) 'Supporting the Family: Lone Mothers, Paid Work and the Underclass Debate', *Critical Social Policy*, 17/4, November, pp. 24–49.

Ellwood, D. (1988) *Poor Support: Poverty in the American Family*, New York, Basic Books.

Erskine, A. (1997) 'The Withering of Social Insurance in Britain', in J. Clasen (ed.), *Social Insurance in Europe*, Bristol, Policy Press, 130–50.

Esping-Andersen, G. (1990) *Three Worlds of Welfare Capitalism*, Cambridge, Polity Press.

——(1994a) *After the Golden Age*, UN World Summit for Social Development Occasional Paper 7, Geneva, UNRISD.

——(1994b) 'Welfare States and the Economy', in N. Smelser and R. Swedberg (eds), *The Handbook of Economic Sociology*, Princeton, Princeton University Press, pp. 11–32.

——(1996) 'Positive-Sum Solutions in a World of Trade-offs?', in G. Esping-Andersen (ed.), *Welfare States in Transition: National Adaptations in Global Economies*, London, Sage, 256–67.

Esping-Andersen, G. and Korpi, W. (1984) 'Social Policy as Class Politics in Post-war Capitalism: Scandinavia, Austria and Germany', in J. Goldthorpe (ed.), *Order and Conflict in Contemporary Capitalism*, Oxford, Clarendon Press.

Etzioni, A. (1998) 'Voluntary Simplicity: Characterization, Select Psychological Implications and Societal Consequences', *Journal of Economic Psychology*, 6.

Evans, G. (1996) 'Cross-national Differences in Support for Welfare and Redistribution: An Evaluation of Competing Theories', in B. Taylor and K. Thomson (eds), *Understanding Change in Social Attitudes*, Aldershot, CREST/Dartmouth.

Evason, E. and Robinson, G. (1998) 'Lone Parents in Northern Ireland: The Effectiveness of Work Incentives', *Social Policy and Administration*, 32/1, March, pp. 14–28.

Evason, E. and Woods, R. (1995) 'Poverty, Deregulation of the Labour Market and Benefit Fraud', *Social Policy and Administration*, 29/1, March, pp. 40–54.

Ferrera, M. (1993) *EC Citizens and Social Protection*, Brussels, CEC, VE2.

——(1995) 'The Mediterranean Welfare State', International Sociological Association, Committee on Poverty and Social Policy, Annual Conference, University of Pavia, 15 September, mimeo.

——(1996) 'The Southern Model of Welfare in Social Europe', *Journal of European Social Policy*, 6/1, pp. 17–37.

——(1997a) 'The Uncertain Future of the Italian Welfare State', in M. Bull and M. Rhodes (eds), *Crisis and Transition in Italian Politics*, London, Frank Cass.

——(1997b) 'The Uncertain Future of the Italian Welfare State', *West European Politics*, 20/1, pp. 231–49.

——(1998) *Le trappole del welfare. Uno stato sociale sostenibile per l'Europa del XXI secolo*, Bologna, Il Mulino.

Flemming, J. and Oppenheimer, P. (1996) 'Are Government Spending and Taxes too High (or too Low?)', *National Institute Economic Review*, 157, July, pp. 58–78.

Flora, P. (ed.) (1986) *Growth to Limits*, vols 1 and 2, Berlin, De Gruyter.

Friedman, M. and Friedman, R. (1980) *Free to Choose*, Harmondsworth, Penguin.

Frobel, F., Heinrichs, J. and Kreye, O. (1980) *The New International Division of Labour*, Cambridge, Cambridge University Press.

Fukuyama, F. (1992) *The End of History and the Last Man*, London, Hamish Hamilton.

Galbraith, J. (1992) *The Culture of Contentment*, Harmondsworth, Penguin.

Garman, A., Redmond, G. and Lonsdale, S. (1992) *Income In and Out of Work*, London, HMSO.

George, V. (1998) 'Political Ideology, Globalisation and Welfare Futures in Europe', *Journal of Social Policy*, 17/1, January, pp. 17–36.

George, V. and Miller, S. (eds) (1994) *Social Policy towards 2000*, London, Routledge.

George, V. and Taylor-Gooby, P. (eds) (1996) *European Social Policy: Squaring the Welfare Circle*, London, Macmillan.

George, V. and Wilding, P. (1984) *The Impact of Social Policy*, London, Routledge and Kegan Paul.

George, V., Taylor-Gooby, P. and Bonoli, G. (1995) 'Squaring the Welfare Circle in Europe. The Working Papers', Canterbury, University of Kent (mimeo).

Giddens, A. (1990) *The Social Consequences of Modernity*, Cambridge, Polity Press.

——(1994) *Beyond Left and Right?* Cambridge, Polity Press.

——(1998) *The Third Way: The Renewal of Social Democracy*, Cambridge, Polity Press.

Glennerster, H. (1995) *British Social Policy since 1945*, Oxford, Blackwell.

Glennerster, H. and Hills, J. (1998) *The State of Welfare: The Economics of Social Spending*, 2nd edn, Oxford, Oxford University Press.

Godfrey, L. (1975) *Theoretical and Empirical Aspects of the Effects of Taxation on the Supply of Labour*, Paris, OECD.

Golub, S. (1995) 'Comparative and Absolute Advantage in the Asia Pacific Region', Working Paper, Federal Reserve Bank of San Francisco, as reported in *The Economist*, 4 Nov. 1995, p. 142.

Goodman, R. and Peng, I. (1996) 'The East Asian Welfare States: Peripatetic Learning, Adaptive Change and Nation-building', in G. Esping-Andersen (ed.), *Welfare States in Transition*, London, Sage.

Gough, I. (1979) *The Political Economy of the Welfare State*, London, Macmillan.

Gough, I. (1996) 'Social Welfare and Competitiveness', *New Political Economy*, 1/2, pp. 210–32.

Gould, A. (1993) *Capitalist Welfare States*, London, Longman.

Green, D. (1995) 'Social Justice in the International Economy', *Contemporary Politics*, 1/1, spring, pp. 55–74.

HM Treasury (1979) *The Government's Expenditure Plans 1980–1*, Cmnd 7746, London, HMSO.

Habermas, J. (1970) *Towards a Rational Society*, Boston, Beacon Press.

Hage, J., Hanneman, R. and Gargan, E. (1989) *State Responsiveness and State Activism*, London, Unwin Hyman.

Hall, P. and Taylor, R. (1996) 'Political Science and the Three New Institutionalisms', *Political Studies*, 44/5, pp. 936–57.

Hantrais, L. (1995) *Social Policy in the European Union*, Basingstoke, Macmillan.

Hassenteufel, P. (1994) 'La réforme Seehofer: vers un abandon de l'auto-administration en Allemagne?', in B. Jobert and M. Steffen (eds), *Les politiques de santé en France et en Allemagne, Espace Social Européen*, special issue 4, pp. 209–20.

Hayek, F. A. (1944) *The Road to Serfdom*, London, Routledge and Kegan Paul.

Headey, B. (1978) *Housing Policy in the Developed Economy: The United Kingdom, Sweden and the United States*, London, Croom Helm.

Held, D. and McGrew, A. (1993) 'Globalization and the Liberal Democratic State', *Government and Opposition*, 28/2, spring, pp. 261–89.

Helleiner E. (1995) 'Explaining the Globalization of Financial Markets: Bringing the States back in', *Review of International Political Economy*, 2/2, spring, pp. 315–42.

Hessing, D., Elfers, H., Robben, H. and Webley, P. (1993) 'Needy or Greedy? The Social Psychology of Individuals who Fraudulently Claim Unemployment Benefits', *Journal of Applied Social Psychology*, 23/3, pp. 226–43.

Hicks, A. and Swank, D. (1984) 'On the Political Economy of Welfare Expansion', *Comparative Political Studies*, 17/1, pp. 81–119.

Hills, J. (1993) *The Future of Welfare: A Guide to the Debate*, York, Rowntree Foundation.

Hinnfors, J. and Pierre, J. (1998) 'The Politics of Currency Crises in Sweden: Policy Choice in a Globalised Economy', *West European Politics*, 21/3, July, pp. 103–19.

Hinrichs, K. (1995) 'The Impact of the German Health Insurance Reforms on Redistribution and the Culture of Solidarity', *Journal of Health Politics, Policy and Law*, 20/3, pp. 653–87.

—— (1998) 'Reforming the Public Pension Scheme in Germany: The End of the Traditional Consensus?', paper presented at the 14th World Congress of Sociology, Montreal, 26 July–1 August.

Hirst, P. (1995) 'Globalisation in Question', Occasional Paper 11, Political Economy Research Centre, University of Sheffield.

Hirst, P. and Thompson, G. (1996) *Globalization in Question*, Cambridge, Polity Press.

Holliday, I. (1992) *The NHS Transformed*, Manchester, Baseline Books.

Howe, Sir Geoffrey (1979) *Hansard: Parliamentary Debates*, 5th series, vol. 968, column 258.

Huber, E., Ragin, C. and Stephens, J. (1993) 'Social Democracy, Christian Democracy, Constitutional Structure, and the Welfare State', *American Journal of Sociology*, 99.

Hutton, W. (1996) *The State We're In*, London, Vintage.

Immergut, E. (1992) *Health Politics: Interests and Institutions in Western Europe*, Cambridge, Cambridge University Press.

——(1998) 'The Theoretical Core of the New Institutionalism', *Politics and Society*, 26/1, pp. 5–34.

Inglehart, R. (1990) *Culture Shift in Advanced Society*, Princeton, Princeton University Press.

International Labour Office (ILO) (1995) *World Employment 1995*, Geneva.

——(1997) *World Labour Report 1997–98*, Geneva.

International Social Security Association (ISSA) (1996) *Developments and Trends in Social Security throughout the World, 1993–1995*, Report I, Geneva, ISSA.

Jessop, B. (1994) 'The Transition to Post-Fordism and the Schumpeterian Workfare State', in R. Burrows and B. Loader (eds), *Towards a Post-Fordist Welfare State?*, London, Routledge.

Jessop, B., Kastendiek, H., Nielsen, K. and Pedersen, O. (1991) *The Politics of Flexibility: Restructuring State and Industry in Britain, Germany and Scandinavia*, London, Edward Elgar.

Jobert, B. and Steffen, M. (1994) 'Introduction', in B. Jobert and M. Steffen (eds), *Les politiques de santé en France et en Allemagne*, Espace Social Européen, special issue 4, pp. 13–19.

Johnson, P. and Falkingham, J. (1992) *Ageing and Economic Welfare*, London, Sage.

Join-Lambert, M.-T. (1997) *Politiques sociales*, Paris, Dalloz.

Jones, C. (1993) *New Perspectives on the Welfare State in Europe*, London, Routledge.

Jönsson, B. (1996) 'Making Sense of Health Care Reforms', in OECD (ed.), *Health Care Reform: The Will to Change*, Paris, OECD, pp. 31–45.

Jordan, B., James, S., Kay, H. and Redley, M. (1992) *Trapped in Poverty*, London, Routledge.

Kaase, M. and Newton, K. (1996) *Beliefs in Government*, Oxford, Oxford University Pess.

Kaletsky, A. (1998) 'Strong Pound Carries the Can for Weak Management', *The Times*, 20 March 1998.

Kalisch, D., Tetsuya, A. and Buchele, L. (1998*) Social and Health Policies in OECD Countries: A Survey of Current Programmes and Recent Developments*, Labour Market and Social Policy Occasional Paper 33, Paris, OECD.

Kapstein, E. (1995a) 'Governing Global Finance', in B. Roberts (ed.), *New Forces in the World Economy*, Cambridge, Mass., MIT Press.

——(1996b) 'Workers and the World Economy', *Foreign Affairs*, May/June, pp. 16–38.

Kasvio, A. (1995) *Re-inventing the Nordic Model*, Dept of Sociology and Social Psychology, University of Tampere, Finland.

Katzenstein, P. (1985) *Small States in World Markets: Industrial Policy in Europe*, Ithaca, NY, Cornell University Press.

Kemeny, J. (1995) 'Theories of Power in Three Worlds of Welfare Capitalism', *Journal of European Social Policy*, 5/2, pp. 87–96.

Klein, R. (1995) *The Politics of the NHS*, 3rd edn, London, Longman.

Kleinman, M. and Piachaud, D. (1993) 'European Social Policy: Conceptions and Choices', *Journal of European Social Policy*, 3/1, pp. 1–19.

Korpi, W. (1978) *The Working Class in Welfare Capitalism*, London, Routledge and Kegan Paul.

—— (1983) *The Democratic Class Struggle*, London, Routledge and Kegan Paul.

Kwon, H. (1995) 'The "Welfare State" in Korea: The Politics of Legitimation', University of Oxford, D.Phil thesis.

Labour Party (1997) *New Labour, Because Britain Deserves Better*, election manifesto, London.

Lansbury, M., Pain, N. and Smidkova, K. (1996) 'Foreign Direct Investment in Central Europe since 1990: An Economic Study', *National Institute Economic Review*, 156, May, pp. 104–14.

Laxer, G. (1995) 'Social Solidarity, Democracy and Global Capitalism', *Canadian Review of Sociology and Anthropology*, August, pp. 287–313.

Le Grand, J. (1997) 'Knights, Knaves or Pawns? Human Behaviour and Social Policy', *Journal of Social Policy*, 26/2, pp. 149–70.

—— (2000) 'From Knight to Knave: Public Policy and Endogenous Motivation', in P. Taylor-Gooby (ed.), *Risk, Trust and Welfare*, London, Macmillan.

Lehmbruch, G. (1982) 'Introduction: Neo-Corporatism in Comparative Perspective', in G. Lehmbruch and P. Schmitter (eds), *Patterns of Corporatist Policy-Making*, London, Sage.

—— (1984) 'Concertation and the Structure of Corporatist Networks', in J. Goldthorpe (ed.), *Order and Conflict in Contemporary Capitalism*, Oxford, Clarendon Press, pp. 60–80.

Leibfried, S. (1990) 'The Classification of Welfare State Regimes in Europe', Social Policy Association Annual Conference, University of Bath, July.

—— (1993) 'Towards a European Welfare State?', in C. Jones (ed.), *New Perspectives on the Welfare State in Europe*, London, Routledge.

Leisering, L. and Leibfried, S. (1998) *Time, Life and Poverty: Social Assistance Dynamics in the German Welfare State*, Cambridge, Cambridge University Press.

Letourmy, A. (1994) 'The Economic Forms of the Regulation of Health Spending in France: Negotiated Waste', in MIRE (ed.), *Comparing Social Welfare Systems in Europe*, vol. 1 (Proceedings of the Oxford Conference), Paris, pp. 295–332.

Leuven, E. and Tuijnman, A. (1996) 'Lifelong Learning: Who Pays?', *OECD Observer*, 199, May, pp. 10–19.

Lewis, J. (ed.) (1993) *Women and Social Policies in Europe*, Aldershot, Gower.

Lijphart, A. (1984) *Democracies: Pattern of Majoritarian and Consensus Government in Twenty-One Countries*, New Haven and London, Yale University Press.

Lijphart, A. and Crepaz, M. (1991) 'Corporatism and Consensus Democracy in Eighteen Countries: Conceptual and Empirical Linkages', *British Journal of Political Science*, 21, pp. 235–56.

Longman, P. (1987) *Born to Pay: The New Politics of Ageing in America*, Boston, Houghton Mifflin.

MacDonald, R. (1994) 'Fiddly Jobs, Undeclared Working and the Something for Nothing Society', *Work, Employment and Society*, 8/4, December, pp. 507–30.

—— (1996) 'Welfare Dependency, the Enterprise Culture and Self-employment Survival', *Work, Employment and Society*, 10/3, September, pp. 431–49.

McKay, S., Walker, R. and Youngs, R. (1997) *Unemployment and Jobseeking before Jobseekers Allowance*, Department of Social Security, Research Report 73, London, HMSO.

McKee, M. (1996) 'The Influence of European Law on National Health Policy', *Journal of European Social Policy*, 6/4, pp. 263–86.

McLaughlin, E. (1991) 'Work and Welfare Benefits: Social Security, Employment and Unemployment in the 1990s', *Journal of Social Policy*, 20/4, October, pp. 485–509.

—— (1997) 'Workfare – a Pull, a Push or a Shove? Balancing Constraint, Opportunity, Compulsion and Autonomy in Individual Experience', in A. Deacon (ed.), *From Welfare to Work: Lessons from America*, London, Institute of Economic Affairs, pp. 79–96.

McLuhan, M. (1964) *Understanding Media*, London, Routledge.

Macnicol, J. (1987) 'In Pursuit of the Underclass', *Journal of Social Policy*, 16/3, July, pp. 293–319.

Marsh, A., Ford, R. and Finlayson, L. (1997) *Lone Parents, Work and Benefits*, Department of Social Security Research Report 61, London, HMSO.

Miliband, R. (1991) *Divided Societies*, Oxford, Oxford University Press.

Milkman, R. and Townsley, E. (1994) 'Gender and the Economy', in N. Smelser and R. Swedberg (eds), *Handbook of Economic Sociology*, New York, Princeton University Press/Russell Sage Foundation.

Mishra, R. (1990) *The Welfare State in Capitalist Society*, New York, Harvester Wheatsheaf.

*MISSOC* (1996) [= *Social Protection in the Member States of the Community*, biennial], Brussels, CEC.

Morris, L. and Llewellyn, T. (1991) *Social Security Provision for the Unemployed*, Social Security Advisory Committee Research Report 3, London, HMSO.

Moylan, S. and Davies, B. (1981) 'The Flexibility of the Unemployed', *Employment Gazette*, 89/1, January.

Murray, C. (1984) *Losing Ground*, New York, Basic Books.

—— (1990) *The Emerging British Underclass*, London, Institute of Economic Affairs.

Myles, J. and Quadagno, J. (1997) 'Recent Trends in Public Pension Reform: A Comparative View', in K. Banting and R. Boadway (eds), *Reform of Retirement Income Policy: International and Canadian Perspectives*, Kingston (Ontario) Queen's University, School of Policy Studies, pp. 247–72.

National Audit Office (1997) *Measures to Combat Housing Benefit Fraud*, London, HMSO.

Nesbitt, S. (1995) *British Pension Policy Making in the 1980s: The Rise and Fall of a Policy Community*, Aldershot, Avebury.

Niero, M. (1996) 'Retrenchment in Expenditure in Italian Welfare Policies (1985–1995)', MS, University of Kent.

North, D. (1990) *Institutions, Institutional Change, and Economic Performance*, Cambridge, Cambridge University Press.

O'Connor, James (1973) *The Fiscal Crisis of the State*, New York, St Martin's Press.

O'Connor, Julia (1988) 'Convergence or Divergence: Change in Welfare Effort in OECD Countries, 1960–80', *European Journal of Political Research*, 16/2, pp. 277–99.

O'Connor, Julia and Brym, R. (1988) 'Public Expenditure in OECD Countries: Towards a Reconciliation of Inconsistent Findings', *British Journal of Sociology*, 39/1, pp. 47–67.

OECD (1983) *Historical Statistics 1960–1981*, Paris.

——(1988a) *Reforming Public Pensions*, Paris.

——(1988b) *Ageing Populations: The Social Policy Implications*, Paris.

——(1992) *Historical Statistics 1960–1990*, Paris.

——(1994a) *New Orientations for Social Policy*, Paris.

——(1994b) *Economic Outlook*, 55, Paris.

——(1994c) *Economic Surveys: Sweden 1993–1994*, Paris.

——(1994d) *Economic Outlook*, 56, December, Paris.

——(1994e) *The OECD Jobs Study: Facts, Analysis, Strategies*, Paris.

——(1995a) 'Effect of Ageing Populations on Government Budgets', *Economic Outlook*, 57, Paris.

——(1995b) *Revenue Statistics for Member Countries, 1965–94*, Paris.

——(1996) *Social Expenditure Statistics of OECD Member Countries*, Labour Market and Social Policy Occasional Papers 17, Paris.

——(1997a) *Economic Outlook*, 62, December, Paris.

——(1997b) *Revenue Statistics of OECD Member Countries, 1965–96*, Paris.

——(1997c) *Statistical Compendium. Labour Force Statistics*, Paris.

——(1998) *Main Economic Indicators*, March, Paris.

——(1999) *Economic Outlook*, 65, June, Paris.

Olsen, G. M. (1996) 'Re-modelling Sweden', *Social Problems*, 43/1, February, pp. 61–71.

Owens, J. and Robson, M. (1995) 'Taxation and Household Saving', *OECD Observer*, 191, December 1994/January 1995, pp. 27–30.

Oxley, H. and Martin, J. P. (1991) 'Controlling Government Spending and Deficits', *OECD Economic Studies*, 17, pp. 145–89.

Palme, J. and Wennemo, I. (1997) 'Swedish Social Security in the 1990s: Reform and Retrenchment', Stockholm, Swedish Institute for Social Research, mimeo.

Pfaller, A., Gough, I. and Therborn, G. (eds) (1991) *Can the Welfare State Compete?*, London, Macmillan.

Piachaud, D. (1997) 'Social Security and Dependence', *International Social Security Review*, 50/1, pp. 41–56.

Pierson, P. (1994) *Dismantling the Welfare State? Reagan, Thatcher and the Politics of Retrenchment*, Cambridge, Cambridge University Press.

——(1996) 'The New Politics of the Welfare State', *World Politics*, 48/2, pp. 143–79.

——(1998) 'Irresistible Forces, Immovable Objects: Post-industrial Welfare States Confront Permanent Austerity', *Journal of European Social Policy*, 5/4, pp. 539–60.

Pierson, P. and Weaver, K. (1994) 'Imposing Losses in Pension Policy', in Weaver and Rockman, 1993.

Pius XI (1931) *Quadrigesimo Anno*, Actae Apostolicae Sedis 23.

Piven, F. Fox (1995) 'Is It Global Economics or Neo-Laissez-Faire?', *New Left Review*, 213, September/October, pp. 107–15.

Piven, F. Fox and Cloward, R. (1982) *The New Class War: Reagan's Attack on the Welfare State*, New York, Pantheon.

Ploug, N. (1995) 'The Welfare State in Liquidation?', *International Social Security Review*, 48/2, pp. 61–71.

Porter, M. (1990) *The Competitive Advantage of Nations*, London, Macmillan.

Powell, M. (1998) 'Great Expectations? New Labour and the "New" UK National Health Service', *Critical Public Health*, 8/2, pp. 167–73.

Ramesh, M. (1995) 'Economic Globalization and Policy Choices: Singapore', *Governance*, 8/2, April, pp. 243–60.

Regini, M. (1984) 'The Conditions for Political Exchange: How Concertation Emerged and Collapsed in Italy and Great Britain', in J. Goldthorpe (ed.), *Order and Conflict in Contemporary Capitalism*, Oxford, Clarendon Press, pp. 124–42.

—— (1992) 'Introduction: the Past and Future of Social Studies of Labour Movements', in M. Regini (ed.), *The Future of Labour Movements*, London, Sage, pp. 1–16.

Reynaud, E. and Hedge, A. (1996) 'Italy: A Fundamental Transformation of the Pension System', *International Social Security Review*, 49/3.

Richards, A. and Madden, K. (1996) 'An International Comparison of Taxes and Social Security Contributions (1984–1994)', *Economic Trends*, 517, November, pp. 16–29.

Rifkin, J. (1995) *The End of Work*, New York, Putnam.

Rinehart, J. (1995) 'The Ideology of Competitiveness', *Monthly Review*, 45/5, October, pp. 14–24.

Ritchie, J. (1990) *Thirty Families: Their Living Standards in Unemployment*, Department of Social Security Research Report 1, London, HMSO.

Robertson, R. (1992) *Globalization: Social Theory and Global Culture*, London, Sage.

Robinson, I. (1995) 'Globalization and Democracy', *Dissent*, Summer, pp. 373–81.

Rodrik, D. (1997) *Has Globalization Gone too Far?* Washington, DC, Institute of International Economics.

Room, G. (ed.) (1991) *Towards a European Welfare State?*, Bristol, SAUS Publications.

—— (1994) 'European Social Policy', in R. Page and J. Baldock (eds), *Social Policy Review 6*, Social Policy Association, University of Kent.

Room, G. and Berghman, J. (1990) *The 'New Poverty' in the European Community*, London, Macmillan.

Rowlingson, K. and Berthoud, R. (1996) *Disability Benefits and Employment*, Department of Social Security Research Report 54, London, HMSO.

Rowlingson, K., Whyley, C., Newburn, T and Berthoud, R. (1997) *Social Security Fraud: The Role of Penalties*, Department of Social Security Research Report 64, London, HMSO.

Ruellan, R. (1993) 'Retraites: l'impossible réforme est-elle achevée?', *Droit social*, 12, pp. 911–29.

Ruppel, F. and King, A. (1995) 'The German Care Insurance and the British Community Care: Comparative Perspectives', *Social Work in Europe*, 2/1, pp. 12–16.

Sachs, J. and Schatz, H. (1994) *Trade and Jobs in US Manufacturing*, Washington, DC, Brookings Institutution.

Saunders, P. and Klau, F. (1985) *The Role of the Public Sector: Causes and Consequences of the Growth of Government*, Paris, OECD.

Scaperlanda, A. (1993) 'Multinational Companies and the Global Market', *Journal of Economic Issues*, 27/2, June, pp. 605–17.

Scharpf, F. W. (1997) 'Economic Integration, Democracy and the Welfare State', *Journal of European Public Policy*, 4/1, pp. 18–36.

Schmähl, W. (1993) 'The 1992 Reform of Public Pensions in Germany: Main Elements and Some Effects', *Journal of European Social Policy*, 3/1, pp. 39–52.

Schmitter, P. and Lehmbruch, G. (eds) (1979) *Trends toward Corporatist Intermediation*, London, Sage.

Schwab, K. and Smadja, C. (1994) 'Power and Policy: The New Economic World Order', *Harvard Business Review*, November/December, pp. 40–53.

Shaver, S. (1992) *Body Rights, Social Rights and the Liberal Welfare State*, SPRC Discussion Paper 38, University of New South Wales.

Shaw, A., Walker, R., Ashworth, K., Jenkins, S. and Middleton, S. (1996) *Moving off Income Support: Barriers and Bridges*, Department of Social Security Research Report 53, London, HMSO.

Shola Orloff, A. (1993) 'Gender and the Social Rights of Citizenship: The Comparative Analysis of Gender Relations and Welfare States', *American Sociological Review*, 58, pp. 303–28.

Skocpol, T. (1995) *Social Policy in the United States*, Princeton, Princeton University Press.

Skocpol, T. and Amenta, E. (1986) 'States and Social Policies', *American Review of Sociology*, 12, pp. 131–57.

Spicker, P. (1991) 'The Principle of Subsidiarity and the Social Policy of the European Community', *Journal of European Social Policy*, 1/1, pp. 3–14.

Stahlberg, A.-C. (1997) 'Sweden: On the Way from Standard to Basic Security?', in J. Clasen (ed.), *Social Insurance in Europe*, Bristol, Policy Press, pp. 40–59.

Standing, G. (1995) 'Labor Insecurity through Market Regulation', in C. McFate, R. Lawson and J. W. Wilson (eds), *Poverty, Inequality and the Future of Social Policy*, New York, Russell Sage Foundation.

Stephens, J. (1980) *The Transition from Capitalism to Socialism*, Atlantic Highlands, NJ, Humanities Press.

Strange, S. (1995) 'The Limits of Politics', *Government and Opposition*, 30/3, summer, pp. 292–312.

Streeck, W. and Schmitter, P. (1991) 'From National Corporatism to Transnational Pluralism: Organised Interests in the Single European Market', *Politics and Society*, 19/2.

——(1995) 'Community, Market, State – and Associations? The Prospective Contribution of Interest Governance to Social Order', in Streeck and Schmitter (eds), *Private Interest Government*, London, Sage.

Supplementary Benefits Commission (1980) *Annual Report 1979*, London, HMSO.

Svallfors, S. (1997) 'Worlds of Welfare and Attitudes to Distribution: A Comparison of Eight Western Nations', *European Sociological Review*, 13/3, pp. 283–304.

Svallfors, S. and Taylor-Gooby, P. (1999) *Responses to State Retrenchment: Evidence from Attitude Surveys*, London, Routledge.

Tabb, W. (1997) 'Globalization is an Issue, the Power of Capital is The Issue', *Monthly Review*, 49/2, June, pp. 20–31.

Taylor-Gooby, P. (1994) 'Postmodernism and Social Policy: A Great Leap Backwards?', *Journal of Social Policy*, 23/3, pp. 2385–404.

—— (1997) 'In Defence of Second-Best Theory: State, Class and Capital in Social Policy', *Journal of Social Policy*, 26/2, pp. 171–92.

—— (1998a) 'Policy Change at a Time of Retrenchment: Recent Pension Reform in France, Germany, Italy and the UK', *Social Policy and Administration*, 33/1.

—— (1998b) *Choice and Public Policy: The Limits to Welfare Markets*, London, Macmillan.

—— (1998c) 'Convergence and Divergence in European Welfare States', in R. Jowell, J. Curtice, L. Brook and A. Park (eds), *European Social Attitudes: The 3rd ISSP Report*, Aldershot, SCPR/Ashgate.

—— (1999) 'Policy Change at a Time of Retrenchment: Recent Pension Reform in France, Germany, Italy, and the UK', *Social Policy and Administration*, 33/1, pp. 1–19.

Teague, P. and Grahl, J. (1998) 'Institutions and Labour Market Performance in Western Europe', *Political Studies*, 46/1, March, pp. 1–19.

Thurow, L. (1996) *The Future of Capitalism*, London, Nicholas Brealy Publishing.

Turner, B. (1990) 'Outline of a Theory of Citizenship', *Sociology*, 24/2, pp. 189–217.

Tversky, A. and Kahneman, D. (1981) 'The Framing of Decisions and the Psychology of Choice', *Science*, 211, pp. 453–8.

Ulrich, W. and Zika, G. (1997) 'Social Protection: An Obstacle to Employment?', *International Social Security Review*, 50/4, pp. 7–27.

United Nations (1995) *World Economic and Social Survey*, New York.

—— (1997) *World Economic and Social Survey*, New York.

UN Center on Transnational Corporations (1992) *World Investment Report, 1992: Transnational Corporations as Engines of Growth*, New York.

Van Kersbergen, K. (1991) 'Social Capitalism: A Study of Christian Democracy and the Post-war Settlement of the Welfare State', PhD dissertation, European University Institute, Florence.

Van Langedonck, J. (1997) 'The Social Protection of the Unemployed', *International Social Security Review*, 50/4, pp. 29–43.

Visser, J. and Hemerijck, A. (1997) *A Dutch Miracle? Job Growth, Welfare Reform and Corporatism in the Netherlands*, Amsterdam, Amsterdam University Press.

Vobruda, G. (1996) 'Social Policy on Tomorrow's Euro-corporatist Stage', *Journal of European Social Policy*, 6/4, pp. 303–16.

Waine, B. (1995) 'A Disaster Foretold? The Case of Personal Pension', *Social Policy and Administration*, 29/4, pp. 317–34.

Walker, A. (1991) 'Thatcherism and the Politics of Old Age', in J. Myles and J. Quadagno (eds), *States, Labour Markets, and the Future of Old Age Policy*, Philadelphia, Temple University Press.

Walker A. and Wong, C. K. (1996) 'Rethinking the Western Construction of the Welfare State', *International Journal of Health Services*, 26/1, pp. 67–92.

Wallace, W. (1994) 'Rescue or Retreat? The Nation State in Western Europe, 1945–93', *Political Studies*, 42, special issue, pp. 52–77.

Washington, S. (1996) 'Globalisation and Governance', *OECD Observer*, 199, April/May, pp. 24–8.

Waters, M. (1994) 'A World of Difference', *Australian & New Zealand Journal of Sociology*, 30/3, November, pp. 229–34.

——(1995) *Globalisation*, London, Routledge.

Weaver, R. K. and Rockman, B. A. (eds) (1993) *Do Institutions Matter? Government Capabilities in the United States and Abroad*, Washington, DC, Brookings Institution.

Whiteford, P. and Bradshaw, J. (1994) 'Benefits and Incentives for Lone Parents: A Comparative Analysis', *International Social Security Review*, 47/3–4, pp. 69–89.

Wilding, P. (1997) 'Globalisation, Regionalism and Social Policy', *Social Policy and Administration*, 31/4, December, pp. 410–29.

Wilensky, H. (1975) *The Welfare State and Equality*, Berkeley, University of California Press.

——(1976) *The 'New Corporatism', Centralization and the Welfare State*, London, Sage.

Wilensky, H. and Lebeaux, C. (1958) *Industrial Society and Social Welfare*, New York, Free Press.

Wilkin, P. (1996) 'New Myths for the South: Globalisation and the Conflicts between Private Power and Freedom', *Third World Quarterly*, 17/2, June, pp. 227–38.

Wilks, S. (1996) 'Class Compromise and the International Economy: the Rise and Fall of Swedish Social Democracy', *Capital and Class*, 58, pp. 89–111.

Williams, F. (1992) 'Somewhere over the Rainbow: Universality and Diversity in Social Policy', in N. Manning and R. Page (eds), *Social Policy Review 4*, Social Policy Association, University of Kent.

——(1995) 'Race/ethnicity, Gender and Class in Welfare States: A Framework for Comparative Analysis', *Social Politics*, 2/2, pp. 127–59.

Wood, A. (1994) *North–South Trade: Employment and Inequality*, Oxford, Clarendon Press.

World Bank (1994) *World Population Projections*, Washington, DC.

——(1995) *World Development Report 1995*, New York, Oxford University Press.

Wriston, W. (1988) 'Technology and Sovereignty', *Foreign Affairs*, 76, pp. 63–75.

# Index